GOING UP COUNTRY

GOING UP COUNTRY

Travel Essays by Peace Corps Writers

EDITED BY JOHN COYNE

CHARLES SCRIBNER'S SONS
NEW YORK

Maxwell Macmillan Canada
TORONTO

Maxwell Macmillan International
NEW YORK   OXFORD   SINGAPORE   SYDNEY

Charles Scribner's Sons
Macmillan Publishing Company
866 Third Avenue
New York, NY 10022

Maxwell Macmillan Canada, Inc.
1200 Eglinton Avenue East
Suite 200
Don Mills, Ontario M3C 3N1

Macmillan Publishing Company is part of the Maxwell Communication Group of Companies.

Library of Congress Cataloging-in-Publication Data

Going up country : travel essays by Peace Corps writers / edited by John Coyne.
    p.   cm.
  ISBN 0-684-19629-8
  1. Peace Corps (U.S.)   2. Voyages and travels.   I. Coyne, John.
HC60.5.G64   1994
910.4—dc20   93-6293
CIP

Macmillan books are available at special discounts for bulk purchases for sales promotions, premiums, fund-raising, or educational use. For details, contact:
Special Sales Director
Macmillan Publishing Company
866 Third Avenue
New York, NY 10022
10 9 8 7 6 5 4 3 2 1
Printed in the United States of America

For Jim Thompson,
who first drove me up the Gondar road.

CONTENTS

FOREWORD

Senator Harris Wofford

Of all the social inventions of the sixties, the Peace Corps has been the most successful, and it is John Kennedy's most affirmative legacy. In accepting the presidential nomination, Kennedy promised "invention, innovation, imagination, decision"; in establishing the Peace Corps, he kept his promise. By serving for two or more years, Peace Corps Volunteers have attended an unusual "university in dispersion," one in which they have been educated about the human condition and about the United States's relationship with the Third World.

That was as Kennedy would have wished it. He established the Peace Corps in 1961 with three goals: 1) to contribute to the development of the country; 2) to promote international cooperation and goodwill; 3) to contribute to the education of America and to more intelligent American participation in the world.

That third goal is surely being fulfilled by the Returned Peace Corps Volunteers (RPCVs) whose work appears in this book. These Returned Volunteers have written about the world from a Peace Corps perspective, which is a unique one.

The overseas experience was so important in their lives that, as novelist Richard Lipez has said of his time in Ethiopia, "Whatever we were before, and none of us can quite remember, that's all gone. Peace Corps life tempers one by its sheer and irresistible intensity."

Peace Corps Volunteers didn't just pass through foreign countries. They unpacked their belongings, they settled down, they set about to do a job, and made lifelong friends.

And having lived and worked at the edges of the earth, and on top of the world, their service provided them with wonderful stories, many of them touching on how the world was turned into a global village by Kennedy's idea for something called "a Peace Corps."

Coleman Lollar, once a Volunteer in Africa, later wrote an essay explaining how the Peace Corps experience had set him on the road to his career as a travel writer: ". . . the first foreign road I ever took . . . was a bush road to an up country village in Sierra Leone, where I would spend two years as one of 'Kennedy's Kids' in the Peace Corps. It was my good fortune that childhood wanderlust segued neatly into the passions of the sixties. There weren't any Alps or Eiffel Towers in a West Africa village with the unlikely name of Port Loko, but I found there confirmation of a long-held suspicion that in no place on earth would I ever feel entirely the stranger. I've long since shed, or had wrested from me, the innocence and idealism of youth. But unlike most politicians and institutions, I have never lost sight of the little gem of truth picked up in the African bush, wherever I have gone."

Peace Corps Volunteers know how not to be strangers. Their experience allowed them to reach through the barriers of culture and tradition and touch other lives.

John Coyne, the editor of this volume, and once a Volunteer in Ethiopia, tells of the time shortly after JFK was killed, when he stopped his Land-Rover in the highlands to give an old man a lift across the high plateau. On the side of the Land-Rover the old man saw the Amharic words "Yeasalem Guad," Messenger of Peace—the Amharic translation of "the Peace Corps." The old man asked Coyne if he had known President Kennedy and John told him no, but he had once shaken Kennedy's hand on the White House lawn just before leaving for Africa. For a moment, as Coyne tells the story, the old Ethiopian looked out across the flat brown land at the distant acacia trees and small tukul villages they were passing, and then he grinned and seized Coyne's hand and shook it, shouting happily over the roar of the Land-Rover engine, "Yeasalem Guad, Yeasalem Guad."

He had shaken the hand that had shaken the hand of John F. Kennedy. Those two—a Peace Corps Volunteer and an old

Ethiopian farmer—on the highlands of Africa, and as far away as one could possibly be from Washington and the Rose Garden, were, for a moment, connected by history.

That is one Peace Corps story. The story of strangers who find that they have much in common with whomever they meet in the world. John Coyne, himself a gifted writer and former volunteer, now has put his fine editor's hand to the production of this excellent collection of travel essays.

The Peace Corps story is also one of adventure. The filmmaker David Schickele, who was a Volunteer in Nigeria in the sixties, summed up the Peace Corps this way: "It is the call to go, not where man has never been before, but where he has lived differently."

Kennedy's New Frontier, or any frontier worth crossing, begins first as a challenge. My friend, the novelist and travel writer Paul Theroux, who was a Volunteer in Malawi, said he joined the Peace Corps after reading Conrad's *Heart of Darkness*. He put his finger on the title page and said, "When I join the Peace Corps, I shall go there." Theroux, like so many others of those first volunteers to go overseas, was responding to a personal challenge to do something different with his life.

Thirty-three years later, the Peace Corps continues to send men and women into the world. Today over 6,000 PCVs live and work in one hundred countries in Africa, Asia, Latin America, and Eastern Europe. Volunteers today are in Russia and China, and a half dozen other countries that have only recently become new nations.

And now, we Americans can share in the experiences of these Peace Corp writers. For after their service, these writers have come home again to tell their stories, and by doing so, are educating America about the world.

GOING UP COUNTRY

THE PEACE CORPS TRAVELER

Everyone knows the difference between tourists and travelers. Tourists move through a foreign country in clusters and in comfort, collecting impressions, snapshots, and most of all, gifts for home. Seldom are they remembered by the people they meet.

Travelers, on the other hand, move at a slower pace and most often alone. They travel by bus and boat, and at times exotically, on camel in the Sudan, for example, or across the Red Sea in an Arab dhow. They seek destinations. They want to journey up the Nile, down the Amazon, across Yemen. They, too, are passing through and focused on their own ambitions and achievements. They leave little of themselves in their wake.

There is, however, another kind of traveler to distant locations: the Peace Corps Volunteer. For three decades Peace Corps Volunteers—PCVs—have been traveling to places difficult to find on a map.

Unlike those who choose the expatriate life, volunteers didn't go to the ends of the earth to escape American civilization or, for that matter, to make money from the labor of others. They went to jobs that took them away from embassies, first-class hotels, and the privileges of being rich foreigners in poor countries. They lived far from the capital, in villages that would never be tourist sites.

The Peace Corps has always attracted men and women of exceptional intelligence and sensitivity, with a very special sense of adventure. An unusual number of these volunteers, after their period of service, have become professional writers.

Thirteen of these Peace Corps writers were asked to return to their country of service or another country in which they had lived, and write about it from the Peace Corps perspective, a perspective gained from long residence in the country, fluency in the language, and very close contact with host country nationals. These writers were asked to relate that Peace Corps experience to their perception of life in those countries today. What is true and lasting in that country? What has changed? What does a traveler, even a casual visitor, really need to know about the place?

Jeff Taylor, for example, a Peace Corps Volunteer in Hungary, writes about the rapid changes there and how it affected him. "I fear I've become a bit of a crotchety, contemptuous, old expatriate here as Eastern Europe gets progressively diluted by more starchy Americans come to see 'all the changes.' I already catch myself beginning too many sentences with 'I remember when. . . .' When every sign still read People's Republic, and my school sat on Red Army Street. When only Germans drove Western cars and Hungarians still bought Trabants new. When an establishment distinguished itself by advertising its private ownership. Most of all, I can remember when Soviet soldiers in Hungary actually wore all the pins and hats and helmets that tourists buy on Buda's Castle Hill. I remember when the Soviet Union was still a monolith on our eastern border, and I traveled through it only months before it slipped away into history."

Other essays in this book are not about just being there, but rather traveling in the ways all Peace Corps Volunteers do.

Jeanne D'Haem, a Volunteer in Somalia who has circled the globe several times, explains it this way: "Traveling requires either money or time. Fortunately, I've never had any money, but I can sleep anywhere and eat anything. I stay where the local people stay. I eat the local food. And traveling this way it is amazing what you can get into."

Kathleen Coskran, who was a Volunteer in Ethiopia and has traveled on her own throughout East Africa, knows exactly what a person can get into. "I was in Uganda in a *matatu*, a local bus, and the guy on my left was smuggling sugar in from Kenya. I didn't know this until he dived out the window at a roadblock. The woman next to me slipped a kilo of the contraband sugar into her basket, then pulled my skirt over the rest just as a soldier stuck his semiautomatic in the window. The *matatu* was packed, but the soldier had eyes for me alone. He took my passport, looked at my picture, looked at me, back and forth three times, then handed it back and walked away. That's what I like. I don't know what's going on and I'm in the middle of it."

The middle of it is where Peace Corps Volunteers always find themselves, and that is what makes their writing so revealing and distinctive. All of these writers bring to their current writing a special insight into human nature and a special concern for humanity gained, in part, during their years in the Peace Corps.

They were too young to have been in Paris during the twenties or to have written the great World War II novel. But now, three decades after the Peace Corps began, they are among a growing list of authors who have had their writings and views of the world shaped by their overseas experience.

Bob Shacochis summed up the kinds of essays, stories, and novels we can expect from Peace Corps writers. "We are torchbearers of a vital tradition, that of shedding light in the mythical heart of darkness. We are descendants of Joseph Conrad, Mark Twain, George Orwell, Graham Greene, Somerset Maugham, Ernest Hemingway, and scores of other men and women, expatriates and travel writers and wanderers, who have enriched our domestic literature with the spices of Cathay, who have tried to communicate the 'exotic' as a relative, rather than an absolute, quality of humanity."

That is the spirit that motivates this book. Here are the Peace Corps writers and the stories they have to tell.

John Coyne
Pelham Manor, New York
October 1993

ON THE PIRANHA TRAIL WITH RUSSELL AND KURTZ

by Mike Tidwell

Mike Tidwell published a book about his Peace Corps experience in Zaire, where he was in the late eighties as a fish-culture extension agent. That book was entitled *The Ponds of Kalambayi.* His second book, *In the Shadow of the White House: Drugs, Death, and Redemption on the Streets of the Nation's Capital,* is about the year he spent counseling homeless drug addicts. Between books he does a lot of traveling, and his next book will be on travels through Latin America.

For Mike there is something about the act of traveling, about motion itself, that clarifies his thinking and sharpens his vision—of himself and his surroundings. He became acquainted with this phenomenon at age fifteen when his family left his native Georgia in a rattletrap, two-tone station wagon to visit an uncle in Colorado for Christmas. For the ride, Tidwell brought along ten very long and very knotted algebra equations to solve for a ferocious martinet of a teacher. Tidwell was failing algebra at the time.

Through Alabama, Mississippi, and Arkansas the equations remained impenetrable. Then, west of Amarillo, Texas, a great afternoon wind blew up from the Gulf of Mexico, causing a wondrous dust storm that nearly stamped out the sun entirely. The station wagon slowed to a walk, and Tidwell stared out in amazement at curtains of blowing dust and cascading tumbleweeds he'd never seen before. After an hour, his eyes smarting from dust seeping in, he noticed the textbook still opened in his lap. Then and there, one by one, the algebra problems began solving themselves as fast as Tidwell's pencil could keep up.

"The feeling of being on the moon is what did it," he told me. "I think the brain works best sometimes when we feel utterly far away from home. In that bizarre storm, I was able to think, to finally find my way."

Over the years such epiphanies have continued to find their way into Tidwell's travel writing in whatever latest version of the moon he has explored—the Congo River, the Amazon rain forest, the Guatemala highlands. Life's toughest secrets, he says, just seem better understood on the road. The pencil can barely keep up.

Thinking back again, he added with a laugh, "If not for the Texas panhandle I might still be in tenth grade."

It's not a good feeling to be lost over the Amazon jungle. Inside
an airplane. During a storm. With the radio equipment down
and visibility virtually zip. Looking for a landing strip the size of
a butter knife.

It's not a good feeling especially when, already, you hate to fly,
and the only reason you've lived to be twenty-nine is that there
happens to be an island in the middle of the Mediterranean
called Crete and your Cairo-to-Athens flight a few years back,
engines barely functioning, just happened to reach the island
before crashing into the drink.

So I didn't feel well that morning sitting in the army C-130
Hercules, circling over the Amazon, those front propellers
whirring overtime against a paint job of jungle camouflage. I
didn't realize at first that we were lost, that the Ecuadorian pilots
were searching frantically for an airstrip called Tarapoa somewhere down there in all those Ecuadorian trees. The scheduled
arrival time had come and gone, the landing gear had gone
down, noisily, and come back up, curiously, and the plane had
begun banking, backtracking, flying in circles.

The few odd civilians who hitchhike into the jungle aboard
these army flights are given seats amid stacks of cargo, between
bare, curving fuselage walls. For the deafening engine noise, the
crew hands out bolls of pink cotton to shove inside your ears. So
there I was on this particular flight, surrounded by cargo at the

very rear of the fuselage, alone except for a crew member next to me in a baggy jumpsuit. His name was José, and he slept most of the way despite wearing headphones that connected him directly to the pilots in the cockpit.

It is my curse that even minor wind turbulence scares me badly when I fly. But my main rule is this: never get totally terrified until the crew starts to look mildly concerned. Yet when José sat bolt upright from his sleeping position just then, pressing the headphones tightly to his ears, listening intently as the plane banked and turned another time, he didn't look mildly concerned. He looked totally terrified, which put me—by extension—in an emotional state beyond known psychiatric borders.

A split second later José ripped off his headphones and thrust them into my hands. "Here," he said in rapid Spanish, "put these on and listen to the pilots. If they call for me, you come and get me as fast as you can."

Then he was gone, off to a starboard window, scanning downward with mile-wide eyes. Glancing out the window myself, all I could see were clouds and an occasional treetop. I put on the headphones as ordered, a draftee, and listened to a conversation I would gladly pay to have surgically removed from my memory.

Pilot One: "It's no good! I don't see *anything!* Let's turn north again."

Pilot Two: "We've tried north! We've tried it! Maybe we're not even close."

Pilot One: "But where could it be? Trees! Trees! That's all I see. *Dios mío!*"

The voices were scratchy, full of that rough electronic sound that somehow makes even routine cockpit communication seem dire and foreboding. As I listened, I realized that not only were we lost, but I was also hearing the only thing investigators would find after the crash. I was getting a grotesque and very unwelcome prescreening of that very terrible thing: the black box.

José was still glued to the window. It seemed academic to ask him the question. His face said everything: "Can't turn around. Not enough fuel to make it back to Quito. Must land. Must find airstrip."

And God, I thought, I wasn't even supposed to be on this flight. It was the classic plane-crash tragedy. There had been a change of plans, a last-minute decision to fly. A series of strange events during the past week had come together to put me on this plane at this moment—and now, in a rush, those events passed through my mind. Why, for heaven's sake, couldn't Russell and I have just had a nice, peaceful trip into the rain forest that first time, without all the intrigue? Why did we have to stumble onto a bizarre and complicated *news* story, one that was sending me back into the forest this second time? Russell was my companion, a crazed genius of a photographer who wore piranha teeth and a light meter on the same necklace and who carried an eight-foot-long fishing pole with him wherever he went. What in the world did Russell and I know about *news?* News was tedious. We hated news. We had abandoned newspapers for travel writing years before, we hated news so much.

Which is how, the week before, we wound up in the Amazon in the first place, deep inside Ecuador's Lower Cuyabeno Wildlife Reserve. Sitting in the lost Hercules, thinking back, I recalled how we had planned to focus on nature, nothing more. How we had traveled by plane, then motorized boat, then walked part of the way, then paddled dugout canoes, then waded through swamps pulling boats behind us à la Humphrey Bogart. Then, when we finally reached the end of the earth, suffocating in the dense greenery and isolation of the Amazon, ready to do a light story on leaf-cutter ants and freshwater dolphins, we discovered the unexpected: something just shy of a shooting war was stirring in the Cuyabeno. Beleaguered forest Indians were using dynamite detonation wire as clotheslines. Rogue oil explorers—from whom the dynamite came—were muscling in illegally on the reserve, lurking behind every tree. Oil production would obliterate the forest, and the Indians, it turned out, were backed into a corner with nowhere left to run. They were making a last stand. A showdown was in the works.

All of which was startling enough even before the Oil Helicopter from Hell swooped down on our canoe that one afternoon, buzzing the water angrily, telling Russell and me, in effect, to split. But just when things couldn't get weirder we heard the rumor about the island up the river where the great white chief lived. The chief was an American, reportedly born and raised among forest Indians, a blowgun hunter since age four, a man gone totally native. With paint on his face and wild-boar eyeteeth around his neck, this bushed-out Caucasian was leading the Indian campaign to keep the oil intruders out. The name Kurtz settled over my mind like equatorial heat when I heard this. I saw a malarial dream of a man. Conrad's antihero fast-forwarded to the late twentieth century.

But Russell and I refused to track the rumor down. The whole jungle situation, in fact, had too many markings of a great news story, so we did the only appropriate thing: we ignored it completely. I went back to Quito when the nature tour ended, leaving Russell behind only to get a few more tree shots. And that's when, inside my head, the whisper started. A voice from my newspaper past. "Find Kurtz," it kept saying. "Find Kurtz." I smote my palm against my temple a few times until word reached Quito that the white chief, back in the jungle, was taking hostages now as part of his crusade. The whisper grew louder. "What are you waiting for, pal? Go on. This ain't no page-20 house fire. Get the story. Find Kurtz. *Find* him!"

And the next thing I knew I was back on the Hercules, pink cotton in my ears, José by my side. I was on my way back. Back to the forest, back to the Indians, back to find Russell, back to find the oil explorers. Back to find Kurtz.

But first, God, the Hercules had to land. We had to find the airstrip. José was still staring, mouth open, out the window. The cockpit conversation was still crackling in my ears. "*Mierda!*" one pilot said. "Let's turn around! Turn around! Try west! Too far this direction!" I learned later that, by the end, there were six crew members and two civilians crammed cheek by jowl in the cockpit, all searching the ground for the butter-knife runway. I had the sudden urge to add my own voice to the black box — "Goodbye, Mom. Goodbye, Dad. I love you, Sis" — when at last the cockpit words hit my ears: "There it is! There it is! There it is!"

Never in my life have I been in a plane that maneuvered so sharply. It banked and dropped like an arrow to the earth, racing madly for the 1500-foot asphalt strip before clouds swallowed it up again. José made his way back to his seat and put on his earphones. I stuffed cotton into my ears, and the plane landed herky jerky on the tarmac, coming to rest, finally, dead still, in the middle of the jungle.

There's a growing consensus among environmentalists that the only way to save what's left of the Amazon rain forest, now on an express train to oblivion, is to make it pay. You have to treat the forest as a sustainable, commercial resource. Rubber tapping instead of ranching. Herb harvesting instead of homesteading. And tourism. Open the door to bird-watchers and adventure freaks. Let in the people who bring binoculars, not chain saws; people who pay top dollar just to look. There's even a word for it now: eco-tourism, or, if you prefer, eco-tripping. It's a new sort of drug experience, recreational in form, more expensive than acid but easier on the cerebral cortex.

Which is how this whole knotted jungle yarn got its start. To begin at the beginning is to begin with that idea, eco-tripping. When, after months of wanting to visit South America, Russell and I learned that Metropolitan Touring, an Ecuadorian company, had begun offering eco-trips into a remote portion of the Amazon, we signed up, wheedling a freelance assignment from an editor in New York. It was nothing too complicated. Just flora and fauna in pictures and prose. We would have fun while being part of the rain forest solution — paying customers. Trouble was the last thing we were looking for. We just wanted to trip a little, ecologically. So we packed our bags, issued our goodbyes, and went off.

The tour began, simply enough, on the banks of the Aguarico River, a moderate-size river flowing down from the Andes and snaking its way into the jungle near Ecuador's borders with Colombia and Peru. Backpacks in tow, after having flown 2800 miles in the past thirty-six hours, Russell and I arrived at the Aguarico with a small group of other travelers. We hopped into aging wooden boats with outboard motors and settled in for the seven-hour journey to our initial base camp.

That first day on the river, moving farther and farther into the forest, was truly an exquisite experience, replete with the sense of being gradually and lastingly dipped into the unknown. As Russell and I did not yet know fully of the oil-and-Indian pyrotechnics about to greet us up ahead, we were able to enjoy with a touch of innocence and equanimity the wonderland unfolding before our eyes. Against a backdrop of mammoth, cottony kapok trees, we began to spy a greater variety of birds every hour than we had probably seen in our entire lives combined. The occasional Quechua Indian huts along the shore, meanwhile, grew fewer and fewer the farther we traveled, eventually disappearing altogether, leaving only river and forest and sky. "I'm in the Amazon," I kept wanting to say over and over to no one in particular as howler monkeys staged vine acrobatics to our right and a sixty-pound peccary—bristle-haired and searching for mauritia fruit—emerged on a muddy bank to our left.

Roberto, our bearded twenty-two-year-old guide with scars on his hands from a slew of scary jungle accidents, was pointing out these gems one by one from the stern as I took notes. Meanwhile, Steve, a nature photographer from Colorado, was taking pictures, and each time I looked he seemed to be urgently reloading his film. This made me nervous because *my* photographer, Russell, was behaving the way he always did on assignments. He was doing nothing. Just hanging out. Dallying serenely.

"What about the monkeys, Russell?" I said finally, deciding to act. "Wouldn't they make a nice shot?"

In his own way Russell was as exotic as anything on the river. He was a hulking, befreckled redhead from Brooklyn who wore shaded eyeglasses and a backward-facing baseball cap and a baggy pair of shorts that hung like knickers to his knees, resting above bulky, overworn hiking boots. My question about photographs seemed to irritate him. He squinted his eyes at the shore, then at the sun, then at the shore again.

"The light's not right," he said flatly, turning back to me.

It was Russell's pat response to such situations, revealing his approach to photography, which was like that of a master surfer. Let others ride the duds. Only when the light was just right, when the perfect wave was cresting right before him, did he make a move. Until then his mind stayed mostly on his favorite subject: fishing. Russell had many gods, and they all had fins. He asked Roberto if the armored catfish of this region would hit a spinner. He asked Roberto if a fly rod was of any use against piranha.

I gave up and went back to watching birds. After two hours my list of sightings was getting quite long, ranging from a pair of boat-billed herons to a red-capped cardinal to a lesser kiskadee flycatcher.

Just then, up ahead, another animal came into view. This one was in the water, weighing a hundred tons, and it was coming straight at us. It was a boat, actually, a floating hotel, a Fitzcaraldo mirage of jungle comfort put together piece by piece on the Napo River and then piloted all the way up the Aguarico to this spot by Metropolitan Touring. As the boat grew closer, Roberto explained that those twenty rooms on three decks were designed for the semirugged jet-set crowd, for people who like to fly in and absorb nature's savagery from a sundeck, drink in hand.

At Roberto's suggestion we tied up alongside the boat and climbed aboard, stretching our legs on the deck and peeing in flush toilets. Sensing this was our last brush with modernity, Russell offered to stand me a drink at the top-deck bar. Afterward, we decided to order a bottle of whiskey for the road. Without blinking, the bartender said, "One bottle, seventy-eight dollars." Supplies were very expensive this far into the jungle, he added. Russell let loose a long gasp at this. Forget the macaws screeching overhead. Forget the evil-eyed caymans (alligators) along the shore. It was whiskey at $78 a bottle that let him know just how far from Brooklyn — or anyplace else — he really was. We told the bartender no and returned to the river.

It took four more hours to reach Zancudo, the isolated and tumbledown Ecuadorian military outpost from which we would set off on foot. A two-hour hike through the forest lay ahead, then a canoe trip across Iripari Lake to our camp.

A doctor was waiting for us at Zancudo. Her name was Dorys, a pretty twenty-seven-year-old Ecuadorian wearing tall rubber boots and a no-nonsense frown. Dorys was a walking first-aid station, hired to protect us from the myriad hazards of this jungle place so far from telephones and hospitals. Those hazards included poisonous frogs and scorpions and, of course, snakes — bushmasters, anacondas, water snakes. I asked Dorys what antivenins she carried.

"I don't use antivenins," she said. "This is better."

She reached into her kit to produce an ominous black "stun gun," the sort people back in Brooklyn use against muggers, Russell pointed out. Dorys pulled the trigger and a blue jag of electricity crackled between the terminal heads — 20,000 volts. Applied to the skin, this slowed the spread of venom long enough to allow a chance to get to a Quito hospital. But the blast treatment was very, very painful, Dorys admitted, and I began to wish we'd coughed up the $78 for whiskey.

The hike through the forest, with Roberto up front and Dorys in the rear, was long and tiresome and sweaty and wonderful. Now that we were off the river, seeing things up close, a

Byzantine universe of Amazon insects came into focus. Leaf-cutter ants streamed across the trail, hurrying toward vast subterranean cities. A gigantic moth, delicate despite its size, lighted on Roberto's shoulder, its wings presenting an exact replica of an owl's face, a trick on would-be predators. And just as we were getting hungry, Roberto led us to a species of lemon tree covered with millions of tiny black ants. The tree and the ants were linked in a complex symbiotic relationship, but more intriguing was the ants' surprising culinary allure. With a wetted finger, Roberto withdrew a few dozen of the insects, popping them into his mouth. The rest of us followed suit, making a small snack of the ants—lemony, through and through—as the sun set and a gentle shower of snowlike cotton fell to our shoulders from a nearby kapok tree.

It was almost dark by the time we reached Iripari Lake to canoe across its glassy water to the camp on the far shore. The camp was a collection of sturdy thatch-roof huts built for Metropolitan Touring by Quechua Indians. Each hut, Roberto explained, was constructed with a special forest tree harvested only at night by the light of a full moon—a Quechua superstition ensuring extra durability. Sleek rectangular solar panels, ferried in by canoe, lay in startling juxtaposition atop each grass roof, feeding batteries that powered small lightbulbs below. This was, after all, an eco-tour. No machinery, no generators, no engines allowed.

I fell asleep that night to the sound of the forest, nothing more.

Soft shafts of amber light streamed through my window, filtering through my mosquito net, reaching my eyes and waking me the next morning. I looked outside. The sun, a stunning fireball, was barely above the trees on the far shore. Just as stunning was the sight of Russell's tripod and camera set up outside, facing the lake. Russell himself was nowhere in evidence, though. He had taken a few sunrise shots, gotten irritated somehow by the quality of the light, and reached for his fly rod instead. Sighing, I fell back to bed, listening to the morning operetta of a hundred different birds and the gentle rhythms—swoosh, swoosh, plunk; swoosh, swoosh, plunk—of Russell's expert fly casting somewhere in the distance.

After a leisurely morning observing pygmy marmosets dangling from vines around camp, we all sat down to lunch and Roberto promptly held environmental court. By definition, most eco-tours have as their objective more than just taking travelers to see pretty things in hard-to-reach places. The point is to educate along the way, to hold forth on the sundry man-made hazards that directly imperil all that's on display.

The overriding environmental threat in Ecuador, of course, was oil. That much I already knew. The jungle oil boom around Lago Agrio, to the northwest, had spread over the years to devastate vast portions of Ecuador's forest. When, in 1975, Metropolitan Touring organized nature trips along the Napo River to the south, that area was largely untouched except for a population of forest Indians living in a virtual state of nature. But then came oil: seismic testing, wells, a pipeline, roads, settlers. Today, seventeen years later, most of the area along the Napo is a rambling ruin of cleared squares and fenced-in rectangles, a checkerboard wasteland. In disgust and defeat, Metropolitan abandoned the Napo altogether in 1990.

The tragedy of this wholesale butchery is made worse, Roberto pointed out, by the uniqueness of Ecuador's rain forest. Indeed, for all the hymns sung to Brazil's magnificent forest, it is less well known that for sheer richness, for variety and diversity of life in a concentrated area, the small portion of the Amazon Basin in eastern Ecuador, southern Colombia, and northern Peru is the continent's true crown jewel, a mecca of biodiversity. It may be the presence of volcanic soil from the Andes, but whatever the reason, this dense forest within a forest is a veritable candy store of tropical plants and animals and insects heaped atop one another—layer upon layer—in ways found nowhere in Brazil. If it makes sense, consequently, to save any one part of the Amazon, this is the place.

Which is why, in 1990, conservationists hired by Metropolitan pulled out a map and drew a wide circle around the lower Aguarico River, around a forest called Cuyabeno—one of the last great stretches of wilderness still untouched by oil and settlement in Ecuador. And this time there would be protection. With lobbying pressure from Indian rights groups, international environmental organizations, and Metropolitan itself, the government of Ecuador in May 1991 established the 1.5-million-acre Lower Cuyabeno Wildlife Reserve, a place off-limits—on paper at least—to everyone except tourists, scientists, and indigenous Indians. The park was heralded internationally as perhaps Ecuador's last and best chance to save part of its exceptional forest.

It was midafternoon by the time Roberto wrapped up his history of the reserve. Russell, who had been listening from a nearby hammock, swinging softly with his boots propped up, had just bolted off to chase Helena, the camp's burly semitame pet tapir. Vaguely pig-shaped in appearance, Helena was a gentle insect eater who also happened to have a sappy soft spot for human beings. Like an oversized puppy starving for attention, she kept loping into camp from the forest and stealing Russell's baseball cap, giving it a light chew each time. She had his cap again now and Russell was gone.

Meanwhile, pouring another glass of water, Roberto returned to the subject of the reserve, and I asked him if he thought the new protected status would succeed in keeping oil exploration away forever. He wasn't sure, he said. There were known oil deposits all along the park's perimeter, and no one pretended to think there was no oil *inside* in the reserve. Less than a month after the park's inception a seismic testing crew had been spotted near the border at Zancudo. Two months after that Indians in one village found dynamite detonation wire inside the park. The Indians confiscated the wire and were using it to make clotheslines. Petroecuador, the national oil company that from the start had opposed the park's establishment, was now saying publicly that it would stay clear of Lower Cuyabeno. But way out here in the park itself, way out here so far from Quito, things were shaping up differently.

The situation was worse than Roberto admitted that first day—much worse. If Russell and I had come seeking only flora and fauna in pictures and prose, we had chosen an exceptionally bad time to do so. A showdown—approaching for months and involving Metropolitan Touring and the local Indians and crews of unscrupulous oil explorers—was about to reach the shoving and kicking stage. It would begin the very next day.

Dr. Dorys, Roberto, Russell, and I were on Iripari Lake when it happened, paddling in canoes. It was late afternoon and we were bird-watching, taking in another superlative dose of biodiversity. Below us in the lake's black water swam manatee and caymans and piranha of several different varieties. All the while

Roberto kept telling us to keep one eye on the muddy shoreline where jaguar prints were visible from time to time.

It was then that we heard the sound, first a hum in the distance, then a growing rumble, then a shattering shriek as the helicopter burst over the tree line. It came out of nowhere, circling the small lake once before spotting us. Within seconds the helicopter was hovering directly overhead, seventy-five feet up, the blades causing ripples on the water. "*Dios mío!*" Roberto shouted above the noise, looking up. "Stay seated everyone! Don't move!" With its bulbous windshield eyes and long mechanical tail, the helicopter had a giant dragonfly look. It stared down at us, creating the effect somehow that we, vulnerable below, were its prey, tiny ants on water.

"It's an oil helicopter!" Roberto cried against the sound of blades. "I've seen it before near Tarapoa. They know they're not supposed to be here, those bastards!" Roberto waved the helicopter away with his hand, but it stayed. I looked at Russell, who had brought none of his cameras, just his fly rod. I wanted suddenly to throw him to the caymans below.

For about a minute the helicopter stayed fixed overhead, long enough for my goose bumps to grow taller with the realization that this oil-versus-reserve business was no damn game. Not in the Amazon, a place long known for its frontier law and violent endings. Nervously, I wondered if the pilots up there were packing guns. But then, just as suddenly, the helicopter banked and flew away, disappearing. The lake was quiet again. There had been no direct communication whatsoever, not even a wave from the pilots.

"It's intimidation," Roberto said, angrily turning the canoe back to camp now. "They know what they're doing. They're telling us to leave, to clear out, because they're coming in. It's bad. This is very, very bad."

That night, in the camp's main pavilion, we gathered under a bare solar-powered bulb and the atmosphere was subdued. With an incongruous lack of fanfare, Roberto did something no one anticipated. He pulled out a detailed map of Lower Cuyabeno park. The map had been given to him during his last visit to Quito, obtained secretly by Metropolitan officials with contacts at Petroecuador. Afraid it would alarm us, he had decided not to show it to us the day before. But now he unfurled it on the table, and when I finally realized what I was looking at I recoiled.

There, running through the heart of the park, stretching out all along the banks of the Aguarico, were thousands of markings for dynamite placements. Virtually every region of the park had been turned into a grid of lines, with Xs spaced every one hundred meters for detonations that would give a seismic reading of any oil deposits below. One line of explosions, according to the map, would run within thirty meters of this very camp. This piece of paper explained everything, the helicopter visit, the detonation wire, and the seismic testing crew near Zancudo. The oil people *were* coming. It was happening now. To hell with the reserve.

"So what are you going to do?" I asked Roberto anxiously, still feeling tremors of shock as I handed the map back to him.

He had already radioed Metropolitan's Quito office about the helicopter incident, he said. Letters would go out immediately to the Minister of Forestry, Petroecuador, and environmental groups. Some sort of legal action was also possible, perhaps a last-minute injunction preventing exploration.

But Diego, Roberto's assistant guide, was shaking his head as Roberto spoke. Diego had been mostly silent since the helicopter incident. He lacked the look of fighting determination still remaining in Roberto's eyes. "No," Diego said, lowering his gaze to the dusty plank floor. "It's over. Nothing's going to stop these oil people now. What happened on the Napo River is going to happen here. I know it will."

Of all the emotions crowding Diego's face at that moment, the most dominant was anger. He turned to me, the American, and boiled over.

"I'll tell you what I think," he said. "I think it's funny how everyone in your country looks down here at rain forest destruction and thinks, How could all those ignorant people tear up such a beautiful place and kill all those animals and make all those medically valuable plants extinct, and then have nothing but a big desert left afterwards? That's the way they think, isn't it?"

I didn't answer. Diego didn't give me a chance.

"But you see what the problem is here in Ecuador?" he went on. "It's oil. We're trying to protect this forest by using it for tours, to let it earn money without being destroyed. But oil is more valuable. Our country needs oil to pay its debt to your banks. Your country needs oil because everyone has two cars.

So my question is, who's really destroying the Cuyabeno forest, Ecuadorians or Americans?"

It was a fair and obvious question, and during the long discussion that eventually followed I did nothing to challenge Diego's conclusion of where the real problem lay. When all the bizarre plots and subplots had played themselves out in the jungle, the final story was rather simple: entire ecosystems were being obliterated in northwest South America to keep shopping-mall parking lots full in Chicago.

But Roberto, for now, was less interested in grand analyses than in sticking to the specific subplot at hand: the growing threat of seismic testing in Cuyabeno. As it turned out, our knowledge of the situation was incomplete. Roberto had until now failed to mention one of the last, key weapons in the fight to keep oil out. "And what's funny," he said, glancing significantly at Diego, "is that weapon happens to be a gringo. He's a man from North America."

It was then that Russell and I learned for the first time about Randy Borman. For the past two days we had seen and heard a lot of unusual things, our imaginations stretched in many directions. But the moment Roberto began describing Randy Borman I wondered even more just what sort of true-life novel we had stumbled into.

According to Roberto, Randy was a thirty-six-year-old Caucasian living on an island up the river, presiding as chief over a band of Cofán Indians. Born in the jungle to American missionary parents, Randy had grown up in virtually every manner like a Cofán, speaking the language, hunting with blowguns. The Cofán were true forest people, not Andean immigrants like the Quechua. They decorated themselves with face paint and flower bracelets, and wore macaw feathers pierced through their noses. In 1981, when his parents ended their forest missionary work, Randy decided to stay behind. And in 1984, when oil production by Texaco Oil had decimated the Cofán's homeland near Dureno to the west, Randy led a band of Cofán Indians to the isolated lower Aguarico. Now the Indians had nowhere else to go. They had migrated once to escape oil and their backs were up against the Peruvian border. As perhaps the only Indian chief in South American history with deep knowledge of both Western and Indian ways, Randy had so far proven adept at defending Cofán rights, and he was instrumental in helping establish the new Cuyabeno reserve. Now, with oil threatening everything again, he wasn't about to yield quietly, Roberto said.

"But what is he?" I asked Roberto, trying to get a better fix on this man. "Is Randy an Indian or an American or both or what?"

"He's an Indian," Roberto said. "He's white like you and speaks English. But he lives in a village and hunts animals and up here"—Roberto pointed to his head—"he's really Cofán, I think."

I have to admit that I was so taken by the Conrad-esque implications of all this that sleep came to me slowly that night, postponed by flights of imagination. It crossed my mind to visit this man myself, to see firsthand what sounded like an honest-to-god Kurtz figure alive and well on the shank end of the twentieth century, digging in at his own final station. But it also sounded, at second blush, a little too much like a news story for my taste and for that of Russell. We just weren't the investigative types. Period. No apologies. Besides, Roberto the very next morning was adamant in saying the tour should go on as planned, with no detours. Despite the awful seismic map and the helicopter scare and everything else, there was much, much more wildlife to see and he intended to show it to us.

Thus instructed, I strung my binoculars around my neck, pulled out my bird- and plant-life guidebooks, and, without too much fuss, let the idea of finding Kurtz pass from my mind.

A long morning of travel took us to our second base camp that next day, situated near the Peruvian border. We began in canoes, leaving Iripari Lake via a swampy blackwater creek. Diego was pointing out a series of strange trails left on the shore's edge by bushmaster snakes when our canoes began to snag and falter in the swampy creek.

"Get out and push," Roberto ordered in frustration. "Don't worry. The piranha only bite if you're already bleeding. Jump in."

With a splash, Russell and I obeyed. Water and mud rose up to our hips. Rechristening our canoe the Amazon Queen, I pushed and pulled and grunted until my legs quivered with exhaustion and my arms were covered with the prickly bites of dozens of tiny black spiders.

Later, paddling again, we reached the Aguarico, then took a left on the Lagarto Cocha, a blackwater river separating Ecuador from Peru. We gratefully reached our second base camp without seeing a single sign of more oil-crew activity. This camp—again a collection of modest huts—was on a lagoon called Imuya, abutting the Peruvian border.

Too tired for bird-watching, Roberto, Russell, and I deposited our gear and went down to the lagoon's murky water to fish for piranha. For bait, Roberto brought a bag of raw beef chunks cut into cubes, pilfered from Manuel, the tour cook. Roberto and I used his gear: bundles of old fishing line wrapped around sticks like kite string. We loaded our hooks and slung them into the water. "You know," I said to Russell, who was using his fly rod next to me, "I don't think I've ever fished with beef chunks before."

Roberto got the first bite almost immediately, pulling in his line hand over hand. The two-pound piranha that landed on shore had beady eyes and reddish scales and teeth just as you imagine: upper and lower rows like the pointy edges of a sharp, lethal saw. It took five crushing blows from a canoe paddle to kill it and finally end the awful reflex snapping of those jaws.

I caught the second piranha. Like Roberto's, mine arrived bleeding from fresh, gaping bite wounds on its back and sides. The wounds, Roberto explained, were inflicted by other piranha in the water who mercilessly cannibalize their struggling, vulnerable peers as they're being reeled to shore.

Russell had yet to make a catch, and in a move both bonkers and highly typical of him, he decided to wade into the water for better reach with his fly rod. Roberto assured him it was okay as long as there were no cuts or sores on his legs. But I was nearly hyperventilating, glancing at Russell's succulent calves and thighs submerged just feet away from where I was pulling in a second and third chomping monster. When at last Russell made his own catch he was so elated and proud he took the piranha and, before it was cleaned for cooking, had its jaws removed to wear on a string around his neck. There the jaws stayed the rest of the trip, large and awe-inspiring, a toothy jungle trophy dangling just below his now jungle-worn baseball cap.

Still, it was with a note of melancholy that Russell and I prepared for bed that night. Try as we might, neither of us could shake off the implications of Roberto's awful map. In our minds we kept hearing dynamite explosions, thousands and thousands of them, following the seismic Xs spread all over that morose piece of paper. Was it already too late for any other outcome? we wondered. Could Roberto and Randy and the river Indians really find a way, at the last minute, to save this irreplaceable place from oil and its attendant settlers? Or was it all in reality just one big, elaborate joke; the idea of forests as sustainable resources—of eco-tourism and all the rest—having arrived far too late in the path of steamrolling Western cupidity to make a difference?

That night, for the first time on the trip, I had trouble sleeping. When finally I drifted off it was to the sound of a lonely guitar being strummed somewhere in the distance. It was a Quechua Indian, one of Roberto's assistants, singing a Spanish love ballad. The song was soft and sad and full of long, slow moans that broke my heart into a thousand pieces.

My last day in the jungle was a blur of arduous travel and fast, strange developments. The plan was to go by motorboat all the way up the Aguarico and reach the Tarapoa airstrip by afternoon. Along the way we would drop Russell off at the Fitzcaraldo riverboat near Zancudo. So much fishing had left him a little short of photographs for the magazine piece. He would stay on the big boat a few days, getting forest shots from the top deck, while I waited in Quito.

"Now remember," I said as Russell clambered onto the riverboat deck, reaching back for his tripod from Roberto. "Just pictures. No fishing. Please don't fish, Russell."

He agreed, but with a throaty chuckle refused all offers to carry his rods back to Quito for good measure.

The rest of us pushed on. We had barely traveled another mile upriver when, with great excitement, Diego began shouting across our small boat to Roberto, pointing to something on the left riverbank. The moment Roberto saw the thing in question, he pounded his fist against a gunwale.

"What?" I asked Roberto. "What is it?"

"See that clearing on the shore over there?" he said. "It's a heliport for the oil people. Indians don't make clearings like that. We know the style. We saw those on the Napo. It's for helicopters to land, and it's *inside* the park."

The clearing had not existed five days earlier during our trip in. Roberto very carefully memorized the location on the river: more information to radio back to Quito. The situation was escalating.

And more was in store. I was already airborne inside the Hercules, having said goodbye to Roberto and Diego on the Tarapoa tarmac, when Pedro, a Metropolitan guide heading back to Quito, took a seat by my side. The first thing he said to me was, "Can you believe what happened to Randy Borman and the Cofán?"

I sat up in my chair. "Believe what happened to them?"

"You mean you didn't hear? They took hostages last night. One of the Cofán on the river told us. They found a seismic testing crew in the forest near their village and they're holding them as hostages to keep the oil people out of the park."

Immediately, I wanted off the plane. I wanted to go back. Hostages? Really? Now this was something too big for even the likes of Russell and me to ignore. But the Hercules was well into the air by then. The Aguarico was getting smaller and smaller outside my window.

That night in Quito I spent long, restless hours trying to decide what to do. Should I really go back? Was the hostage story true? Did this guy Randy, this Kurtz figure, really exist or was he, as almost seemed the case, some sort of bizarre forest myth dreamed up by the Cofán, a great white protector spirit hovering only in the upper branches of a few superstitious minds?

But a Quito newspaper settled everything the next morning. The hostage story had filtered into the capital. A back-page article said twenty-three oil workers hired by Petroecuador had been detained for twenty-four hours and released without harm by Cofán Indians and their chief—there it was in print—Randy Borman. The Indians were protecting their land against oil exploration, the article said. Immediately, I put down the paper and booked a flight back to Tarapoa.

Which is when the Hercules got lost. It got lost in a storm, in the clouds, above the trees, its radio equipment down. While José stared out the side window, scanning the ground, I listened in stark terror to the cockpit communication until, finally, we dive-bombed in a panic to the airstrip and the ordeal ended. I wobbled off the plane and set out to find the Cofán.

Russell was very surprised to see me on the Aguarico again. He was also a bit disappointed, having planned to stalk mountain trout in the Andes that weekend. I convinced him to change his plans.

"This man Randy, whoever he is, has taken hostages, Russell. Grab your equipment."

A guide named Philippe offered his services, and the next thing we knew we were in a canoe pulling up to a village on an island near where Sabalo Creek flows into the Aguarico. Philippe told us to stay in the canoe while he went ashore to find Randy. The Cofán weren't expecting us and things had been tense the past few days. Philippe returned ten minutes later accompanied by a man who—in some ways, at least—could have just as easily sashayed right out of a Des Moines cafe: white skin, blue eyes, thick mustache, baseball cap. But there were differences—profound ones. Randy was barefoot and wore the thin, gownlike cotton garment typical of the other Cofán men standing around him. He was also holding a blue-headed parrot in his calloused hands, one he had found lame in the forest and was nursing back to health.

"So you're journalists?" Randy said to Russell and me in perfect American English, handing the parrot to a child. "We don't get many journalists here, but I think we might need you now. Can you stay with us overnight?"

Russell and I looked at Philippe, who agreed to return the next afternoon to pick us up. Some men were gathering rocks along the riverbank to build a village well, and Randy, their leader, asked them in rapid Cofán to prepare a guest hut for us.

Now that I was finally in the presence of this chief, fascinated by him in every way, I had to overcome the urge to ask a thousand different questions all at once. I focused instead on the immediate situation.

"So what happened with the oil crew the other day, Randy? Did your village really detain them?"

He waved his hand in the air at this. "We'll discuss all that later," he said. "It's a long story. First I have some fishnets I need to check. Want to come?"

We said yes, very much, and off we went, heading in a canoe up narrow Sabalo Creek. Whatever crisis had come with the oil crew, whatever sword of Damocles hovered over this Cofán world, it didn't seem to matter at that moment. The sky had broken clear, the sun was shining bright, and some fishnets some-where needed checking.

Randy's Cofán brother-in-law, Alonzo, a short man with deep brown skin and flowing black hair, joined us. Along the way, Randy and I talked. He confirmed what I had already heard, that he had been born to missionary parents and had spent almost all his years in the forest. After taking a Cofán wife a few years back and fathering two children, he had made a final deci-sion never to leave. Never.

Alonzo tied the canoe to a bank, and we set off through the forest toward what Randy called his favorite fishing lagoon. With nimble hands, Randy began gathering leaves and vines with which to carry whatever fish we caught. I asked him if checking the nets was a routine, something he did every day at this time. As I spoke, I noticed the only thing on his left wrist was a collection of colorful glass bead bracelets.

"Time?" Randy said, looking at me rather puzzled. "No, there's no set time for this. We just do it. When you're hungry you check your nets or you hunt a peccary. You just do it. There aren't schedules for anything here. Sometimes the whole village loses track of what day of the week it is and we have to have a meeting just to try to figure out what it is."

As I listened to Randy say this, and watched him pick another leaf in the process, I felt myself drifting deeper and deeper into one of the strangest cross-cultural experiences of my life. I was beginning to feel seriously off balance around this man. Forget the Des Moines face and the American accent. This guy was dif-ferent — foreign. He wasn't like me. Being with him was like watching a poorly dubbed movie: what you're seeing and what you're getting don't match up. It was more than just Randy's comment about time. The difference was there in his use of mostly simple sentences, in the grace and ease with which he moved through the forest, without shoes, picking leaves. Written all over both Randy and Alonzo was a demeanor of utter open-ness and guilelessness I've learned to associate only with very traditional people in developing countries.

Alonzo plucked two peacock bass from the lagoon nets and Randy began wrapping them up. I decided to ask Randy about his knowledge of medicinal plants. "I know a few," he said. "Maybe fifty or sixty that I use a lot. But don't ask me the scien-tific names because I don't have a clue."

He added that his knowledge in this realm was marginal compared to other Cofán. Everyone in the village had a particular expertise. For some it was medicinal plants, for others basket weaving, for others spearfishing.

"What's your expertise?" I asked him.

Randy thought for a second. "Blowguns," he said. "I probably make some of the best blowguns."

We returned to the village and went to Randy's house. Though decidedly rough-hewn, his was the largest house in the village and the only one with a tin roof. Randy's wife, Amelia, twenty-two years old and beautiful and breast-feeding a baby, began gathering plantains to accompany the fish.

"I wouldn't say they were hostages," Randy said, finally turning to the subject of the seismic oil crew as we settled onto the porch. "It was more like an arrest situation. We arrested them."

As he shifted to this serious matter, Randy simultaneously began doing a few odd chores. He pulled out a bundle of long knives, sharpening each one on a whetstone, stroking back and forth.

"One of our people saw the crew workers on the river. They were clearing one of our banana fields for a heliport. I showed up with six men behind me. I was prepared to go back and get more men and maybe an unloaded shotgun if necessary. But it wasn't. We asked the workers if they knew they were inside the reserve. They said yes. We asked them if they had permission from the Minister of Forestry. They said they weren't sure. So we told them they had to put down their equipment and come with us to the village. They didn't resist. We gave them a place to camp, and the next morning they got a radio message from their superiors in Quito telling them to evacuate, they didn't have permits. They got in their boats and we waved goodbye and they left."

Everyone was greatly relieved by the outcome, Randy said. It was, in the end, a rather gentle, Cofán-style operation—with results. But would it work the next time? I wondered. Surely there would be a next time.

"Enforcing the laws of this park is our only hope," Randy said. "So it's got to work the next time. The reserve's charter explicitly forbids the import of explosives or toxic chemicals of any kind. We may not have a title to this land, but we have legal standing within the charter to do what we did."

Now that the conversation had turned to oil, an entirely different side of Randy was emerging, and it was fascinating to watch. It was the side of him nurtured in a Quito high school and honed by a few years of college in the States. His mind, out of abrupt necessity, was making a sharp Western turn right before our eyes.

"The problem," he continued, "is that there are conflicting laws here. The Ministry of Energy and Mines claims a theoretical legal right to drill wherever it wants to. The Ministry of Agriculture, on the other hand, has set up laws to safeguard this forest. Then there's the economic pressure to drill. It's enormous. And no money is being spent to enforce park laws. So we have to be the stewards. We have to uphold our set of laws."

It sounded like a tall order given all the circumstances, I said.

"Maybe it is," he replied. "But the least we can do is get delays. We can force the workers to get permits, if they can. Then we'll push for an environmental impact study. Then we'll use the time we gain to publicize the issue, to get more Ecuadorians and foreigners to realize that after ten years of pumping you don't have oil *or* a forest."

And what if the delays and the publicity don't work and encroachment continues?

"Then we'll draw a line," Randy said emphatically. "There are no other pristine areas left for us to go to. We have to draw the line *here*."

Did that mean, in the end, resorting to violence? Was that a real possibility?

A silence fell and Randy's face hardened when I asked this. He was still sharpening his knives, checking one now by running his thumb along the blade in a way that almost made me fear he was cutting himself.

"No," he said finally. "The lesson has been learned abundantly well by the Indians of Latin America: you can't fight Western encroachment physically. We have to stay within the spirit of the law. I wouldn't rule out some sort of civil disobedience, though. Definitely not. Sitting in front of bulldozers or something."

Randy decided to backtrack at this point. He described how seven years ago he had led this group of Cofán to the Cuyabeno forest. Four years after that he was officially voted chief. Two years after that, as chief, he helped secure establishment of the reserve, the clan's dream.

He pointed out that in the year 1500 there were an estimated 15,000 Cofán Indians in the Amazon rain forest. By the 1930s, because of the introduction of European diseases, that number was down to an astonishing 350. Today, a majority of the surviving members live in Dureno, surrounded by the Texaco oil boom, succumbing to a familiar Indian pattern: youth flight to the cities, rampant alcoholism, cultural disintegration. The Cuyabeno Cofán, eighteen families in all, were some of the few remaining members living the basic forest life of their ancestors. Thousands of years of cultural knowledge rested on their survival. And their survival rested on an intact forest.

I decided to push things still further. "Let's say civil disobedience doesn't work," I said to Randy, "and the testing and drilling start."

"If it doesn't work, then we'll have no choice but to just watch and hope and pray they don't find oil or that the oil is of a poor quality not worth extracting. In the end it may come down to that: luck."

And if the luck is bad, if the oil turns out to be good, and all the destruction kicks in?

Randy didn't rush to answer the question. "I don't allow myself to think that way," he said. "I just don't. I guess we've come too far now. We've tried too hard for us to imagine the worst really happening. We've just tried too hard."

An unmistakable note of sadness, laced with foreboding, infused his last sentence. It hung on the porch like the midday heat, threatening to saturate everything until, turning away, Randy suggested we walk down to the river.

Reaching the riverbank, Randy squatted down. With one of his just sharpened knives he began cleaning a very large fish speared earlier by his father-in-law, Alfonso. I sat on a stone next to Randy, and our talk continued, turning more personal. Despite the language and the dress and the cultural knowledge, I asked him if he ever felt a little odd, a little out of place, living this way day to day as the Caucasian chief of a clan of forest Indians. Was perhaps part of it some sort of Western fantasy come true? A way of dropping out along Robinson Crusoe lines? Or did he really feel legitimate? Really feel authentic?

His answer came without hesitation. "The only reason I'm chief here is because these people absolutely see me as a Cofán. That's the only test that matters. Many of them were my childhood friends. I grew up with them. And as long as I'm one of them in *their* eyes and they want me as their leader, then that's enough for me. The rest of the world can say whatever it wants.

"And it's not a fantasy," he went on. "I don't wake up in the morning thinking, Wow, this sure is better than being a lawyer in Pittsburgh, or anything like that. I usually wake up thinking about the fishnet I need to mend that day or the banana field I need to clean. It's not that romantic.

"But to be honest, for many years, when I was younger, I don't think I really knew who I was or what I was. I went to a mission grammar school as a kid, while I was spending all my free time with my Cofán friends, doing what they did, growing up like a Cofán, playing in the forest.

"I think it really began to dawn on me just which culture was truly my own when I tried to go to college in the States. I missed the Cofán while I was at Michigan State. I missed the forest. I was also broke, so I did the only thing I knew how to do: I hunted and gathered. My Cofán impulse took over. I had a pellet gun, and I would go out in the morning and kill pigeons and rabbits in other people's yards before dawn. I would cook them and eat them with fruit I gathered, like mulberries and blackberries and damaged apples from orchards. I also had a bicycle, which is how I got a lot of my food. I would ride it around on roads near my house and keep track of road kills every day. Whenever I spotted a fresh road kill I'd pick it up and bring it home and cook it—raccoons and stuff.

"It was a real culture shock. I always felt like a foreigner in the States. Everyone is such a busybody there. No one slows down. I don't think I ever really got the hang of it."

In 1974, after three years of school, Randy returned to Ecuador an "unreformed Cofán." He went back to the forest, living mostly around Dureno until 1984, leading this group here. I asked him what he liked most about Cofán life, what he would miss the most if it ended.

"Sometimes," he said, beginning slowly, "some of the men make expeditions, where we set off in a direction and walk for two or three days, hunting and camping as we go. And the whole time we won't see another human being. Not even the sign of another human being. The whole time. There might be a hill or a rise somewhere and you can climb to the top and look out and see nothing but forest in every direction, as far as you can see.

Just trees—on and on and on. Then we'll come upon something simple, like a waterfall on a small creek. We've never been here before, never seen this waterfall, and it's beautiful. I look at it and I know there are other waterfalls in the world that are bigger and more spectacular. But we're probably the first human beings ever to see this particular one, after thousands and thousands of years. I don't know how to explain that feeling. I guess it's just knowing you live in a huge, huge forest and you live there in a very simple way. That's what I like. There's a joy in that."

The afternoon sun was sinking fast as Randy said this. He had finished cleaning the speared fish and was sitting on the bank, staring out across the waning river light. He had had enough of talking for now. "Come on," he said. "Let's go eat."

After a meal of fish stew, Russell and I retired to the guest hut. The next morning the sky turned cloudy and Russell grew excited. Something about the diffuse light made him eager to shoot pictures.

Randy obliged our request by disappearing into his house and returning in full Cofán costume. He looked positively resplendent with the stripes of red paint across his cheekbones, the flower-laced armbands, and the numerous bead necklaces that hung down across his traditional gown, topped off by one necklace made of nothing but wild boar eyeteeth, thirty in all. Alfonso dressed similarly, adding a long and brightly colored macaw feather that protruded, startlingly, from his pierced nostrils.

We went next to the home of Lorenzo, whose sons and daughters were Randy's godchildren. Burly and good-natured, with a round, full-moon face, Lorenzo sat straddling a hammock, applying face paint and beads and piercing his nose with a macaw feather.

At last everyone was ready. Russell set up his tripod on the riverbank, aiming the camera back toward Lorenzo's long grass hut on stilts. His subjects gathered together. Knowing little Spanish and zero Cofán, Russell promptly employed the same quirky English commands that somehow served him photographing people around the world. "Scrunch in, everybody," he said. "That's it. Scrunch in closer." He was looking through the lens, gesturing with his hands, and everyone was scrunching in.

The Cofán men, with their beads and face paint, stood resolutely tall while children and scrawny dogs and chickens roamed about their bare feet. As I watched all of this from behind Russell's shoulder, taking in the village scene, an unbidden feeling came to me. It came quickly and with inexorable force, like the flow of the Aguarico River fifty feet behind me. I had the distinct, sad sense that Russell and I were recording—had been recording all along, despite Randy's hardbitten words of hope—a world that truly would not be here five years hence. These trees, these houses, these people would be gone if we chose to return later. It was odd, but everything about the village seemed ancient and temporary at the same time, giving the moment the feel of a very old memory even as it was happening. The feeling grew stronger after Russell completed his work.

"Okay, you on the end, perk your chin up some," Russell said, walking around now, organizing a final portrait. "Perk it up a little. That's it." In his soiled hiking boots Russell strode back to the camera, his long hair swinging as he moved, his piranha necklace swinging.

The last shot had been taken when we heard the hum of a motorized canoe on the river. It was Philippe, our guide, coming back to get us. As he stepped ashore, Philippe had an urgent, agitated look on his face. He walked straight toward Randy. "You have to come to Quito tomorrow," he said to the chief. "You have to fly to Quito and hold a press conference."

Philippe quickly explained: During the past few days Petroecuador had begun blitzing the Quito media with lies, telling reporters it had conducted negotiations with the Cofán and had gained the Indians' full permission to explore for oil in the Cuyabeno forest. It was a falsehood so great, so outrageous, that it required Randy and the other Cofán leaders to go directly to the capital to deny everything firsthand. Metropolitan Touring would pay for the trip.

After conferring with Lorenzo and Alfonso, Randy agreed that the three of them would go, taking their families. They would do whatever was needed. The campaign would not be allowed to flag.

So we all left the very next day, settling into boats for the long trip up the Aguarico. The Cofán traveled in style, wearing the same beads and woven headbands and face paint of the day before, the only change being the shoes they put on—reluctantly—for the hard city sidewalks ahead.

At the Tarapoa airstrip, the Hercules was already waiting, its propellers whirring loudly, prepared to go. Russell and I crossed the tarmac with the others, backpacks in tow, notebooks and film stored away as a chronicle of the endangered forest we had come to know and the clash of human wills we'd found in its dense, faraway clutches. Now we were returning home, our tour so brief as to seem nearly a form of voyeurism, a window opened and shut on a people and place we would not soon forget no matter what outcome prevailed.

Lorenzo was first to enter the plane, blood-red macaw feathers rising like horns behind his ears. Then, one by one, the other Cofán followed. Everyone looked grave and expectant and proud at the same time, everyone ready to sit before microphones and TV cameras in the capital, trying to escape one more time—with a white man as their chief—a fate imposed on them by other white men beginning nearly five hundred years before.

Randy's son Philippe, five years old, took my hand as we entered the plane. We took seats side by side, but just before takeoff the rumble of engines frightened him and he pulled free of my grasp, scurrying off in search of his mother. I said goodbye, but he didn't hear me.

Suddenly the plane began to taxi. Everyone buckled in, and bolls of pink cotton were passed around. Then, noisily, too soon, the hulking Hercules flew away, off to Quito, out of the jungle.

AUTHOR'S POSTSCRIPT:

Despite the best efforts of environmental groups and the Cofán themselves, Petroecuador began seismic testing in the Lower Cuyabeno Wildlife Reserve along the Aguarico River within weeks after Russell and I departed in November 1991. To date, no drilling has begun and no roads have penetrated the region, but Petroecuador has designated several areas as potential oil sites within the reserve, and exploratory wells are planned within the next two years. The Cofán, meanwhile, continue to resist in every way feasible, and they have no intention of relocating.

JUMPING INTO THE RAINBOW

by *Richard Wiley*

A Peace Corps Volunteer in Korea in the late sixties, Wiley wrote about that experience in his novel *Festival for Three Thousand Maidens*. He has also lived in Japan, and his PEN/Faulkner Award–winning novel, *Soldier in Hiding*, is set there.

It was this novel that got him safely through Kenya airport customs in the mid-eighties. He had arrived in Nairobi to begin a new job, and the airport customs inspector asked him what was in one of the suitcases coming off the conveyor belt.

"Only clothing, I think. Personal effects."

"Ah ha!" the customs officer said, reaching for the case.

Wiley was asked to open it, and when he did so, though there was indeed a layer of clothing and personal effects, underneath all that was his computer, small and large pieces both, lodged among his shirts and pants.

The customs officer stacked the computer on the bench beside him and began to calculate the duty that was owed.

"But I am a writer," Wiley said. "For me this is personal effects. Without it how will I be able to do my job?"

"Writer? What writer?" the customs man asked.

"You brought this in to sell. You want to double your money every time you come in."

With that, Wiley pulled a copy of his book *Soldier in Hiding* from his briefcase and showed the official his photograph on the back.

"See, that's me," he said. "I wrote this book."

The customs man called a couple of other customs men over to look at the photograph and the book.

"You wrote this?" the man asked. "Using this computer here?"

Wiley smiled broadly. "Yes, I did!" he said. It was the first time he'd ever been publicly recognized as a writer, the first time the book had done him any practical good.

"Okay," said the customs man, "you may take it in. But in order to assure that you take it out again I am writing a note about it in your passport."

Wiley lived in Kenya for two years after that. The note in his passport was long and detailed, but the passport expired before he left Kenya and he got a new one at the U.S. embassy there. The new passport had no note.

When Wiley left Kenya in 1988 he sold his computer and thought, for a while, of the customs man. He doubled his money and was able to buy a better computer when he got home.

I was sitting with my friend David Bartholomew in the bar of the Heron Court Hotel, planning a safari. I had just returned to Nairobi in order to research a novel-in-progress and needed not only to remember the city, but also to travel out of it, to the Masai town of Narok and the farm country north of there. My novel was a mess of early ideas, three hundred pages of long, undisciplined chapters, with no end in sight. I hoped that this trip would bring it into focus, begin to teach me what my book was about.

David, a friend of mine when I'd lived in Nairobi four years before, had been a teacher at the International School for eighteen years. He was thin as a refugee, caustic and brazen, startlingly passionate at odd moments, and avid about photography. He also seemed excited about my research and willing to come along.

"What we need is a car and driver," he said. I had already rented a little Daihatsu Charade, intending simply to travel out of Nairobi in that, but David said it had been raining in the Mara for a week and I wouldn't be able to go off the road. He also told me he had a friend with a safari business and would make a call.

We had been in the Heron Court bar since late that afternoon, and by early evening young women were everywhere, walking about, staring at us, stopping to chat and ask for beer. The

Heron Court is one of the most infamous bars in Nairobi, but for several years now, for these young women at least, business had been slow. AIDS was on everyone's mind, and at the end of each evening most of them went home alone. Many of them, in fact, no longer came to the bar. When I asked a bartender where they had all gone he said, "Back to the village to die."

The bar had a Wild West decor, booths had cloth tops, making them look like covered wagons, and there were Marlboro stickers on the big glass doors. I remembered the place as having been better fitted before, with antlers on the walls and saddles on the stools at the bar, but now, like the girls, even the stools were gone. David and I were sitting in one of the covered wagons with a half dozen girls who pushed us to the wall, smiling whenever we looked their way.

"She is my cousin," said the girl next to me, and when I looked at her she pointed across the table at a young woman on David's side.

Though neither of us had suggested they were not, the other girl immediately spoke up, sternly insisted that they really were cousins, and that they had not seen each other since leaving their village to come to town. "That is why we are celebrating," she said. "What a coincidence!"

The girl sitting next to David was especially beautiful. She worked as a hairstylist during the day, and her cousin, who was far less talkative, worked in an office. By the time an hour passed we had bought several rounds in honor of their accidental meeting, and once David briefly escorted the cousin next to him across the street while she checked on her children. "They are studying," she said, "and I want to tell my neighbor where I am."

As soon as they left, their places in the covered wagon were taken by other young women, breasts straining forward from across the table and from beneath the thin white T-shirts that they wore. Like almost everyone in the bar their eyes projected energy and light, their faces animated and full. Of course I thought of AIDS again. In 1988, 54 percent of the prostitutes in Nairobi were reported to be carrying the disease. The figure came from Nairobi Hospital itself, but whatever the statistic, these girls were the picture of health, most of them unjaded and kind. If they were like lambs to the slaughter, the slaughter was certainly an insidious and well-hidden one. As I looked around I counted at least one hundred women in the bar, laughing and carrying on. One hundred women. Fifty-four of them, then, were infected with HIV. And the figure was four years old.

When David came back he was feeling sad and suggested that we go home. "She's living in this shitty little room with two of the most beautiful kids," he said. "When we got there her son was studying an atlas and I helped him find Kenya and the U.S.A."

The mother of the two children had come back with David and was sitting with her cousin once again. They were both clearly sorry to see us go. They wrote their names on scraps of paper, stuffing them into our hands.

Outside, leaning against the driver's side of my rented car was another young woman, gorgeous and slender and wearing a tighter T-shirt than the ones inside. "Here I am," she said. "What kept you? I waited all evening long."

I smiled, but moved her aside, unlocked the door, and got into the car.

"I have many condoms," she told me. "More than you will ever need."

I couldn't argue with that, and when I unlocked the other door David got in and laughed. "Rubbers are everywhere now," he said. "I suppose that's a good sign."

When I rolled my window down the girl stuck her head in. "Safe sex," she said. Then she added, "Okay, forget it. How about a ride downtown?"

A couple of mornings later, the day before David and I were to leave on our safari, the cook in the house where I stayed asked me to go into Westlands and get some coffee. When I wondered what else we might need she said, "If you happen to see any sugar. . . What we had is entirely gone."

Perhaps it was only jet lag, but Nairobi, the beautiful jewel of East Africa, had been looking tarnished to me since my return a few days before. Everything seemed overly damp and heavy, the buildings crumbling, the roads worse than before, and pencil-thin Somali refugees everywhere in the street. Even the roses and the bougainvillea were lackluster. The upcoming long-promised elections were constantly in the news, but it was clear that President Moi would not allow them to proceed fairly, and, in any case, opposition candidates were too numerous and factional to win. Still, Moi's reputation for being oafish and dictatorial had grown, and people were more vocal. Rumor had it he had killed his old vice president, that he had enough money in Switzerland to rival Marcos.

When I got to Westlands, however, my mind was not on Moi but on buying coffee and sugar, after that perhaps a doughnut or a roll. The coffee would be easy to buy, but I had seen long sugar queues the day before. For ordinary Kenyans it was in short supply. Still, I went into a favorite store of mine, stepped past the sugar queue, and found some coffee on the shelf. Since the only sugar was coming from a box at the front of the queue, I went to a cash register with the coffee and a two hundred shilling note. When the Indian salesgirl smiled at me I whispered, "Do you have any sugar I could buy?"

I was embarrassed by the question and expected she would quickly say no, but instead she called her father, in loud Swahili no less, saying something like, "Daddy, can you bring a bag for this guy?"

Since the sugar queue was directly behind me, I was afraid to turn around, but the girl's father immediately stopped what he was doing and brought over a couple of two-kilo sacks, placing them on the counter by the coffee. "Yes sir," he asked me, "anything more?"

My price for the sugar was twice what those in the queue were paying. It made little difference to me whether I paid one dollar or two dollars for a two-kilo sack, but it was suddenly quiet in the store, clear that those in the queue had stopped talking to watch. Did they hate me for what I was about to do? I expected they might yell, that one or two of them might even get out of line and come over to try to take the sugar back, but when I chanced a peek at them the men in the line were only staring in a narrow-eyed way, and even the women, who were far more numerous, seemed content to damn me quietly among themselves. I remember thinking that had I been in West Africa, in Nigeria where I had also once lived, such an act would have meant taking my life in my hands, but East Africans were a slow-brewing lot, still allowing a colonial moment, a frame from their occupied past. I had bought the sugar because I wanted to be a good houseguest, because the cook had requested it, because another person in the house liked sweet coffee. But wasn't this the stuff from which revolutions came? Wouldn't sugar buying be a good last straw? I worried about it all the way home. When I walked into the house, however, I got my reward, first in the cook's dismay and then in her unquestioning delight.

David had recently returned from a Red Cross trip to Somalia, and as we waited at a petrol station for our safari car to arrive he showed me photographs of what he had seen there. In every photograph were starvation and guns, two things that were still, thank God, foreign to the people in that sugar queue.

"Somalia is apocalyptical," David said. "They're digging the fucking telephone cables out of the ground and selling them to agents from Dubai. In six months it will be the Stone Age all over again." In the photograph he held I could see the telephone cables, Somali laborers hefting them, and I imagined the Duba'an agents just outside the picture frame, the sudden deadness of telephones all over town.

When our safari vehicle arrived I was surprised to discover that our driver was a white Kenyan named Stuart Cunningham, who, since it was the off-season, had been eager to take us out. He had unexpectedly brought a friend along, a rumpled but hip-looking young Palestinian named Naheem, who had a safari business of his own and who also wasn't busy at the time. Stu was a short, athletic-looking man of about fifty, with neat black hair and a ready smile. Naheem, on the other hand, was twenty years his junior, and wore sunglasses to cover a black eye that he'd gotten in a fight at the racetrack the night before. Stu's vehicle was a 1961 Land-Rover with tents on top, a refrigerator in the back, and windshield wipers that you had to turn by hand from inside the car. But though the tents were on the car we wouldn't be using them. David had made reservations at Keekorok Lodge and at Cottar's Camp as well. Cottar's was an old favorite of mine, a hunting camp that had turned to tourists when hunting was banned. It had a new name now, but would forever be Cottar's to me.

When I asked Stu how business had been he allowed that it wasn't good. "It's the off-season right enough, and the bandits are doing their share, too, to keep the tourists away."

Stu was talking about Somalis again, gangs who had been coming over the border with their weapons and their nerve. Such bandits were nothing new, but until recently they had been content to poach elephants and rhinos, selling the ivory and aphrodisiac horns. Now, however, they were robbing tourists on the road, and, according to Stu and Naheem, every incident made the international news. On the day we left Nairobi a van full of tourists had been stopped in Amboseli and their Kenyan driver was killed.

"It only happens once a fortnight," said Naheem, "but the Americans and Brits don't come. They think it happens every day."

There was a lot I needed to learn in order to make my novel work, but of singular importance was discovering whether or not coffee could grow in the farmlands above Narok, overlooking the Mara Plains. At 6000 feet the land was certainly high enough, but no one grew coffee up there. They grew wheat, and the characters in my book were irreversibly committed to making coffee grow.

Since Narok was about a three-hour drive and we'd gotten a late start, our plan was to stop there for lunch and then take a side trip up into the farmland to sniff about. When we arrived in Narok, however, Masai were everywhere, not only herding their cattle along the main street of town, but also hanging out at the petrol stations or squatting down in circles in the dust.

Stu parked the Land-Rover in front of a butcher shop that had two-inch tenderloins for half the price they were in Nairobi. Although David and I would not be camping, Stu and Naheem certainly would. Each of the Mara lodges had drivers' camps near them, so when David and I were inside buying overpriced beer, eating our six-course meals, and sleeping under starched sheets, Stu and Naheem would be resting, too, cooking these tenderloins over an open fire and getting their beer from the refrigerator in the Land-Rover's back. Surely David and I had the better deal.

Since the Land-Rover didn't lock, I was leaning against it, waiting for Stu to come out. Naheem was off buying cigarettes and David had run into someone he knew, the father of a girl he had taught years before at the International School. I was brooding about my novel again, about forcing the wheat land to grow coffee, and wondering how in the world I had ever made a novel work before, when two Masai *morani* walked by. *Morani* are "warriors," but though I had seen them by the score before, I had never seen the likes of these two guys. Most Masai, however beautiful to look at, have the unthreatening countenance of folk dancers, but these guys were darkly dressed and looked seriously bad. They wore togas and skirts that were thin and clinging, slightly wet looking and identical in color to their skin, which had been dyed the dark red of a barroom floor the morning after a bloody fight. Their faces seemed brushed very lightly white, like a half day's accumulation of dust on the hood of a black car, and they carried long sturdy spears. They were straight out of the deepest bush, lion hunters in the wildest throes of their ancient youth. They were so unusual in town that even the other Masai stopped to watch them as they passed by.

When the others came back I said, "Did you see those guys?" David had his camera with him, and it occurred to me that he might have chanced a shot, but when I asked him about it he said, "Hell no."

Stu's face took on an owlish expression, his eyes in the middistance where the *morani* had most recently been. His voice seemed outright reverential. "Bloody Stone Age teenagers, those! A rarity. They aren't supposed to have spears in town. I don't reckon anyone is going to point that out to them, though."

Since we weren't hungry, we decided to ride up the Narok-Nakuru road for half an hour, then come back into town to eat before heading off to the Mara and our night at Keekorok Lodge. Getting out of Narok took no time at all, and as we turned up the first hill we were into such deep greenery that the blood-red hue of those two Masai soon left my eyes.

"Ah, I love this road," said Stu. "Sometimes I bring my tourists out this way. A night at Lake Nakuru, then down here to Narok and the Mara. That's the ticket. It's a beautiful drive."

Though we could no longer see the town, there were still people on the road, hands raised slightly in the hope of a ride. Most of the children up here wore school uniforms. The women were wrapped in *kikois* or *kangas*, the men all dressed like door-to-door salesmen, in their peripatetic African uniform of threadbare suit over the open collar of a multicolored shirt. The fields on both sides of the car were incredibly rich looking and grand. "Surely they can grow anything here," I said. "We might even be high enough for tea."

"No we are not," said Naheem. "For tea you need seven thousand feet. The best you can hope for here is six thousand two."

We rode quietly after that, each of us lost in private thoughts. Though the land was stunning I nevertheless remember wondering why I loved it so much and why I always wanted to come back. After all, AIDS and corruption were everywhere, and life for ordinary people had become an impossible series of daily battles, my experience at the sugar queue the very least of them all. I had needed to come for my research, of course, but I also knew that here, and in Nigeria and Korea and Japan as well, I could somehow find my real self waiting to take me up again. Does that make any sense? Expatriate life is the drug I am addicted to, but why? Is it because, unlike all the other drugs I know, it gives me clarity of mind and a kind of traction that I can't seem to find on American soil?

I must have lost track of time, for when I looked at my watch a full hour had gone by and we were in the heart of wheat country, still driving along. "There's a village around one of these bends," said Stu. "Let's ask about coffee and turn around."

There was no village around the next turn or the one after that, but we did finally come to a widening in the road, a low country school on the road's east side. Since there were children and teachers everywhere, Stu stopped the Land-Rover and stepped out, greeting the nearest adult.

"Tell me, sir," he asked formally, "where does coffee grow? Where does coffee grow around here?"

It sounded like a code, the kind of question one spy might ask another, and the man was bewildered.

"Say again?"

"Coffee," said Stu. "There are wheat farms, but are there any growing coffee? A small one, perhaps, tucked in among the wheat?"

The man took his time but finally said, "Coffee doesn't grow around here. We have a store, however, if you want to buy some."

"Ask him about feasibility, Stu," I said. "Ask him if he thinks coffee might grow. I mean if someone tried. I don't care if it actually grows, but it has to be possible to grow coffee here."

"Can coffee grow on this land?" Stu persisted. "What do you think?" Stu's manner was pressing and a little gruff, as if demanding a positive reply.

The man looked at each of us and then seemed to make a decision to join in the spirit of the day. "I don't see why not," he said forthrightly. "This is fine land. If a farmer wanted to he could certainly grow coffee here." He paused, as if incensed that no one had ever tried it before, and then he added firmly, "If he was a good farmer he might even be able to grow tea."

"No he could not," said Naheem. "For tea he would need seven thousand feet."

Though we had been talking to this one man, we were surrounded by children, and David tried taking photographs of them. He hadn't gotten out of the car, but each time he raised his camera the children took off, screaming and running up toward the school.

I thanked the man, and when Stu and I got back in the car we headed down the road again. And as the children streaked after us, barefoot and fast on the soft green ground, I remember deciding that feasibility was in the eye of the beholder and that though my characters would certainly have to work at it, I could put their farm up here. I looked to the west. On the stretch of land that I saw just then, far down a side road and overlooking the Mara Plains, they would make their coffee grow. That would be the least of their worries, in fact.

By the time we got to Keekorok Lodge it was after five and getting dark. A layer of thin gray clouds had shouldered in above us and it had begun to rain.

David and I had one half of a duplex cabin with twin beds in it and two chairs on a low cement porch outside. We were far from the lodge proper, from the dining area and the bar, but it was a pleasant walk, and it was also somehow good to know that we were at the end of things. If the Keekorok cabins formed a horseshoe, with the main lodge at its center, then we were at the horseshoe's far left end. That meant that if we stepped out of our cabin and turned away from the lodge we would be walking directly into wilderness, and that if we continued, unchallenged by the lions and the cape buffalo that were there, we could walk to Tanzania in about an hour and a half. I had been to Masai Mara many times, but I had never been to Tanzania, and it struck me that I could go there now, on foot and without the hassle of border guards, if only I turned that way.

For a moment the idea seemed fine, but in the end we showered and went to the bar instead, where we found Stu and Naheem, ice-cold lodge beers in their hands.

"Listen," said David, "while we still have light let's go for a quick game drive, take our drinks along."

It was clear that the last thing poor Stu wanted to do was climb into his Land-Rover again, but I wanted to go for a drive, too, and since Naheem was Stu's guest and didn't get a vote, in a minute we were in the parking lot. There were safari vehicles everywhere, but all of them were coming in.

"We won't go far," Stu warned. "We'll make a small loop and come back for another cold one before dinner."

As we drove out the Keekorok road we saw a smaller one leading to the drivers' camp and canteen. A pretty young Kenyan woman was standing at the fork, an off-duty desk clerk or a maid who had just walked down from the lodge. As we passed her she looked up and smiled. Though all of us stared at the woman, Naheem stared the most, and when we lost sight of her he leaned forward, whispering to Stu. "I've got an idea, Stuart my friend," he said. "Why don't we go to the canteen tonight?"

Though it was not yet dark, it was nevertheless difficult to see. Those low clouds had come even farther down, connecting with the land in such a seamless way that I got the feeling we were inside a dark and colorless balloon. The place was surreal, like Dorothy's Kansas half an hour before the wind came up. But though Stu was the one who hadn't wanted to come, quite suddenly he seemed energetic and happy again, his mood a perfect counterpoint to the world outside.

"Let's move toward that clump of yonder trees," he said. "I've seen lions there quite often at this time of day."

The trees had no road leading to them, but Stu found a place where the grass had bent to other tires, and he quickly turned the Land-Rover into it, bringing grass up to the bottoms of our windows, but with deep mud underneath.

"Oh shit," he said, "the rain has done its job, hasn't it? Hold on!"

Suddenly the Land-Rover leapt forward, hunkered down and leapt again, bucking like a bull in a rodeo. "I think all this dampness has made the game lie low," said Stu, and once we were clear of the mud, sitting properly above the earth once more, he added, "It's a pity the migration hasn't begun. In a fortnight there'll be wildebeest going through here by the thousands, never mind the bloody rain. Zebra too. I'll tell you, that's something to see. Have you seen it, David? Have you seen the migration that comes through here? It's a pity to have lived your life in Kenya and never seen that."

David admitted that he hadn't, but resolved to come back in two weeks to see the migration, come what may.

"We can camp down at my place," Naheem told him, "pull up the flap and watch them roar by, for the tent's inside. I've got a good plot of land down by the river, at the other edge of the park."

It was clear that Stu had been right, night was falling and there were no animals around, but we pushed through the soft ground anyway, finally finding a road. Stu and Naheem were carrying on about the migration and what a wonderful sight it was to see, when suddenly as we bounced around a corner we saw a sight of our own, directly in front of us and fifty meters away. A Suzuki Samurai jeep was up on two wheels and careening sideways. When it finally came down on all fours again, the engine died and the right front wheel deeply embedded itself in the mud.

"My God, the bugger almost did it that time," laughed Stu. "Those little Suzukis will drive you out of trouble sometimes, but they're top-heavy, they'll go over if you aren't careful. Ha. It's getting late, though. We'd better stop and give these buggers a hand."

As we approached the jeep two men got out and stood in the rain looking our way. They were so soaked and chagrined, so unhappy looking, that it was suddenly clear they'd been out of the jeep before. The two men were tourists, the jeep was rented, and they were obviously Japanese.

"I speak Japanese," I said. "Let me see what's up."

When I got out of the Land-Rover the two men gave me bedraggled smiles.

"Hey," I said, "are you guys Japanese?"

"Haw?" the nearest one said, but the second guy immediately answered, "Yes, yes. We are Japanese!"

"What's the trouble? What problems do you have?"

"The engine is dead and the tire is stuck," said the second guy. "And now when we turn the key we don't get a sound."

"Not only that, but we can't find the hood latch," the first guy admitted.

I translated everything for Stu, who had opened his door and was standing out of it, smiling hard. "Tell 'em the hood latch is in the glove box," he said. "And my guess is that when they landed just now they knocked the battery cable off."

When I told the two men where the hood latch was they looked irritated, but quickly found it, and when the hood was up Stu came over and hit the positive pole of the battery once with a large wrench. After that the jeep started up. And when David and Naheem joined us we had it out of the mud in nothing flat.

"Oh thank you, thank you," said both young men. "Now, can you tell us how to get to Fig Tree Lodge?"

Stu pointed the way, and the four of us stood with mud on our shoes, watching them go.

"Fig Tree Lodge," said Naheem, shaking his head.

"By God, they'll be lucky if they find it," mused Stu. "There are twenty minutes of daylight left and it's a forty-minute drive."

When we got back in the car David looked at me and smiled. "I don't know about you," he said, "but I'm having the time of my life."

We headed back to Keekorok then, quiet until Stu started laughing. "Can you imagine those poor blokes trying to tell the story? Here they are, out in the middle of nowhere, deep in trouble and facing nothing but the quickly falling night, when along comes a Land-Rover and out jumps a *muzungu* speaking Japanese!"

When we all laughed Stu shook his head. "The bloody glove box! After all, it's their own damned fault. Who else would think of putting a hood latch in the glove box but the Japanese?"

The next morning when we awoke and checked out of the hotel the rain was gone and the Mara, in its aftermath, had the lightest shade of new-growth green under its otherwise constant brown. The grass was higher than it should have been at this time of year, hindering our vision some, and I could not shake the idea that all the animals were still in Tanzania, waiting for some internal alarm clock to sound, that mysterious something that told them it was time to ford the river, migrating north again.

It seemed to me that everything was at hand for a daytime drive that exactly mirrored the one we'd had the night before. There weren't any animals in sight and the sky was still gray, threatening another rain. When we were only ten minutes out, however, I began to understand that I was wrong.

"Look there," said Stu. "Hyenas in the road."

David and I both looked, and we could see well enough that the brown plane of the road before us was broken in some way, but as far as I could tell it was only a discoloration, something as easily caused by puddles of leftover rain as by hyenas.

"Right-o," said Naheem. "Must be something happening nearby."

The spots in the road were a mile away, so I looked at Naheem quickly to see if he was putting us on. He was, however, lighting a cigarette, his face as rumpled as his shirt, a sleepy look in his eyes.

As we got closer the puddles in the road became bumps and the bumps became hyenas, several dozen of them, stirring slightly, but otherwise unmoved by our approach. Stu drove right in among them, cut the engine, and sat back.

"Filthy buggers," said Naheem, coughing at the first smoke of the day. "Better not breathe through your nose."

Though I had opened my window to stare at the beasts, I had somehow not noticed the odor until Naheem spoke. After that, however, it was if someone had changed the actual makeup of the air. The rancid thickness of feces and rotting flesh was suddenly everywhere, overcoming me and making me cry. Breathing through my mouth didn't help. It was like the atmosphere on Mars, perhaps, or at the bottom of a putrid and gaseous sea.

"The hyena is an odd creature," Stu said mildly. "In all of nature he seems to be the one with no self-respect at all."

The hyena nearest me certainly seemed to bear that out. His eyes were narrow and his mouth was open, with lines of drool hanging down. His neck was long and tightly corded, sloping to a horribly broad chest and to a shag of such tangled and matted hair that it seemed fashioned for only the devil to wear. He really did seem evil to me, the way his front legs were strong under the muscles of his chest and jaw, yet his back legs looked atrophied, weak, and almost withered, as if God had finally intervened there to keep the competition from getting too strong.

As I watched him I was suddenly sure that the thick and horrible smell invading my mouth and nose was coming from this one beast alone, and that he wanted me to step from the car so that he could claim me, closing his jaws around my body and all my past sins. It was as if he knew me, as if the spiritual deprivation apparent in his eyes made it easier for him to see.

When Stu suddenly started the car again my hyena moved a step back and the modern world returned.

"I fear we've stopped for too long," said Stu, "but if we've missed the kill it will only be by a minute or two."

Maybe I had been too busy facing the devil down to look around, but when I finally did so I had no idea what Stu was talking about. We were at the center of plains and grass and empty land. The clouds stood over us in vague recollection of wildebeests, perhaps, but otherwise we were quite alone. There wasn't any kill to be late for, nothing, all the way to the horizon, in any direction I chose.

Stu saw the skeptical look on my face and pointed vaguely off at a couple of trees at the very edge of my sight. "Those hyenas are waiting their turn," he said. "They'll be heading this way in an hour or so, about the time the buzzards come. By then, though, tourist vans will be everywhere and it won't be any fun."

It took five minutes to get to the trees Stu had pointed at, but when we got there things were so much as he had intimated that I suspected he might have heard about it in the morning before leaving the lodge. A huge male lion, no longer hungry, was sitting on high ground watching countless others tear a zebra apart.

Stu turned the engine off again, and this time we sat for ninety minutes watching the lions eat. The zebra had been torn in half, its torso and rear legs getting the attention of most of the pride, its head and part of a shoulder fought over by cubs and half-grown males. David moved a little in order to take photographs from the various windows of the car, but otherwise we were captivated and quiet, watching and breathing the morning air, the hyena smell completely gone. The lions ate fastidiously, thirty-six of them magically making the zebra disappear.

There is a lion in my book who kills a baby elephant, making its mother mad. I had written the scene in a personal kind of way, from the point of view of my best female character, and emotionally. Yet the lions outside our car worked at the zebra with the expressions of house cats in their eyes, the thunderous violence of their attack completely gone. Seeing them somehow brought those warriors from Narok to mind again. When they hunted lions what did they do when the lion was dead? Did they smile at each other, did they shake hands? Or did they hunt alone, meeting up only later to walk back into town?

I don't know why, but the Masai, the lions, and those hyenas back there suddenly made me think of Nairobi again—of the Somalis in the street, the prostitutes, and the people in that sugar queue. Was there a linkage, something I could find to put in my book to make me proud? There was, of course, but the problem was to find it, to write it, to see it well. And for that I would need better equipment, a stronger and more analytical mind—either that or Stu's miraculous eyes.

The day, as I remember it, got very strange after that. Everything I have mentioned took place before ten a.m., after which I have various pictures of us (in my mind's eye, though perhaps in David's camera as well): parked on a stretch of land as vast and empty as a moonscape, utterly barren and forlorn, overlooking an expanse of wildly growing grass with five hundred wildebeests in it, the forward observers for the migration, perhaps; and at just around noon, standing beneath a mammoth jacaranda tree at a desolate turn in the Mara River, eating lunch and watching the long gray backs of sleeping crocodiles in the near gray sand. I also remember a one-armed Frenchman in a car with three pretty girls. "Where are you camping tonight?" Naheem asked them all.

We spent the entire afternoon following two cheetahs around. We had spoken little to each other since leaving the lions, but Stu suddenly stopped the car on an empty road saying, "Look over there, underneath that tree."

"Oh, right," said Naheem. "Cheetahs."

David and I glanced at each other and then out the window where Stu was pointing. Ah yes, now we could make out a tree, or foliage anyway, about three quarters of a mile away.

"There it is again," said Stu. "They're sleeping, but one of them has his tail sticking up."

It took a long time for us to drive to the tree, and when we got there a tourist van had arrived before us, but sure enough, two cheetahs were lifting their heads off the ground as cameras came out of the other van like guns.

"These two are brothers," Naheem said, and Stu looked at his watch. "It'll be crowded here soon. And these guys won't go hunting until around two o'clock. What say we drive on over to Fig Tree? Put our feet up, have a beer? We'll find 'em again when they start to move about."

I didn't think our chances of finding the cheetahs again would be very good, but the morning had otherwise been so full that none of us objected to getting out of the Land-Rover for a while. So we spent the next two hours at Fig Tree Lodge, perched at the edge of a veranda, watching a hippo in a far-off pool.

It was interesting to me to contrast the beauty and utter wildness of the Mara, with its strict and unbreakable laws, to the city, indeed, to all human life, whether it be in Nairobi or Moscow or Wichita. Perhaps this is the linkage I was after before. Here the world was in tune with itself, though harshly so. If an antelope sprained an ankle, for example, death was inevitably near. It was simple, it was absolutely clear, and there was no anticipation in it at all. But half the population of Nairobi, it seemed, were antelope with ankle sprains of their own. At the Heron Court young girls walked around with animal grace, breaking your heart. But in what wild animal could you find a T-cell count so low, an internal sprained ankle, like a time bomb ticking away? And where was that inward-looking "I"? If anticipation of our own death is what sets us apart, then why were those girls still smiling and walking around?

When we left Fig Tree Lodge David said, "This is where those two Japanese were headed. I wonder if they ever found their way."

Stu looked casually about saying, "Maybe we should ask," but we didn't ask about them or anything else. They had made it, I didn't have any real doubt about that, but when I thought of their hood latch and their battery cable fallen away, I somehow got back to sprained ankles once again. With people, of course, a mere sprained ankle did not mean that death was near. Since we had language and intelligence it didn't mean anything of the kind. With people nothing was clear, and that is why those girls kept going back to the bar. Though the disease might be within them, they wanted companionship and community. And though the disease might be within them, at the Heron Court they could argue the point endlessly.

Back in the Land-Rover Stu said, "Those two cheetahs will be up by now, heading toward that herd of tommies on the hill back there, no doubt."

We were on a narrow and scarcely used road when he spoke, and immediately after that we turned a corner and there were the two cheetah brothers, walking along.

"I'll be damned," said David, and Stu looked pleased. "I get a bit lucky sometimes," he allowed.

But though we followed the cheetahs throughout the rest of the day, nothing much happened. It was as if we'd simply added another couple of members to the quiet company of our car. When the cheetahs stopped we did too, when they slept we parked in the distant grass as an animal might, and since Stu hated the idea of drawing other cars, when the cheetahs moved again, we did not. Rather, we waited with the engine off, until they were completely gone. We did this six times, and each time, though I was positive we'd never be able to find them again, Stu would finally start the Land-Rover and drive right to them, as if they were signposts in familiar ground, as if they were not wild and roving animals with random minds of their own.

We invested four hours in following the cheetahs along. Twice they crouched a hundred yards away from the gazelles, beginning a low crawl, but no one was limping and both times the tommies skittered away. And as the sun started down and another van finally found us, Stu lost interest and we started home.

"It's no bloody fun anymore," he said. "Those guys have radios now, so when one sees something you've got about a minute before everyone else arrives."

When we left the cheetahs I was disappointed, for I was greatly hoping to see the death of one animal at the hands of another. Does that seem strange? I held onto this hope, though for most of the day the two cheetahs, just like the four of us, weren't doing anything at all.

When we got to Cottar's Camp it was dark and we were late checking in. At Cottar's there are tents on cement foundations, with rifle-toting security guards to walk you to them, lest a beast jump out. Though I am a man who is rarely at one with the moment, as David and I walked to our tent that night, in the pitch-black wilderness, I felt incredibly calm. This was the feeling I had waited for, the one I'd often had when living in Africa before. I don't know what caused such a feeling, but after I had showered and was heading back up to the dining hall alone, no guard this time and with only a flashlight in my hand, I paused at the edge of an invisible pond. What a place for solitary thought, what a place to be alone. I tried clarifying the random thoughts of my day, I tried thinking of my novel again, but my presence was unwanted, for it suddenly stopped the voices of a million frogs who, before my arrival, had been furiously singing to the stars.

When I got to the lodge David, Stu, and Naheem were in the bar, surrounded by a dozen South African travel agents, up from Johannesburg and busily packaging tours that they could sell back home. South Africans in Kenya! I could not help remembering the day, surely only a year before, when not only could South Africans not come to Kenya, but also no one who wanted to come to Kenya could ever go there.

Naheem and Stu were chatting with a couple of the travel agents, even buying a round of beer. "Kenya is nice," I heard one woman say, "but the parks at home are better organized, and our roads are all paved. What Kenya needs is a proper infrastructure, you know, competent people in charge."

The next day, the last one of our short safari, was as remarkable as the first, so it doesn't require telling. We were kept from arriving back at Cottar's Camp much earlier than we had the night before, however, by two events that do require telling. First, though we hadn't seen any, I had been mentioning elephants two or three times a day, not in an insistent way, but tacitly presenting Stu with a challenge nevertheless. "Find them," I somehow seemed to say, and at about four o'clock on the final day we did.

"Nice group of elis over there, Stu," Naheem noted mildly.

"Ah yes," said Stu. "Let's take a look."

David nodded and I did too, but this time I was quite bereft. Believe it or not, for another minute or so I couldn't see them. These were elephants. A nice group of them, no less, but though I looked and looked, all I could see was empty land.

And then suddenly there they were. They came out of the shapes of trees, like hyenas out of rain puddles. Even after three days I was still using my city eyes, which were good for finding trouble ahead but not for finding elephants in vast and empty land. Did that mean, I wondered, that were I to take Stu and Naheem to the United States, their adjustment would be as clumsy as mine? Would they miss the guy sleeping at the bus stop or under a cardboard box? Would they miss the nuance of three kids in Raiders jackets, frowning and coming their way?

Elephants had been holed up in my imagination during all the time I'd been working on my book, so when we got close to the real thing I tried to see them with a clear yet calculating eye. There were about fifteen in the herd, grazing and walking around, and Stu stopped the Land-Rover near the largest one. This elephant was taller than the one in my book, perhaps ten feet at the shoulders, which were thick as steam engines and half as strong. It was female, and though she had legs that might be singularly unattractive on a human form, it was her legs that first let my eyes see well. These legs did not bevel, but were as thick at the ankle as they were at the knee. They were as sturdy as redwood stumps, and I suddenly remembered once seeing an elephant leg quite like one of hers in a shop window in Harare. What I had seen was a monstrosity called an elephant-foot stool, or an elephant footstool, I can't remember which, but the leg that made the stool had been cut off at about midpoint between the ankle and the knee, a well-crafted piece of richly grained wood glued or nailed to its top. It was the sturdiest of stools, the best you could buy, but when I looked at the moving legs in front of me I tried to forget about the stool and concentrate on this living elephant's tusks. Though she was certainly fully grown, she was just as certainly no more than about twenty-five years old, for her tusks were still small. An elephant's age is told by its tusks, not by its size, but though I had tusks in my book that were as high as this elephant's eye, this elephant's tusks would barely top the footstool that I was hopelessly trying to purge from my mind.

"No," Stu said, when I asked about finding an elephant whose tusks touched the ground. "We don't see tuskers like that anymore. You should go to the national museum. Ahmed is there, of course."

When we left the elephants a light rain began to fall. We were alone on the road between Masai Mara and Cottar's Camp. The sun was over by Uganda somewhere, ready to go down, Stu was driving fast, and I was thinking about dinner and about listening to those South African travel agents again, when we came upon a Masai village at the side of the road. We had seen this village before, but it had a sign at its front inviting tourists to stop by, so we had hardly registered its existence at all. Now, though, it was easy to tell that whatever connection these Masai had with tourists was finished for the day. The village consisted of an enclosed circle of mud and dung huts. Masai cattle were sometimes placed inside the enclosure to protect them from lions at night, but right now, as the sun went down, there was a group of men outside the enclosure, standing in a circle of their own, chanting and dancing and jumping in the air.

"My God, would you look at that," said Stu.

He stopped the Land-Rover and we all stared, David readying his camera but keeping it low.

"There's a rainbow, too," said Naheem. "Pretend you're taking a photo of that, point your camera at the rainbow and then turn it quickly when they jump up." That made us all laugh, but David actually tried it once or twice.

The Masai were holding their dance on the southeast side of the road, so we were all looking that way and did not immediately see two more Masai boys coming from the northwest, walking toward the dance. Stu saw them first. "Put your camera down, David," he warned, "and get a load of these two guys."

Stu greeted the two boys, who said they were fine, but that was the extent of their Swahili. They seemed surprised to see us and they circled the car, smiling shyly and finally coming up to the window on my side.

"Hallo," said the nearest boy. Both boys were about fourteen and were dressed plainly, in loose brown togas like Roman boys of two thousand years before. I mentioned as much and Naheem said, "Well, you know the rumor. Some say the Masai are the lost seventh division, Roman soldiers who marched down through Egypt and were never seen again. They even carry their spears like Romans. Hell, these guys will wrap themselves in Italian tablecloths, given half a chance."

"Aren't they bloody marvelous, though?" said Stu, turning to me. "Do you understand how far up in the hills these boys must live not to understand any Swahili in this day and age? They might have been walking for days. Where else in the world can you run across blokes like these, that's what I want to know?"

"What's your name?" I asked the nearest boy.

"Bloody Stone Age," said Stu, but the boy said, "My name Sosio."

"My name is Richard," I replied.

Though he didn't understand, Sosio laughed, and I did too. Sosio's friend was gently pulling on him, worried that they'd be even later than they already were for the dance, so David gave them each a couple of empty film cannisters and they went away.

We drove up the road, but after fifty meters or so we stopped again. David put a larger lens on his camera just as we got to a place where the position of the car put the end of that rainbow directly over the Masai. As they jumped and chanted they went up into the rainbow, making it seem, in the flashes of remaining light, as though their hair was on fire. It was the photographic moment of a lifetime, perhaps, but while David shot his pictures, madly turning in his seat, my imagination failed me for a while and I sat back. And after that, for the longest time, all I could seem to think of was Roy G. Biv.

A few days after our return to Nairobi, David and I stopped at the Heron Court just after we had met Stu and Naheem at another hotel bar off Ardwings Kodek Road. Though Naheem looked just as he had on safari, rough-and-tumble and fresh from sleep, Stu was dressed nicely. He wore pressed pants, his hair was oiled and combed, and he seemed like a city man, with ordinary observations to make about the world. He was quiet, actually, and when he glanced across the courtyard to try to find our waiter to order more beer, he couldn't seem to find the man in the expanding crowd.

The safari had done me a world of good, not only unbinding me from my normally muddled life, but radically changing my novel as well. Without exception all of my questions had been answered. By the end of my safari I knew that my characters could grow coffee to their heart's content, never mind what other farmers grew, and I knew how a lion and an elephant might act when facing each other over the body of a dying calf. I had even invented a Masai character who would occasionally come around the farm. Sosio was his name, feasibility his game. Everything was feasible, everything was in order. Wasn't that what I had been after all along?

But it was something Stu had mentioned quite offhandedly that had really changed my book, sending me to the national museum as soon as I got back to town to look at Ahmed the elephant, the one with the mammoth tusks. I knew about Ahmed, of course, had seen him several times, but my God he was magnificent. His tusks were twice as long as any I had seen before. One was nine feet six inches long and the other was nine feet nine! During the last years of Ahmed's life he had become a national symbol and had been under twenty-four-hour guard, lest the poachers come around. But though he was without question a symbol, what, I wondered, was he a symbol of? As I stood there looking at him I began to see my book changing in ways that might try to answer such a question, in ways that would, I hoped, work themselves out once I got home. All I really knew, as I reached across the cordon and touched one of Ahmed's tusks, was that my book, after all this time, finally had a name. Ahmed's Revenge. My book would be called Ahmed's Revenge, though as yet I had no idea what it meant at all.

In the Heron Court, David and I sat in a covered wagon again, many girls sharing it with us and many more walking by. They were Luo and Abaluya and Kikuyu. Some of them were Somali—pretty, leonine, and thin—and seeing them made David pull out his photographs again, the ones from his trip to Somalia a couple of weeks before. On top was the picture of the torn-apart street, the telephone cable dug up and sold to Dubai, and I remembered David's comment when he had shown it to me before. "Somalia is apocalyptical," he had said. "In six months it will be the Stone Age all over again." Stone Age. Sosio and Somalia, Ahmed the elephant and those terrifying warriors with the spears. In the States, perhaps such a phrase could find meaning only in books, but as I sat there I resolved to try to alter its meaning in mine.

FROM INCA
TO INKA KOLA

by Ron Arias

A Volunteer in Peru in the early sixties, Ron Arias used his Peace Corps experience to write *The Road to Tamazunchale*, a comic novel about life and death in Los Angeles and Peru. Published in 1975, and still in print, this novel was nominated for the National Book Award. Arias is a senior writer for *People* magazine, and a lot of what he writes about for the magazine occurs in remote places—from the Aussie Outback to the Canadian Arctic.

"Mostly," he explained, "my stories are about people in poor places, like Haiti, Somalia, Nicaragua, or a Rosebud Sioux reservation in South Dakota."

I asked him to tell me what piece took him on his most remote journey. He thought a while, then answered it was a story about a young woman in Philadelphia named Yárima, who was a Yanomamo Indian from the Amazon. She had married an American anthropologist and had literally gone from a Stone Age, naked existence in the jungle to a life of wearing clothes and shoes in a world where everything was alien to her. "With her husband translating," Arias related, "I tried to get the story of her journey so that what I saw would be an America through her eyes. Yárima's journey was probably the strangest trip I've ever taken."

America — or life outside the forest — surprisingly turned out to be a "world of too much silence," Arias said. "Yárima told me that in the forest there is always laughter and people talking and children playing on the vines in the trees. Here, she heard only sirens. 'At night,' she said, 'when everything is dark, I hear the crying. The sound is like people crying for help.'"

In the end, several years later, Yárima missed her friends and family so much that she left her husband and returned to the Amazon. "That was the closest I've come to time travel," Arias said. "We're the ones always trying to go back to original states, to the remote and exotic. But just try the reverse — putting on clothes as an adult for the first time, flying in an airplane, riding in a car, using a flush toilet, looking in a mirror . . . all for the first time as an intelligent nineteen-year-old. Now that's a trip."

Over my desk at home in Connecticut hangs a sixteenth-century map of the New World. It's a cheap reproduction, but I have it there for occasional inspiration, sometimes for a little travel into uncharted places. Though the coasts are dotted with tiny, insect-like words showing all that was known, I usually fix on the blank interior of South America; it is large and dominates the map's center. If I want, I can cruise the Amazon, or make friends with Patagonia natives, or hike up onto the continental spine to touch the snow, watch a sunrise, look around.

South America, especially in the 1500s, lent itself to dreams and exploration. For example, I've placed myself in an area the map labels Peru. In Gothic-style capital letters, **P E R U**— largest of all words except the names of the oceans—stretches from the Andes halfway across the Amazon Basin. Once the world's richest source of gold and silver, greater Peru became a household word in Spain and wherever else people had heard of the wonders of the New World. "To be worth a Peru," as Europeans used to say, was to be rich beyond dreams.

Today, of course, only drug traffickers after the coca leaf think Peru is rich. History and mapmakers have greatly reduced its size and importance. Say Peru and most people probably think of Machu Picchu, flutes, llamas, women in bowler hats, bombings, cocaine, and the Shining Path. Fair enough. Every place seems to have its exportable pop images. However, long ago I carried away my own images, having lived there — south of Cuzco — for several years.

Sometimes when I look at my funky old map, with its dispro-portionately wide rivers and exaggerated mountain peaks, instead of imaginary places I see a different place, an actual place. I close my eyes and I see people I know. I see faces; among them, I even see my own. It's the same haggard face in a picture someone had taken of me crawling across a log that bridged a stream in the jungle. I look at the snapshot now and I remember how wet, dirty, miserable, and tired I felt. For a week or so I had been tramping along squishy, overgrown trails many miles downriver from Machu Picchu, where the Andes Cordillera meets the Amazon vastness. I was with three other young men and we were trying to find the "lost" city of Vilcabamba, last refuge of the last Inca. Until now, the outpost had eluded discovery, hidden by centuries of tangled growth.

My friends and I were eager and willing, but our map was vague and too general. We had lost our way and run out of food. It was late afternoon when we heard dogs barking. Machetes in hand, we hacked our way toward higher ground and came out into a clearing. In the fading light we saw a rambling, mud-walled house with what looked like a powerful ham-radio anten-na sprouting from a corrugated, metal roof. Three or four German shepherds kept up their barking and snarling behind a shoulder-high picket fence. Over the closed gate, I noticed a few chickens in the shadows near the house. Then a woman appeared and started toward us. She was a frumpy old crone in dark skirts and a dirty apron. When she reached the gate we asked her if we could buy some eggs from her.

"Wait here," she said. "I'll go ask the *patrón*."

We dropped our packs, sat down on them, and listened to the beasts bark. The Spanish word *patrón* means "boss," or "employ-er," but in Peru it can imply a kind of ownership, as in master and slave. I was wondering if the *patrón* would be a generous master. I figured he might fit the master category because the woman had Indian features and was overly polite and deferen-tial.

After a while she returned, quieted the dogs, and asked us in. "The *patrón* invites you to have dinner."

Surprised and very grateful, we filed in through the open gate, lugging our packs to a screened-in patio. A long table with benches occupied the center, and at the far end instead of a chair stood a tall partition of framed cloth. After we washed ourselves with water out of a barrel, we sat at a long wooden table under a hanging kerosene lamp. The heavy air, burdened with darkness and the incessant whine of a million insects, became ominous, gloomy. We were so exhausted that none of us said anything beyond a few profanities about the day's trek.

Eventually the servant woman appeared from the shadows and placed bowls of a meat-and-vegetable stew on the table. About the same time a deep, German-accented voice startled us from behind the screen. I could just make out the shadow of a standing figure. "Welcome," the voice began in English. "I apologize for not eating with you. I hope you like the food and that you reach wherever you are going. Again, please excuse me for not sitting down with you. Good night."

Someone said thanks, then the figure was gone. I don't remember if any of us mentioned how strange it seemed that our host did not appear in person, but at the time we probably thought he was sick or too tired for conversation. And we were busy eating. It was only later, after my hiking buddies and I were packing our little tents and gear in the clearing the next morning, that it struck me: there was only one reason in 1964 for a German to hide away in a South American jungle with servants and guard dogs. He didn't have to fly a swastika from his radio antenna to identify himself.

Over the years I've wondered what kind of man he was, this war criminal on the run. What did he look like? What had he done? Was he truly evil? Did he feel any guilt, remorse, or shame for what he did? I've also thought maybe he wasn't a Nazi. Maybe he was a simple recluse, seeking the secrets of the primitive world, like Conrad's mysterious Kurtz, an upriver figure living in darkness and retreat.

We eventually found our way back to the beaten trail and to Urubamba, the town we'd started from. I remember many details of those ten days, from the bow and single arrow of the Machigenga tribesman we saw to the climb through a cloud forest in which black, stunted trees emerged weird and twisted in the cool, sweeping mists. However, the strongest, most recurrent image I have of the trek is of that grim and brooding presence in the jungle clearing—the darkened house, the flickering shadows on the walls and ceiling. And at the heart of it all is our phantom host—vague, mysterious, perhaps evil. I remember thinking I'd felt the breath of danger and was glad to move on.

The sepia-tinted map sometimes draws me into that other world of shadows and memory and bits of history. It was the same when I lived there, except then I didn't need a map to put me into that murky, adventurous frame of mind. I had the feeling that I'd traveled to a place so infused with the mystique of mountain gods and lost cities, of deserts and tropical forests, and of people living paradoxically on a new frontier in an ancient land, that I believed I had entered another, more permanent reality than anything I'd known in California. It was a world that many would call third, but one that I soon believed undergirded all humanly conceived worlds. I say human because people have created these ideas of first and third worlds, of rich and poor. They are convenient terms that obscure the common everyday, struggling-to-get-by world, which I believe encompasses all our realities and doesn't limit itself to wealth, power, or whether or not everyone has a flush toilet.

For years I'd been wanting to return to Peru, if only for a short visit. What coaxed me into finally making my travel arrangements was a colonial-era painting I saw in a New York gallery. The painting presented a mountain valley town seen from a hillside above the town. In the foreground was a plaza surrounded by adobe-walled buildings with red-tiled roofs. Beyond that, a river ran from left to right, and across the river rose a massive brown fortress. The town was identified as Sicuani, only the scene dated from about two centuries before I had arrived there as a Peace Corps Volunteer.

I stared at the moundlike fort, all of it oversized and out of proportion to the town itself. What intrigued and puzzled me was that it stood just about where I used to live. Yet I never knew or saw remnants of such a structure, which a gallery note explained had been built by the Spaniards to control Indian revolts. I thought I knew everything obvious about Sicuani. Why not the fort, something I had practically lived on? Right there, in the gallery, I hatched my plan, my little quest: take leave of my understanding wife and son, fly to Lima as soon as I had a week or so free, catch a plane up to Cuzco, then head south to find the mysterious fort. This time I'd go without a map.

❊   ❊   ❊

Mario, a friend of a friend, met me at the city's international air-port. I had missed the flights to Cuzco, which all depart in the early morning, so I would have to stay overnight in Lima. I must have been described to Mario, or else my newcomer's roving eye tipped him, because he spotted me as soon as I emerged from customs.

"Ron?" he said, pronouncing my name with a trilled *r* and a nasalized *o*, transforming the word into the Spanish for "rum."

"Mario?" I answered, nodding that I was Ron. We shook hands, then he grabbed my sportsbag and we hurried outside under gray skies toward the parking lot. He apologized for dri-ving a Volkswagen beetle, which was borrowed and difficult to start. "My wife has the Volvo," he explained in Spanish as we zoomed through traffic.

Mario himself, I discovered, was stuck on overdrive. He walked fast, drove fast, spoke fast. Restless, impatient. On the way from the airport to my hotel a guy in a battered Ford cut him off, and suddenly Mario stomped on the pedal and nearly rear-ended the offender. We pulled alongside the guy once, and the two traded gestures and insults. As soon as the Ford veered off where the road split, Mario hurled one last expletive, then he downshifted, jockeyed around a semi, and stopped for a red light. "I won't be intimidated," he announced. "My family's been here for hundreds of years. They came with Pizarro."

Okay, I thought, it's his family pride and a few terrorists in traffic; the Ford guy could have been a guerrilla. Then I realized Mario wasn't talking about the Ford but about his family's forti-tude when he added, "We're not giving up. It'll take more than bombings and terrorist threats to scare us off. Many families did leave, but we're staying."

It took about a half hour to reach Miraflores—where my hotel was—and throughout his monologue I would nod and make sympathetic, guttural noises, once making it clear that I had lived in parts of Latin America and that I had more than a tourist's understanding of Peruvian history and culture. By now I was so focused on my fair-skinned, blue-eyed host that I wasn't paying much attention to our surroundings, which were vaguely generic, busy Big City—a blur of figures at the sides, crowded minibuses, and now and then skinny palm trees, factory walls, billboard signs, and newspaper boys hoisting headlines amid the traffic.

Mario and his family belong to the entrepreneurial class that has run Peru for centuries. And though they lost land and business during the socialist-military regime's tenure of the seventies, he and his clan feel they have enough of a stake in Peru's future to stick out the hard times. Their nisei president of the moment, Alberto Fujimori, because he's sort of an outsider—neither white nor Indian—is in their minds the uncompromised leader who can turn the country around. Of course, Mario and his two sons—all with American M.B.A. degrees—are primed for the boom.

After I got settled in Miraflores—which resembles Santa Monica with its tidy lawns, trendy shops, and palm-shaded palisades overlooking surfers bobbing in the shimmering Pacific swells—Mario took me to his country club for lunch. I had never seen this side of Peru before. I knew such oases of pristine luxury existed, but I had never before sat down to a sumptuous *corvina* and shrimp salad lunch preceded by exquisite shots of pisco sours and served at a fancy clubhouse next to a lush carpet of putting-green grass. I also glimpsed rows of tennis courts occupied by kids in whites competing in a club tournament. I could only imagine everything else that comes with club membership. Beyond the white tablecloths, pools, and miles of rolling fairways were the connections, the traditions, and the family pedigrees. As in all Latin American countries except those populated by Europeans, such as Argentina, life is usually stratified according to race. In this sanctuary of the rich, fair was the prevailing skin tone. The rest of Peru, like Mexico, tends toward the darker shades.

At any rate, I did enjoy the meal and the talk with Mario (who kept racing off for hurried chats at other tables) and his elegant, well-groomed wife. She explained her business of exporting designer alpaca sweaters, then described her passion for golf.

As we were leaving, looking south away from the club, I saw a giant sand hill that cut everything else from view. Yet I knew from the drive here that just over the crest, no more than several football-field lengths away, began the other Peru, miles of what Peruvians call *pueblos jóvenes*, or young towns. Entire books have been written about how these squatter settlements grow from collections of stick shelters to actual municipalities with electricity, sewer lines, mayors, soccer teams, and beauty contests. Built on fifty years of steady migration of poor folks from the mountain valleys of the interior, the towns have spread around Lima in a semicircle like a dusty, brown apron. I asked Mario for a quick tour.

An hour, start to finish. Rocks and sand . . . shacks of woven, straw-matted walls . . . dirt streets and trails; paved streets and stairway paths . . . lots of people coming and going, hanging out in clusters or waiting for buses . . . skinny dogs and fat hogs . . . noisy, banged-up cars and water trucks . . . a soccer game, four people on one bike, teenaged girls in plaid jumpers coming from school . . . slogans on walls, metal signs blaring the logo names of Inka Kola and Bimbo bread. . . .

After Mario left me at my hotel I hopped into a crowded mini-van jitney for a ride into the center of Lima. When I jumped off near the Plaza San Martin, I joined the crowds on the sidewalks and barricaded shopping streets where vehicles were forbidden. Wallet and passport in my front pocket, I felt as safe or safer than I do walking in, say, Manhattan, Miami, or Los Angeles. This is probably because I'm dark-complexioned, short by American averages, walk fast, and try not to gawk like a tourist. Actually, I was walking mainly for exercise, I looped around the plaza once, passing a group of Romanian Gypsies at one corner. All women in long skirts and lots of jewelry, they were money changers. Each held up a calculator in one hand, the other hand usually buried in an apron pocket full of dollar bills and soles, the Peruvian currency. They seemed to be doing a fast business, a black market one but out in the open, as I'd seen elsewhere.

I bought some peanuts, took a last glance at the gray, monumental buildings and at the Liberator on horseback in the square's center, then began the long hike back to Miraflores. I counted at least four tanks along the Avenida Arequipa, parked by the major Western embassies, and dozens of armed guards posted in front of homes and businesses. It wasn't enough to have a private bodyguard, Mario told me. If you could boast that your bodyguard wore a bulletproof vest, then you could consider yourself important. He added that fortunately kidnappings of the rich were starting to fade.

At the hotel I ate pasta, drank a glass of a good local red wine, watched a little CNN news, then peered through my twelfth-floor window. It was taped with a giant X in the middle as a precaution against flying glass in case of a car-bomb explosion. These, too, I learned, had been on the decline, perhaps as a result of a new military offensive against the Shining Path and other armed groups. I was gazing across the smoky spread of rooftops toward the Andean foothills, imagining the trip up out of the coastal soup of fog, smoke, and smog.

I had brought along Peter Matthiessen's *The Cloud Forest: A Chronicle of the South American Wilderness*, published in 1961, about the same time as his novel *At Play in the Fields of the Lord*, which is set in the high jungle east of Cuzco. I remembered being taken in by both books years ago, and somehow I wanted to take a parallel journey reading *Cloud Forest* as I traveled in Peru. What I forgot was Matthiessen's low opinion of *serranos*, or people of the highlands, and his coziness with the less spoiled people of the jungle. Having lived among *serranos*, I never felt this way. They are strong survivors of the most awful oppression—centuries of de facto enslavement, death and disease while working the mines and land. I put down the Matthiessen paperback and wondered if I would change my mind about my two other Peru favorites, Ciro Alegría's elegiac novel about a Quechua Indian village, *El Mundo es Ancho y Ajeno* (translated as *Broad and Alien Is the World*) and John Hemming's *The Conquest of the Inca Empire*.

Before bed, I settled for a turn around Miraflores Park. A folk band was playing Andean music to a packed audience in the little amphitheater. At one point the MC pleaded with spectators to come down into the circle and dance. No takers, except a toothless old man everyone cheered on as "*Tío*." Well, Uncle was just about the only white man in the audience. The rest looked Indian or of mixed blood. Yet the music was more theirs than his. Maybe they wouldn't dance because they saw it as a step backward, something that might tag them as Indian and therefore backward. But they liked the old man's spunk. When *Tío* sat down, everyone applauded.

Cuzco tilted into view as the plane dipped its left wing and veered into the valley site and toward the city the Incas called the Navel of the World, center of the four quarters of their empire. I had spent most of the flight alternately peering out my porthole window at the many snow-covered mountains and practicing my list of Quechua phrases with my neighbor, a plump secretarial-skills teacher in her forties who had offered to coach me. After almost thirty years I remembered a half dozen phrases—helpful bits, like "Let's eat," "I don't have any" (for beggars), and "Just because I'm a gringo, don't cheat me, little mama."

On the ground, at the new airport, the teacher suggested I stay at a moderately priced hotel next to the cathedral in the main square. As the cab moved up the long valley slope toward the old part of town, I didn't recognize anything. However, after I saw my first Inca-wall stones, with their large, contoured smoothness and their tight fit all around, I suddenly felt as if I'd arrived at the real city, the ancient city. A traveler on a pilgrimage to Rome might feel the same sense of awe and permanence, of being in a place where you can walk into the past at every corner and down every cavernous cobblestone street. In the original old section that spreads out around the main plaza, the massive stone foundations of Inca structures still rise five to ten feet high, and support most of the wood and adobe-walled buildings. The Spanish and even modern parts struck me as puny when compared to the ancient base.

But I wasn't in Cuzco to sightsee. I had my mission, which so far was providing the weakest of spines to my sojourn. I checked into the hotel and immediately asked for a cup of coca-leaf tea, which is supposed to offset the effects of the city's 11,000-foot altitude. I drank it, then pulled myself up three flights to a small room with monklike furnishings—a bed, table, and toilet—but a great peek of a view out the tiny window overlooking a jumble of angled red-tile roofs.

I napped for an hour. So far, no headache, which is an early sign of altitude sickness. At fifty-one and with a high-cholesterol history, I wasn't taking any chances.

Out on the streets, I stepped slowly, trying to conserve oxygen. Unfortunately, I spent an hour or so trying to find an old friend with whom I'd exchanged Christmas cards for years. Efraín was a dentist trained in Brazil but, as he wrote, "stuck in this piece of shit existence." A bitter man, nothing seemed to have ever gone right in his life. His yearly cards always feigned cheerfulness. He had married a beautiful woman, a doctor, and soon after the birth of their daughter the marriage went sour and they were divorced. His ex-wife then suffered a stroke that left her paralyzed and unable to speak. He also had a string of failed business investments, lawsuits against him, and other problems he only hinted at. About six years ago I stopped receiving his cards, and after several more years I stopped sending mine. What had happened? Had he died? Apparently not, for according to the phone book there was a current listing for Efraín Negrón, *dentista*.

I knocked on the door of his office, located above the open market near the Machu Picchu train station. I wasn't sure if my heart was racing from the altitude or from the anxiety of not knowing if he was still a friend. I hadn't seen him in more than two decades. What would we look like to each other? When I knew him he lived in Sicuani. A suited, dapper figure, he was quick to laugh and endlessly curious about things foreign, especially American. We were talking friends, for ideas. What sort of man would I find now?

A young woman answered the door, listened to my request, then asked me to take a seat in the waiting room while she went into the next room. In seconds Efraín appeared, dressed in a lime-green smock, beaming the same impish smile I remembered. He was grayer and stouter but still the same small, dark, round-faced figure with the Asian eyes. We embraced, I told him I'd come on a whim of nostalgia, and then he provided the answer to the card mystery. He had one returned—wrong address—and then he moved, so mine never got to him. As he was talking, his hands had returned to some poor guy's open, bleeding mouth; we chatted over the man's moans. Efraín also explained that booze had almost killed him. He had recovered, but I noticed the bitterness spilling out with each wrenching twist of the patient's molars. This time Efraín bemoaned Cuzco as a provincial prison. At least, for him it was.

Later, as he exhausted me on a stroll up to a pleasant lookout spot above the city, he admitted it wasn't the city itself he abhorred; it was a lot of judgmental people he always wanted to escape from but for one reason or another never could. For a while it was his wife, then his daughter, then his aging parents, then all the legal problems. "I used to dream I could leave anytime I wanted," he said, trancelike. "But I'm trapped, cursed."

We stopped in a coffee shop for tea (mine coca leaf) and some sandwiches. Efraín reminded me of Jimmy Stewart in *It's a Wonderful Life*, except there was no Clarence in his life. Before we parted, we hugged each other again, and this time got our addresses straight.

By now all the emotion and exertion had brought on a headache and some audible heart-pounding. I needed to sleep before my bus trip south to Sicuani. Unfortunately, I first had to drag myself up three flights of stairs. I rested on the landings, sucking air like a sprinter. In my room I collapsed on the bed, wriggled my way, fully clothed, under the covers, and gradually calmed myself.

I awoke at four in the morning, sweating, my heart doing leaps, my brain trying to burst out of my skull. I wrote in my notebook: "I want to leave a record of what's happening to me. Chest pressure. Taking aspirin. I suppose I shouldn't have taken that walk. What's happening? Hang on, heart."

I survived. At noon I was peering through a window toward the rear of a midsize bus bound soon for Sicuani. The headache had eased, but I was still wary of activity. Sicuani is higher than Cuzco, more than two miles above sea level.

Thirty years ago this same trip was made either by bus on a dirt road through roiling dust clouds or by train without the dust. If you could afford it, you traveled in clean, civilized fashion—that is, first-class by train, which simply meant cushioned instead of wooden slat seats. But nowadays, I discovered, a paved highway reaches nearly all the way to Sicuani, so most people prefer to make the four-hour trip by bus. Fares are cheap and the buses leave every half hour.

Once all the bundles, boxes, and luggage had been stored on the roof rack and the aisle filled with standing passengers, we chugged off, heading south through suburbs lined with rows of new apartment buildings and condos. Rain clouds hung low over the valley, and it was just cool enough for people to need a jacket or sweater.

"Going to Sicuani?" I asked my seat neighbor in Spanish. She looked about twenty and wore a sheeny, baby-blue sweatsuit. Like most of the passengers, she had black hair and predominantly Indian features.

She nodded, smiling in a friendly way. I asked her if she lived there, and she said only temporarily; she was going to start a new job as a clerk for a driving school. I told her I remember when the town had only about a dozen vehicles.

Before I could continue, the bus stopped and took on two young men, one tall, the other short. The short one pushed past the standing passengers until he reached the rear. Then the two men began shouting insults at each other, some in Quechua, the lingua franca of the countryside. Passengers were either amused or pretended to ignore the exchange, which was a back-and-forth between a cheating husband and a vengeful wife. At one point, to start another long joke, the tall fellow looked directly at my seatmate and asked for a pretty female volunteer to "dialogue" with him. No one answered the call, so the short comic played the part by putting a scarf over his head and talking in a high-pitched voice. My neighbor and I laughed a few times, but neither of us dropped coins in the hat that was passed around before the two men hopped off the bus.

For a time we were also treated to a poet who recited verses with sweeping, exaggerated arm gestures, difficult to do in such a crowd. By the end of his performance he was making tiny finger gestures.

At the town stops along the way, food vendors would surround the bus, holding up to the windows bottles of soft drinks, corn-beer *chicha,* grilled goat meat, bread rolls, and boiled Andean ears of corn, or *choclo.* I bought a steamy ear of *choclo* and began plucking off huge white kernels the size of my thumb. I offered some to Wendy Zúniga (actually Gwendolyn, probably a testament to her mother's taste for gringo-pop names), but she had already begun munching a cornmeal *tamal* laced with beef strips and *ají,* the Andean chili.

About an hour into the trip we finally pulled into a town I could recognize in some detail. Urcos had the same tilted plaza on a slope, the same steep streets, the same little herds of tassel-eared llamas and alpacas being coaxed along by Indian girls in tire-sole sandals, black homespun skirts, and fringed, red-and-black, flat-topped hats. For the tourists, they might be walking postcards, but to me, at that moment, I felt I'd returned to a part of my past that hadn't changed. Long ago I was used to seeing shepherd girls in traditional dress, shy and giggly, bearing on their backs bundles of firewood, cornstalks, or a baby sibling.

So when we rolled into Urcos, the setting seemed so familiar, so comfortable, that I almost felt proprietary toward it all. It was something I'd known before most of the people on the bus were even born.

As we headed up the Vilcanota River valley, I started boring Wendy by announcing the name of every town we came to. I tested myself, caressing the words I'd learned so long ago: Quiquijana, Combapata, Tinta, Rajchi, San Pedro, San Pablo. Though parts of these adobe and metal-roofed towns had been spruced up, the idyllic landscape was as benignly beautiful as I remembered it: the Vilcanota flashed silver and white in its rockier, shallow stretches; the steep, mostly treeless mountain walls receded; the valley widened, and through breaks in the clouds, sunshine poured onto the green square fields of ripening corn, bean, and potato plants.

By late afternoon, with dusk coming on fast, I recognized a particular railroad crossing. We were now on the unfinished part of the highway, so we were hitting the old washboard ridges I used to maneuver, hurtling along in my blue PC jeep, deftly riding the gravel tracks, aiming for the smoothest ride possible. In the town where I used to deliver bread rolls to a one-room schoolhouse—part of a nutrition program I helped run—there now rose an imposing Inka Kola bottling plant. "The new Peru," my neighbor observed proudly.

About a half hour later I blurted out, "Sicuani!" Wendy woke from her doze. I saw nothing recognizable until we passed the small hospital located next to the train tracks. The bus followed alongside the tracks and stopped by the old bridge spanning the river. At this point the Vilcanota is really only a stream thirty miles or so from its headwaters.

"Last stop!" the driver shouted, opening the door. As everyone shuffled out, I wished Wendy good luck. She smiled, and as she moved into the crowd I could still spot her blue sweatsuit a block away.

I crossed the tracks and started up a ramplike street leading to the main square. Again, I walked slowly, remembering the thin air. On the sidewalk I stepped around a few shawled women in bowler hats squatting behind neatly piled mounds of potatoes and little displays of plastic combs, cheap knives, and hand mirrors. A mix of voices and radio music—mostly Colombian *cumbias*, Indian *huaynos*, and coastal *marineras*—came pulsing from open doorways.

Just beyond a tailor shop and a small grocery store, my stomach was drawn to the smell of cooking coming from a hole-in-the-wall eatery that had beads hanging in long strings over the doorway. I stepped in and sat down at an empty table next to a couple hunched over large glasses of *chicha*. In the dim light I spotted several guinea pigs—*cuys*—scrounging for scraps under the tables. The little hairy scavengers were an Andean delicacy since before the Incas. I ordered a bowl of beef stew.

I was just thinking I'd almost reached my goal. End of the road. I'd come all the way back to this rustic, remote town complete with domesticated rodents still underfoot. Just then a young man with a dirty white apron wrapped around his waist rushed out of the kitchen, crossed the uneven wooden floor, and turned on the big color TV set. "Michael Jordan," he explained, "*Los* Bulls."

I was soon watching an NBA game, listening to the play-by-play in English. Where was I? When I was last here the town had one weak-signal radio station. Today, I learned, TV sets proliferate. Even without a satellite dish, or *parabólico*, you can receive at least four channels, one local and three via relay transmitters from Cuzco.

I also learned Sicuani now had more than 50,000 inhabitants. When I left there were 15,000.

After dinner I walked along the main street and noticed the liveliest places were video stores packed with boys at the controls of Sega games. My head was again in full throb, so I checked into the first recommended hotel, one of three in town.

Next morning, after much rest, I opened the shutters of my third-story room and looked across the rooftops to the snow-covered peaks in the distance. Spectacular view, but my ears were hurting. Less than a hundred yards away, the church's bell-tower carillon bonged out an uptempo version of Beethoven's Fifth, or at least the most dramatic parts. This wakeup blended into the noise below—motorbikes, vendors, a few drunks, dogs, radios, and pickup trucks with bad mufflers.

After coffee and rolls in the plaza (new church and new city hall), I went looking for the home of Jaime O'Brien, a long-ago friend and the descendant of a far-flung survivor of the last century's Irish diaspora. At the house I was told by a stranger that O'Brien and his wife had died years ago.

I also knocked on a few other doors, only to learn that former friends had died, moved to Lima, or were not even known anymore.

Finally, I hit pay dirt. Jeanett Hasbun, owner of a hardware and appliance store, saw me enter and approach. "*Hola,* Roe-nahl [Ronald]," she said brightly, as if I'd been in the store yesterday. She looked a bit like a fairer-skinned, mature Indira Gandhi.

I kissed her on one cheek—the custom—then told her I was vacationing. Between customers she told me what had happened to most of the people I knew. "You can't even find them in the old cemetery," she said. "They moved all the deceased to a new cemetery. It was awful. They dropped bones and skulls everywhere. I had my father's remains burned to ashes. Now he's safe on a table in my bedroom."

Jeanett's parents were Christian Arabs who had left Jerusalem in the forties, come to Peru, and started several dry-goods stores, first in Lima, then here.

I asked her about the Spanish fort I'd seen at the exhibit in New York.

"If you mean the *huaca* on the other side of the river," she said, "well, some people call it that. But I don't know." (*Huacas* are sites of precolonial ruins.)

About then Jeanett's nephew, another Mario, dropped by and invited me to a sauna session at one of the many public baths I'd seen signs for. With a jolly clap on my back, he also insisted I join the Hasbun clan for lunch. I'd last seen Mario when he was eight, and now he had grown children himself.

At the sauna there were four of us, all men, sitting around on benches in our underwear. I asked the trio of relatives what was the most memorable time in the city's past thirty years.

"The week television came," replied Omar, who looked to be about thirty. The others smiled. What had happened was that in 1978 Peru was scheduled to play Scotland in a televised early round of soccer's World Cup games. It didn't matter that Sicuani still could not receive any TV signals; local fans started buying TV sets in Cuzco by the dozens on the promise that a Cuzco station would erect a relay transmitter on a nearby mountain to service the Sicuani area.

Two weeks before the game the antenna plan was scrapped because the builders needed a road up the mountain to deliver their equipment. Not a problem. In a cooperative spirit worthy of their industrious Inca forebears, hundreds of men, women, and children, armed with shovels, picks, and wheelbarrows, carved a five-mile road right up to the summit in eight days. By game time, the antenna was operating, and everyone saw Peru beat Scotland.

After lunch Jeanett suggested I ride to the *huaca* in one of the many tricycle taxis that were cruising around the plaza. I felt like a pasha, or some brocaded mandarin, being wheeled through the crowded streets in my own rickshaw. My peddling chauffeur, an enthusiastic but spindly young man named Willy Quispe, sped across the bridge and delivered me to the *huaca*. Located behind a new church-run school for handicapped children, the barn-size mound of mixed dirt and rock looked like a chunk of the fort I'd seen in the painting.

"Some people come here to pray," Willy explained. I knew the Spaniards often built over indigenous shrines as a matter of policy in their zeal to convert natives to Christianity.

"Wait here, I'll have a look," I said. Climbing down from the *tricitaxi*, I approached the mound, found a path to the top, and started up. I had lived several blocks away, yet I still didn't remember this site. At the end of the climb I noticed an Indian woman sitting alone on the ground at the center of the mound. I passed by her and we exchanged nods. She wasn't doing anything but sitting quietly.

Scanning the valley from this height—about thirty feet above the street—I realized Sicuani, the valley, Peru itself, was no longer a faraway place in my mind or on a map. All of it was here and now—the cool breeze, the mountains, the snow-covered peaks, the green fields, the river, the clean, clear sky pocked by puffy clouds floating westward from the Amazon, the music, the Sega games, the street stalls, the wafting smells of *choclo* and skewered chunks of beef hearts, the market crowds, the lovers and mothers, the bonging church tower, the alpacas and llamas and the single mournful flute heard in the distance. This was the feast I wanted and found.

I picked up a stone, thinking I'd return to my Connecticut home with a souvenir, a reminder. Just then the Indian woman across the way glanced up, curious. After one more scan around the valley I dropped the rock and found my way down to the street.

"Willy," I announced, climbing back into my canopied, wheeled wonder. "Let's get going."

"Where to?" Willy asked, hopping onto his seat.

"Anywhere," I said. "I'm not in a hurry."

SHIFTA

by Jeanne D'Haem

Jeanne D'Haem returned from Somalia in 1970, obtained her Ph.D. in school administration, raised a family, and worked as a school administrator in several states, but she never got over her fascination with Somalia. One story that she loves to tell is about the reaction in her village to the moon walk in 1969.

"The Somalis believe there is a tree on the moon, and each person is represented by a leaf. When your leaf falls from the tree you will die. Many feared the American rocket would kill all the Somalis when it landed. My students saved me from being stoned to death when I showed a movie to the village about the moon walk."

This piece is about the *Shifta*, the Somali bandit one encounters in the Horn of Africa. She met these renegades while returning to her small village in up-country Somalia.

The stars are bright and held in place by the overturned bowl that is the sky in Somalia. You can clearly see the constellation of Cassiopeia in the autumn sky. The shores of the Indian Ocean around Somalia are part of the legendary land of Queen Cassiopeia and King Cepheus. In Roman mythology, Cassiopeia bragged that she was more beautiful than the sea nymphs and they complained to Poseidon. He sent Cetus to waste the shores of Somalia. To stop him, Cassiopeia sacrificed her daughter, Andromeda, to Cetus by chaining her to some rocks. Perseus saw her plight and rescued her, then he turned Cetus to stone with Medusa's head. Many travelers to Somalia describe the land as if it had been laid waste by Cetus. Audrey Hepburn described it as a "moonscape" when she visited in the fall of 1992. Somali women are, however, noted the world over for their beauty, and I could understand why the sea nymphs were jealous. The men are also physically attractive but often quick to become angry. The best trait of the Somali people, independence and a strong will to survive under any circumstances, has been honed for centuries in the difficult, unforgiving climate. Unfortunately, this strength is also their weakness as they confront the modern world, where machine guns have replaced sticks and shouting. Aggressive tendencies ensured survival in the nomadic societies of the past, but these tendencies, tangled with tribal obligations, have played a large part in creating the current chaos in the country.

Sir Richard Burton was one of the earliest Europeans to travel among the Somali, and only travelers as bold and adventurous as Sir Richard have followed. He called his book about his experiences *First Footsteps in East Africa*. Sir Richard notes in 1882 that the natives in Berbera, a northern port on the Gulf of Aden, liked to attract bats to live in their houses. They had noticed that bats eat mosquitoes and do a good job of keeping the insect population down. They had also observed that malarial fever coincided with the mosquito season. Sir Richard dismissed this connection between mosquitoes and malaria as a native superstition, much to the suffering of many.

Burton has my sympathy, however. It is not always easy to understand what you see in Somalia. When I cried in frustration about this to my friend Asha, she told me: "Listen and watch, listen and watch. When you finally think that you understand, don't say anything because you don't understand. You need to listen and watch some more. You cannot speak until you have learned to listen." She pointed to her mother pounding grain in the courtyard of the house and continued: "Somali women no longer wear the black cloak of purdah, but they see the world through the veil of their experiences. You cannot communicate with them until you understand the way they see things."

When I knew her Asha had just returned from England, where she had been sent to study nursing. At first the British called her "that dirty African," but as she learned to emulate the ways of the English, they began to consider her delightful and beautiful. Asha also found the habits of the British very confounding. She described how a person would be in the middle of something, or just about to start, or even just about to finish. Rather than continue with what was happening, they would suddenly leave and go to have a cup of tea. Asha could never figure out why they just got up and left. I couldn't imagine this myself until I finally determined that it must have been "break" time. When Asha learned to stop trying to complete the job at hand and joined the others at tea, they stopped considering her "dirty."

I was a Peace Corps Volunteer in northern Somalia in 1968. I won't say that I was a good volunteer; Somalia was not an easy place to live. There were few modern amenities and life was occasionally dangerous, but usually it was very quiet. This lulls one into complacency and dims the powers of observation. During the long afternoons I heard the muted echo of the wooden camel bells on the necks of doe-eyed camels that passed my house. Nomad women would sometimes stop at the Bis Corpus house on the outskirts of town and ask for water. They had heard that the Saad Musa had adopted a white woman, and therefore members of the tribe had a right to ask me for water. The camels would stand patiently in a line, loaded with the aqual or portable Somali round house and the bags of supplies they had come into the town to buy in the souk, or market. If, by some off chance, my refrigerator had been running long enough to make ice, I would put an ice cube in the glass of water I brought out to the women, just to see the reaction. Oh, I was perverse.

"What is this?" the willowy women would ask, eyeing the clear floating object with suspicion.

"It's ice," I would tell them, in a well-practiced Somali phrase. Most people had heard of ice, and would eagerly reach into the glass and take it into their hand.

"No, this is hot!" they would shout. "It's burning me!" they would cry, dropping the opaque cube, frightened by the first touch of the modern world.

"*Wallaahii,* it's just a little water," I would explain oh so innocently, as it melted into a little circle on the hot earth.

The African clock is internal. It keeps time with the daylight and the starlight, the hunger of the people, and what needs to be done. It is not an external clock that hangs on the wall and compels us to eat even if we are not hungry, or to leave because it is time and not because we want to go. Sometimes time passes slowly, sometimes so much happens in an instant that it takes years to understand it. I had such an instant on a truck one sultry afternoon. I wanted to get from Hargeisa to my school in Arabsiyo.

This intersection between the Western conception of time as absolute and exoteric, and the African sense of time as meaningful, can pose serious problems for the traveler to Somalia. It is especially troublesome when one wants to know what time the transport truck or car will leave for the desired destination. "*Enshallah,*" or When God wills, is the cheerful answer. It does not make the least amount of sense to the driver that (given the uncertainty you perceive in his answer) you choose to stand next to the lorry as it is being loaded and wait. He does not understand that you are fearful it might leave without you, or that it is the only way you have to get where you need to go. To the Somali, the truck will not leave until it has been loaded, and that is the time when it will leave. If you are part of the load, it is obvious that it will not leave until you are on the truck. Instead of fretting about nothing, I was told to go have some tea in town. The answer to my question, "What time should I come back?" was equally obvious to any Somali: "When you are finished with the tea."

In Somalia one begins to live in the present. The sun always sets at precisely six-thirty because it is so close to the equator. The sun rises at the same hour each day and casts its shadow in the same places in the room at the same time each day. It reached the left end of the table that stood by my bed at seven each morning. If I got up when the sun reached the third tile from the wall in my bedroom and left when it reached my door, I would be on time for school, which always began after the teachers had finished drinking their morning tea.

Freed from watching hands endlessly chasing each other around a numbered dial, I began to consider time in terms of the unfolding drama of life: I knew that the trade truck would leave only after it had been loaded. If it were the rainy season, the driver would want to reach his destination before the late afternoon when the rains come. Therefore, he would leave the marketplace in Hargeisa before the midmorning prayers.

Salat, the prayer of the faithful, is one of the five pillars of Islam. It takes the place of a wristwatch in the life of Somali believers. It offers the real timetable for the day, and reminds the faithful that humankind is intended for more than working and eating. In Hargeisa, as in all major towns in Somalia, the call to prayers is given by the muezzin. His call drifts over the crowded camel market like the distant pealing of church bells. He tells the faithful, and the unfaithful alike, that God is great, Mohammed is his prophet, and the time for salat has come. All the business of the town ceases at the call to worship (so the driver will want to have the truck loaded by that time).

> O ye who believe! When the call is heard for the prayer of the day . . . haste unto remembrance of Allah and leave your trading. (Sura 62:9)

There are forty-seven boxes, fifteen sacks of grain, seven baskets of oranges, and four chickens that have to be loaded on the truck. If I go to the tea shop and have one cup of spiced sweet tea, the truck will be loaded and ready to leave when I get back. Allah only knows what time that will be, but that is God's problem, not mine. I understand when the truck will leave, and it has nothing to do with numbers and everything to do with life.

Trade trucks in Somalia are the central means of transportation. Boxes of rice and flour, cloth, tins of kerosene, bags of grain, boxes of fruits and vegetables are piled into the back of the truck. Human cargo rides on top of the supplies. The riders stand or sit, depending on the size of the load. For a few extra shillings I could ride in the cab with the driver, but there is only one such seat. Usually I was exposed to the burning sun and endless dust curling its insistent way into every crevice of my body as I sat on the back of the truck.

Trucks are not plentiful in Somalia. Working trucks that run with four intact tires are even more rare. Most trucks are held together with wire, and then rope when the wire runs out. Spare parts are difficult to obtain and frequent breakdowns far from help are inevitable. Given this situation, everyone is eager to get their produce or passenger on a working truck, and loading it is a mission. Stuff gets piled right up to the top of the sides of the truck bed. Filling every conceivable space with the maximum amount possible is the most important goal of the driver and his helper. Several relatives stand around to watch while they lean on sturdy canes. They comment on the efforts of the laboring workers like a Greek chorus, suggesting improvements and predicting doom. Eventually the bed of the truck is filled with crates placed so carefully together that they rival the Inca stonework in the Temple of the Sun. Bags of grain are piled on top of the crates, meticulously balanced, until they tower over the walls of the truck. The truck bows under this weight but retains just enough resiliency to hold the thirty-five women and children who climb up over the sides holding eighteen dhills or baskets that are so tightly woven they hold milk. The men will clamber on just as the lorry begins to move, searching for a comfortable place to sit that is not too precariously close to the edge of the truck, yet can allow a hasty exit should the need arise. From a distance, a fully loaded truck looks almost like a hot fudge sundae sprinkled with nuts on top.

One morning I spied an especially attractive place on a truck I was taking back to my teaching post near the border between Ethiopia and Somalia. It was a big wooden box placed next to the front side of the truck with nothing on top of it, although boxes and bags were piled on the three other sides. There was even enough room to tuck my legs over the side of the box so I wouldn't have to spend three hours with my feet curled under and no place to stretch them when they fell asleep. For some strange reason this particular spot had room to spare. I expected my friend from school, Subti, and several other travelers to sit on the box next to me, but no one did. I had often longed for something to lean against on other truck rides, so I leaned back gratefully. However, my pleasure at having a backrest was quickly unraveled as this overloaded omnibus disheveled its way over the rough terrain. There was nothing to prevent the persistent bumping of my back against the bare side of the truck as it bumped over the dirt track that only pretends to be a road in Somalia.

When we left the dusty field near the market, I wrapped myself in my *goa*, or Somali cloak, to keep off the already burning sun and fashioned it into a hood about my face to keep out the blowing dust. Perched on the truck top near eight milk dhills and four fat women, I was tremendously glad, as always, when the truck began to creak forward—immensely glad that the thing actually started and shocked that we were, in fact, moving.

Of course, progress doesn't last long. We must stop just outside town in order to pay for the ride. All the men jumped down and squatted in the shade of the truck. The women were left to gossip and roast in the desert sun. The driver counted his money and his passengers, haggled, joked, pissed, and prayed. At last we started to move again, and the cooling wind against my face was marred only by the stinging dust in my eyes. By one or two that afternoon we would be lucky to reach Arabsiyo, thirty miles from here.

The sky is a large bowl overturned on the earth. It keeps everything in its place and ensures that the future will be much like the past. Despite the crumbling road and persistent (but reassuring) drone of the engine as it edged itself over the desert, a truck is not a quiet affair. The conversation is lively and continual. This is a social occasion and the Somalis take full advantage, especially when a strange foreigner has joined the group.

"HiiYea," said a toothless but smiling old woman, pinching my arm. Her skin looked like an old paper bag rescued from the trash and smoothed out to be used again. "How can this woman be rich if she is so thin? If she had some fat it would improve her looks." She ran her hand up my backbone to show that my bones protruded and, having proved her point, turned triumphantly to her audience.

Another equally toothless old woman joined in the fun. "Howa, Grandma, I doubt that more fat would do her any good. Who would marry anyone so ugly!"

"I wonder if she has a disease or was born with this dreadful white skin," the first murmured.

"Mother, this is a very strange situation," teased Subti, who loved to play this game with unsuspecting nomads as we walked back to town from school. He liked to tease the women who watered their livestock at the wells we passed. "This woman is my sister," he said and waited to hear the gasp that always followed.

"*Wallaahi!*" they both responded, loud enough to attract the attention of several other travelers.

"I was born like this, she like that, and we both had the very same mother. My hair is black, hers is red. My eyes are black, hers are blue. It was quite a shock to our poor mother, Allah protect her."

"*Wallaahi!*" chorused the truck travelers.

"Your mother must have offended a jinn," replied the oldest woman, looking me over with obvious pity. "Only a spirit would play such a trick. Making a live person the same color as the devil!" She shook her head in sympathy and poked me gingerly to see if any of the terrible whiteness would come off my skin onto hers. To the Muslim believer, and in particular the Somali, the fire-born jinn are spirits, considered below the lowest of the angels. They can inspire, mislead, or even possess a man or woman who has faltered in the path of the faithful. Some jinn are good and others are not, but all serve to remind the faithful that the universe has its secrets hidden from the minds of men and women. Surely, my white skin, in contrast to my "brother" Subti's perfect dark features, must be the work of a mischievous jinn.

My red hair was not considered so terrible by the Somalis, who are devout Muslims. In Muslim tradition, the angel Jibra'il, or Gabriel to Christians and Jews, is spoken of as a shining figure whose saffron hair is as luminous as the very stars in the night sky. Many Somali women use henna on their hair to beautify themselves. Men will use it on white beards for the same reason. It was agreed, however, by my sympathetic fellow travelers, that even my auburn hair would not help to dispel the ugly effect of my colorless skin. It was hopeless, no one would marry me. It was a good thing I had a job and could support myself.

An American friend had presented Subti with the gift of a necktie when I had introduced them during our trip to Hargeisa. Subti pulled the tie out from his little bundle and began to show it around to those on the truck.

"It's American," he said proudly. Everyone fingered the soft silk and admired the colors.

Finally, an intrepid soul risked the important question, "What does it do?"

"The American men wear it around their necks," replied Subti. He showed how the tie was put on and I helped him to tie the slipknot. Everyone tried it on then, working the magical knot open and closed about their necks. Somali men wear a sort of skirt folded about the waist called a *ma'aweiss* and a short-sleeved shirt. Because of the relentless desert heat, the top shirt button is never closed. The men on the truck placed the tie about their necks as Subti and I instructed them, and sat wearing it, looking rather silly and terribly uncomfortable. Again, the insistent questions began: "What does it do?"

Subti looked at me for help. "It doesn't do anything," I explained. "It is only for decoration." This was met with incredulous disbelief by a people who own nothing that is not useful. Possessions, for those who live in the desert, are only those items that have many uses.

The Somalis have been nomadic travelers for centuries. They have learned how to move quickly and efficiently because their lives and the livelihood of their families depend on quickly moving the herds of camels, cattle, and goats from the grasslands where they eat, to the wells in the dry season. For nomads, emphasis is on economy and simplicity in the design of their utilitarian possessions. Practical concerns override any others in the acquisition of clothing and anything else that must be carried. The idea that the tie served no purpose at all was totally unacceptable in this culture. The men refused to believe me, and Subti, although he knew it was true, was also at a loss to defend the concept.

The best example of what the Somalis take on trek is the ubiquitous *goa*. This is a colorful cloth about the size of a sheet which
everyone wears. The women have a smaller version called a *chal-
mut*. Originally called a "Mericany" since the cloth was made in
America, this piece of apparel rivals anything in the L. L. Bean
catalog in its versatility and suitability for desert travel.

During a dusty trip behind your camel herds or on the back of
a truck, one wraps the *goa* over one's head and mouth like a
shawl. Thus, the dust and dirt are kept out of your hair and
other clothes as well as your mouth. If the day is fine and not
dusty, you can sling the *goa* around your neck loosely like a
scarf, where it will be out of the way. Should you stop for
prayers, you can dip a corner of the *goa* in some water and use it
as a washcloth to wash your hands and feet. If you are a heathen
and don't pray, you can use it to wash your face and hands anyway. If the sun gets hot in the afternoon, you can wind it into a
turban and use it to keep the sun off your head. Later, if it gets
cool in the evening, you can wear it like a cape to keep warm. If
you sold the goat you brought to market, you can tie the money
in one corner of the *goa* and use it like a change purse. If the goat
is unruly, you can tie him in the *goa* and keep him from wandering off. If you are trying to visit a girlfriend and her father is not
too pleased about your visit, you can wrap yourself in the *goa* so
only your eyes will show. Perhaps he will not know it is you
slinking around the camp, trying to catch his daughter at the
well. On trade trucks, when you are sitting on a hard box, you
can fold it into a pillow and hope that it will cushion your bottom.

Despite all my efforts at explaining to my fellow travelers that
the necktie had no earthly purpose, they still looked back at me
in disbelief. Then, an enterprising young man pulled his *goa* up
around his head. He put the necktie around his neck, over the
goa, and tightened it. This served to keep the *goa* in place despite
the blowing wind on the back of the truck, and a resounding
"*Saah*," or voiced assent, came in unison from the truck voy-
agers. Western men must use the necktie to keep their *goa*'s
securely on their heads when it is windy. They were obviously
relieved to find that the strange item of apparel had a use, and I
decided not to disabuse them of what they thought. I was being
distracted at that point and was quite alarmed.

As the truck strained to cross the desert, I kept feeling hot air next to my left ankle. I assumed it was a little breeze wafting around the truck's cargo. However, the hot air puffs continued even when the truck was not moving. It was a sweltering morning and I was tired, too tired to bother with a little puff of hot air. I moved my foot closer to the box to avoid the draft. It stopped for a moment, but then I felt an utterly strange sensation on my ankle that could not be ignored. It was the unmistakable wetness and roughness of a lick.

It is impossible to jump very far when one's legs are wedged between a wooden crate and bags of sorghum and the truck is pitching over another rough spot in the road. I tried to move my foot into the bags next to the box and doubled myself into a paper clip. I peered into the holes crudely cut into the top of the crate. As my eye slowly adjusted to the darkness within, I discerned the shape of a large beige animal. It was a lion, and he was licking my ankle.

There are some situations where one reacts differently than one would in other circumstances. It was very hot and dusty. I was very hot and tired. There was no place to move to, and as the truck was lurching down into a dry riverbed I had to hang on the side so I would not be pitched out. The lion was also very hot and tired. He looked up at me in abject misery. I felt the same way. In addition to the pitching, rolling truck ride, I could tell that he and I shared a particular physical characteristic — we can't eat when we are upset. Knowing this, I knew without a doubt that I had nothing to fear from the poor beast. That is how I came to have an adventure while sitting on a lion.

The lorry continued its courageous labors all during the torpid and dusty afternoon. As we traveled, I realized that the lion was not about to move because he must have been shipped from the south, the only place a lion could still be found in Somalia. He was, most likely, on his way to the northern border of Djibouti, and I wondered if he would live to see it. He had been throwing up and was covered with ooze. He probably had licked my ankle in a desperate attempt to find some liquid. I was afraid he might die of dehydration. The Somalis are quite cautious about cats, big and small, and keep their distance. They do not keep pets other than their own herd animals. At last I understood why my cheerful companions had not taken a seat with me on the box. They would not sit anywhere near the lion, nor would they offer it food or water. The other travelers had known we had a feline passenger and kept a reserved distance. They had reserved that seat for me.

Without warning, several men on horses appeared out of the bush and blocked the road. They signaled for the driver to stop and shouted something in Somali that was unintelligible to me. The truck creaked to a halt and people began to climb out of the back. I took off my sandals and stretched my legs out over the bags of grain. I was hoping for a peaceful moment alone while the Somalis said their afternoon prayers. I had decided to try to give the lion something to drink.

After everyone left the truck, I slowly pried up a section of the top of the box with my pocketknife. As I had suspected, the lion hardly moved despite the disturbance. I wet a corner of my *goa* with water and lowered it to the suffering animal. At first he seemed not to notice the water dripping into his panting mouth, then he took a few licks, but I feared it was too late.

Angry with the abuse of this poor miserable animal, I sat up and leaned out over the side of the truck to see what was going on. The driver was talking to one of the men on the horses. No one had even started praying yet, but they were just standing in little groups talking quietly. I assumed the horsemen were relatives of the driver and were asking for a ride, or *quat*, or something. I took one of my dusty sandals and banged it on the side of the truck. "*Wham-a hii?*" I asked. "What is this?"

The horseman talking with the driver seemed surprised. He left the conversation he was having and rode over to the side of the truck. He looked at me and my red hair blowing in the hot wind of the early afternoon. "*Muga-Ah,* what's your name?" he asked jauntily. Our eyes met boldly, since to look at a man directly is forbidden to Somali women.

"Jeanne," I replied. "*Muga i goo waa Jeanne,* I'm Jeanne." He returned my upturned gaze, and we appraised each other. His face was the color of mahogany, smooth with perfectly spaced features and large calm eyes. He tightened his hands on the reins of his horse when his eyes suddenly recognized the shape of the lion, which had been revived by the water and began to stir in the open box I was sitting on. "*Muga-Ah?*" I asked him, enjoying his obvious surprise at the truck's cargo and his very handsome face. "Who are you?"

"*Shifta, Wa Shifta,*" he replied quietly, looking deeply into my eyes. Then, for some strange reason, he handed me his hat. It was made of little brown burrs all stuck together to form the shape of a hat with a bill. I was looking at it when he signaled to his men. They rode off over the rolling hills into the desert and disappeared almost as quickly as they had come.

The other travelers climbed back into the truck, and the driver drove on without any further delays. This episode was discussed in great detail in highly animated conversation for the rest of the trip. I could not follow the Somali because it was much too fast and too excited, and I was very tired from the exhausting heat and the rolling ride. I draped my *goa* over my head and dozed.

Later that night, back home in Arabsiyo, Abdillahi, the headmaster of my school, came to visit me with the two other teachers. He was one of the only Somali men I ever met who could be considered plump. He had a round belly and a pudgy face, and I liked him despite his often pompous attitude.

"The town is talking and talking about you again, Jean," he said. The Somalis had trouble saying Jeanne, but not Jean. "Do you Americans know what the Shifta warriors are?"

"No."

"They are bands of guerrillas who are fighting in the border dispute between the Somali and Ethiopian governments. The British gave some of the Somali lands to the Ethiopians when they drew the maps of the two countries at the time of our independence in 1960. You were near the disputed territory today and some of these Shifta stopped the truck and were going to rob it. They are renegades. Didn't you see the guns they were carrying?" he asked incredulously.

"No." I never knew when to believe Abdillahi. I hadn't been looking for guns. I suppose I had thought they were waving sticks.

"You were fearless, they are saying in town. You banged on the side of the truck with your shoe and insulted the leader right to his face."

"I didn't mean to insult anybody. I was banging the dust off my sandal."

"Showing the bottom of the shoe is highly insulting to Muslims; don't you know that?"

"Oh." Another faux pas.

Then Abdillahi's eyes twinkled and he laughed. "This Shifta is from the interior. I think he had never seen a white woman closely before. The Shifta saw your white skin, and those blue eyes of yours, and your hair uncovered. He saw that you were not afraid of him, and then he saw that you were sitting on a lion. He was worried that you might be the actual devil herself and has run back into Ethiopia, the hyena." Abdillahi was obviously pleased with himself for figuring out what happened during my encounter with the Shifta.

"That's not what happened at all," interrupted Subti, who never minded contradicting Abdillahi. "There is a story in the Koran about Mohammed and a prostitute at a well. She had seen a dog who was very thirsty, but could not draw any water up from the well. She dipped her shoe into the water and gave it to the dog. Mohammed said that all her sins would be forgiven because of her kindness.

"Jean," he continued with a little smile, "everyone thinks you are a prostitute because you are not closed [infibulated]. When the Shifta asked who was sitting on the truck, the driver told him it was the American prostitute living in Arabsiyo. That Shifta remembered the story from the Koran when he saw that you were giving water to the lion. I think he decided not to rob the truck for fear of offending Allah. He thought you brought a message from God."

In Somalia there is never one version of an event, there are always at least three that are endlessly discussed and reconsidered. This was no exception. "I heard this in town," said Abdul Kader, who had not been on the truck. "The Shifta went up to the truck and saw this very strange woman. He wanted to know who this is. "Jean, that's Jean," everyone from the truck told him. He thought the people were telling him it was a jinn. He didn't believe it until he went up to see this spirit, and you said, "I'm Jean." Everyone heard it. Then he got scared since everyone is telling him there is a jinn on the truck, and the jinn even admits she is a jinn. He gave you his hat as an offering to protect his men from this bad truck spirit."

Abdillahi's eyes rested on the new torch I had just purchased that morning in Hargeisa. "I will need this torch to patrol the town tonight in case they decide to come back. Thank you for the gift," he said, taking the torch from my table. "I think you should write a letter to your father and tell him what good care I am taking of you here in Somalia. He should send me a present."

"Taking care of what?" I asked. This was the second torch that Abdillahi had taken.

"I'm seeing that no one is fucking you."

"Abdillahi," I said, "that is a very rude word in my language." Subti shook his head and rolled his eyes behind Abdillahi's back. Abdul Kader leaned forward and looked as if he hoped I would explain a little more about this American fucking.

"That's the problem with your language," Abdillahi retorted. "You have only this one word in English, *fucking*. In my language we have so many words I can talk for days about fucking."

Listen and watch, listen and watch, I thought to myself, remembering Asha's advice. You cannot be heard until you learn to listen.

Abdillahi left with my new torch. I could see the three of them walking through the dark street outside my house, safe in the little circle of light. Abdillahi was still discussing the day's events with Subti and Abdul Kader. He wanted my torch, and he wanted to boss everyone around and feel important and powerful. However, he did not want the Shifta hat, which I still have and will always treasure.

I have often reflected on the handsome Shifta and why he decided not to rob the truck. I wonder if, in the brief moment we shared, he saw that I was a renegade like him. I had obviously left my family and had gone off in search of a greater adventure, alone, and outside the reach of my own people. He and I were both wild enough to have insisted on doing something that was very dangerous. I lived alone in Africa in the name of world understanding, he was fighting for the reunification of the Somali people. We were both young, idealistic, and adventurous. I like to think that he gave me his Shifta hat, not because he feared that I was a jinn, or the devil, but because he saw that in my own way, I, too, was a Shifta.

ON RECOVERING KYOTO

by John Givens

Going back to a place that was once important to you
is always risky. It may have changed, for one thing. Or,
worse, it might not.

John Givens got his first taste of what trying to
recover Kyoto might entail in a dingy East Village
sushi-ya. He had overheard two Japanese men arguing
about what had happened to a cheerful girl pop star
named Amachi Mari. That Mari-chan's career had long
since fizzled out was not in question. The excruciat-
ingly buoyant creature had specialized in saccharine
tunes, such as "My Boyfriend Is Left-handed," and
although Japanese pop music can be numbingly bland,
with cute girl singers replacing cute girl singers, all as
alike as cupcakes popping out of a bakery hopper, the
uncertain fate of the particular incarnation seemed
suggestive.

The fellow smoking Short Hopes as he picked his
way through a *supeshiaru nigiri* insisted that Mari had
ended tragically, driven mad from grief at her sputtering career until she was reduced to sitting alone in a
darkened room, weeping uncontrollably. The other fellow disagreed. Mari-chan had accepted fate's fickle
thumb in the eye and gotten a job teaching kinder-
garten in a bedroom community outside Tokyo.

Whichever was the case hardly matters. Givens,

who had been a Peace Corps Volunteer in Korea in the
late sixties and is the author of three novels, had
worked in advertising and marketing for twelve years
in Japan before returning to the United States. Now
he had a sudden appreciation that life had gone on in
Japan without him. Heading back there was the only
solution.

Your train comes out of the long tunnel back into hazy daylight and a cheerful arrival jingle alerts the drowsy. You roll slowing past the shimmering river, past the tile roofs of poor houses huddled together and rusted to the color of dried blood by years of iron rain from the tracks; then, as you reach the giant but impotent bowling pin on the roof of the venerable bowling alley, you simply cease to be moving. The sky over the low city is the soft gray of old cellophane wrap, crumpled into clouds above the rim of the surrounding mountains. All the doors hiss open at the same instant, and people stand up and start hitting you with their luggage even though you're getting off, too.

"*Oy! Watanabe-kun?*" a man calls. "*Kore wa Kyoto ka?*"

Kyoto? Young Watanabe sits up and looks around blearily. An empty pair of miniature black Suntory Old bottles beside his seat indicates the source of his befuddlement. Is this Kyoto? He doesn't know.

The elevated Shinkansen station platform is a ponderous edifice of concrete, steel, and glass that floats above the low-slung city like an elongated aircraft carrier. You get only a glimpse of the Eastern Hills in the distance before the long escalator sucks you down toward the exit wickets. This modern station always seemed an inappropriate gateway for the 1200-year-old city. And now there's a gleaming new subway system that glides smugly up the length of the city, following under a main north-south boulevard that had once been a thoroughfare for closed-in black lacquered oxcarts containing Heian aristocrats too refined to endure being seen. The new subway is adorned with plastic statues of a cute cartoon humanoid theme character draped with informative sandwich boards but blinded under an oversized top hat that covers its eyes and nose amusingly, and thus focuses attention on the ovoid cartoon cheeks and chin and grinning crescent of lipless mouth, so that the thing looks like the sliced-off end of a length of baloney that somebody jammed a garden trowel into.

No. This is not Kyoto.

I was in the Peace Corps in South Korea. Children threw stones at us, and we carried little identity cards that listed the diseases we had acquired while trying to make a difference and the medications we were taking to ease our doubts. I managed TB conversion, full-blown chronic amoebic dysentery, and a brief infestation of lung flukes. Getting lung flukes carried a certain cachet. The TB was no big deal. You could convert to positive in Brooklyn or the Bronx, still can. The dysentery, too, although debilitating, was less impressive. Everybody in-country who ate experienced alimentary ructions of one sort or another.

Sickness occupied the slots in our lives that had formerly been the property of sitcoms or college pranks or organized sports. Diseases of all sorts were acceptable as general-purpose dinner table conversation. You took your medications with OB beer or with one of the potent Korean fermented rice beverages, the quality of which could be stipulated in terms of the dimensions of the meshes of the sieve it was poured through. You would discuss the most revolting things over grilled tripe or fermented cabbage or dog soup. Even cold pepper-sauce noodles, which had to be consumed without breathing since air combined with the pepper sauce agonizingly silenced you only for as long as it took to dine—took to suck down the slimy red mess in a single, determined inhalation, that is—and then wait, sweating, attentive for the first signature quiverings of apoplexy, until the spasms in your digestive tract passed.

Queasiness was a fundamental condition. Nausea could be separated into two broad families. "Lesser nausea" made eating

Korean food unpleasant while "greater nausea" also placed even the smorgasbord at the Swedish hospital cafeteria in Seoul or the hamburgers at the Seaman's Club in Pusan out of reach. We became like silver seniors boring each other on sunny benches in Miami Beach. As a greeting, "How are you?" was always answered in vivid detail. You could tell people you hardly knew that you: do ❏, do not ❏ have worms in your stool. Hook? Tape? Pin? Dead or still wriggling? We relished how disgusting we could be.

Chronic depression was another widely shared if unexpected response to having seen the glass as half full. Many of us medicated ourselves with alcoholic beverages. Some smoked the dried leaves of an indigenous plant, the stalks of which Korean farmers sometimes stripped then flattened and twisted into crude rope. One poor, isolated male volunteer became so depressed that his body refused to obey the most basic commands. Get up, eat, drink, pee over there, stop weeping, speak, roll over—all were beyond him. He went home early.

I stayed the full two years. Plus one day extra due to flight scheduling. Life in Korea had created an appetite for the exotic, however. So still hungry for the thrill of self-discovery if not that of volunteer service, I moved to Kyoto and lived there for four years.

Kyoto was the capital of Japan from 794 until the Meiji emperor was officially moved to Tokyo in 1869, an event that stipulates the advent of modern Japan. On the day he left, the citizens of Kyoto stood in the streets with empty hands and wept as the Imperial procession passed by. But Kyoto had actually ceased to be the capital in anything but name by the beginning of the seventeenth century, and Tokyo's preeminence as the center for Japanese culture as well as Japan's political and business capital had long since become irrefutable.

Today, Kyoto can be thought of as the repository for Japan's premodern soul. Japanese schoolchildren come to Kyoto en masse to discover what being Japanese used to mean. During the spring school travel season in particular, Kyoto is inundated by a roiling sea of uniformed students. Drawn from all over the country, wave after identical wave of them flow through the most famous shrines and temples, gazing dutifully at whatever they're told to gaze dutifully at, then lining up for the obligatory group photograph before moving on to the next gazing venue.

The students travel in prodigious bus caravans, and the ancient shrines and temples of the old city shudder with the massed power of their diesel engines. They all go to the same places and see the same things. Late in the afternoon, the covered shopping malls of downtown Kyoto resound with their chirruping cries of delight as they photograph one another buying cheesy souvenirs that are not dissimilar from the cheesy souvenirs that their parents photographed one another buying in their own happy school days.

Kyoto profits hugely from tourism. The city functions as a kind of "living museum." Or, given the dewy youth of the preponderance of the visitors, perhaps "cultural petting zoo" might be more accurate. Yet despite the city's singular beauty, many serious people dismiss Kyoto as being little more than a quaint but irrelevant backwater. It's *too* antique. Much of what seems most characteristically Japanese developed during the Edo period, when Japan was closed to other countries. And this mostly took place in Edo, the city that became modern Tokyo. Proponents argue that while Kyoto has retained more old buildings, Tokyo maintains more of the spirit of the "real" Japan. They might be right.

Nevertheless, I have never loved a place the way I loved Kyoto—not San Francisco, a city awash with its own picturesqueness, not power-drenched but benign Tokyo, not even fervid New York, with the staggering multiplicity of occurrences that can befall one there.

Now, fifteen years after having left Kyoto forever, I had come back to rediscover what it was about the city that had so engaged me. Despite my determination not to expect too much, I was aware of the risk. The world moves on without asking your permission. People rip out the quaint trolley tracks that run down the middle of old boulevards and throw them quaintly into the sea. Shrines that used to let you enter freely now charge an admission fee that covers the salaries of those stationed at the gates to prevent you from sneaking in without paying. Popular gardens become crowded. Parking becomes a problem. Parking lots replace less popular gardens, enabling even greater crowds to crowd into the popular gardens. Temples prized for serenity set up a system of loudspeakers with a recorded voice chattering unendingly about how serene it all is. Beverage vending machines sprout in malignant clusters, scattering empty beverage cans like evil seeds. Television occurs. Cable television occurs. Satellite cable television occurs. A priest in an ancient shrine so pure, so perfect, so self-contained that a thousand years of famine and mayhem haven't been able to alter it could now watch CNN and ponder the previously imponderable: *Dō yū imi, desuka? Kono NCAA basukketo-boru fainaru foru?*

No. You don't go back to your past indifferently, particularly not to a period of your life that seemed determinant.

But disappointments come in different grades, as if yearnings were like soy sauces, classifiable by degree of pungency. And the taxi ride to my *ryokan* inn let me know that I might be onto a rare one. Because something had happened to Kyoto that I hadn't anticipated: it had stayed the same.

Oh, there was a new building here or there, a glossy department store on the main crossroads where one didn't used to exist. (For the life of me, I couldn't remember what *had* been there.) But once I got into Gion, the central part of the city just east of the river, the past came surging back. I gazed out at a world I had known. Here was where I had first wanted whatever it was that had eventually become sufficiently unattainable to send me scurrying for refuge in what has to be the exact opposite of Kyoto: Iowa City, Iowa. (The merry tune "I know all I owe, I owe Iowa" is not, apparently, in my case, at least, true.) This was the soul of downtown Kyoto. The *geta* clog maker's shop was still there. So was the paper-lantern maker and the oil-paper–umbrella maker and the wooden-comb maker and the cedar-bucket maker. Even the grubby old *chankonabe* stew restaurant that catered to visiting sumo wrestlers was still on the corner, a *noren* curtain of braided ropes hanging in front of the door. Once again, the serene Eastern Hills formed a backdrop to this most traditional section of the antique city. It was as it had always been, and I stood alone with my baggage on the edge of the narrow lane and ignored the careening taxis and delivery trucks. Despite the obvious impossibility of doing anything of the sort, I was flooded by the desire to live there again. And *this time get it right* —whatever that might mean.

Nostalgia persisted as I settled into my inn. The thick tatami mats were still new enough to smell grassy, and the far walls were composed entirely of sliding rice paper *shoji* doors in front of a narrow veranda. Sunlight glowed on the opaque white paper panels, creating the dim, muted interior that the Japanese prefer. Furnishings were limited to a low black lacquer table in the middle of the larger room and floor cushions with separate backrests. A *tokonoma* alcove held a faded calligraphy scroll with a simple flower arrangement placed before it. *Futon* quilts would be spread out tonight when the inn's maid decided it was time for me to sleep. There was a tall, spindly bamboo rack to hang a kimono over but no closets, no chest of drawers, no place to put anything away. I slid open the *shoji*. Beyond were sliding glass outer doors that opened onto a tiny enclosed garden. The garden was a green space not much bigger than the room I was in. You could sit out on the veranda and feel the spring day heating the rocks and the moss and the camellia bushes, and listen to ducks splashing in the shallow canal just beyond the garden wall. The outside world was incorporated as if it were another design element. The ambience created instant contentment.

I sat on the veranda and listened to the suitably splashing ducks, with the rumble of city buses creating a drone note behind them. I had a large bottle of Kirin beer, dripping and icy, and a dish of dried *soramame* beans mixed with a few rubbery squid tentacle tips. I had brought my worn copy of *The Ambassadors* by Henry James as the reading matter most appropriate for Kyoto. Strether would once again tell little Bilham to "live! Live all you can! It's a mistake not to," and once again, I would agree.

A wind bell clinked gently in the May breeze. I could hear the approaching squawk of the tofu peddler's horn. Old Kyoto had appropriated my room with the languid ease of a friendly cat.

It was as if everything was the same.

But if everything is the same but you aren't, then everything isn't the same.

The Kamo River runs from north to south and divides Kyoto into unequal halves. The main entertainment and shopping districts are found in the streets and lanes along both banks of the river, and the city's two most famous geisha quarters—Gion and Pontocho—regard each other warily from either side of it, as if

the river were necessary to keep apart geisha who might otherwise fall to squabbling with each other.

The Kamo is a narrow, shallow, docile river, crosshatched
with bridges and low weirs and held firmly between parallel concrete embankments. Nothing commercial is ever asked of it. The
Kamo is for looking at. The massive embankments suggest a
response to a history of flooding that today's shallow flow hardly
credits. Kyoto was laid out in the eighth century on the T'ang
Chinese model of an ordered grid of broad boulevards enclosing
narrower interior alleys and lanes, and the Kamo looks something like another boulevard, maintained in perfect parallel with
the others that run north and south — wider and lower and wet-
ter, of course — but still very much in keeping with the overall
design. In warm weather, people stroll along the banks after
work or on Sundays, and at night lovers sit there huddled in
pairs that are spaced at intervals so regular one suspects a late-
arriving couple must create peristaltic ripples up and down the
river bank. The winter river takes on a hard, flat, metallic blue
quality under the icy sky, and weeds at the waterline become fili-
greed with silvery rime. In summer, children wade in the river
and catch trout fingerlings with homemade gauze nets, but in
May when I was there, the only threat faced by tadpoles or min-
nows were the patient white egrets stalking the shallows near
the pools formed under the stone weirs and peering into the
bright, sparkling water.

Geographically, Kyoto is in a basin surrounded on three sides
by steep, low, heavily wooded hills. Much of the newer downtown area looks like a typical large modern Japanese city. Yet
Kyoto was never bombed during the war so large swaths of the
city still retain the ambience of old Japan. The Gion district, in
particular, is a grid of narrow lanes lined with lovely old Kyoto-
style town houses. It would be hard to imagine an urban setting
more conducive to leisurely strolling.

It was only a short walk from the river to the Gion Yasaka
Shrine, where the fabled Eastern Hills begin. I stayed on an
inner lane rather than go up the main boulevard. The difference
between the two is unmistakable. The hand-carved wooden-
comb shops on the main boulevards cater mostly to tourists now,
but the hand-carved wooden-comb shops on the smaller inside
lanes still cater primarily to the people who live around there. To
buy freshly roasted coffee beans, you go to the main street. For

the best tea, however, it's the shops on the inside lanes that you want. Even an interior downtown lane no more than a few meters from a big street will nevertheless still maintain its antique quality.

People on the boulevards walk differently from people in the interior lanes, too. The boulevards are crowded with pedestrians, so even though there's lots to look at in the shop windows, the crowds make you want to move faster and push through them. On the other hand, the narrow interior lanes are usually empty, so you can go as fast as you want, which inevitably seems to slow you down. It's as if you're responding to that sweetly *personal* sense of well-being that arises when you are in a neighborhood where people are glad they live where they do.

Traditional Kyoto houses and restaurants present a blank face to the street. Narrow, closely spaced wooden bars cover street-level windows and loose bamboo blinds hang over those of the second floor. Space is at a premium in Kyoto. Buildings extend right to the edge of their fronting roads, but the structures face inward, focused on the garden in the back. Yet there is no hint of New York paranoia in operation here. The wooden bars over the street-level windows are held in place with nails so flimsy even an inept thief could probably gain access. It's privacy that's wanted here. Prying eyes are to be kept out, not prying robbers.

There is plenty of street life. Doors get left open, things are placed outside to dry in the sun. Neighbors stop and gossip, kids play in the lanes, and toys get left behind so a driver trying to work his car through has to stop and clear them out of the way. If the city can be disparaged as a living museum, it's certainly one overseen by caretakers who are untroubled by their alleged vitiation. Kyoto people live comfortably within their past, often considering some antique custom or practice worthy of comment only if some foreigner is there looking for an explanation. Their emperor abandoned them for the power and glory of modern Tokyo. Yet the people of Kyoto present nothing so much as an unqualified sense of satisfaction.

Was that what had so drawn me when I lived here? The easy grace of those who have accepted themselves as they are?

A kind of aesthetic susurration occupies the old Gion geisha district. You just get hints of it while walking through the streets, glimmers on the periphery. It's the sound of someone practicing a samisen upstairs, a bright flash of a brocade sleeve disappearing behind a sliding paper door, a red oil-paper umbrella open and drying on top of a bamboo gate. You are tantalized but left unsatisfied. You keep trying to seize phantoms. A sliding door standing open invites you to peer into a shadowy entry hall. But there's always another door farther back, deeper in the shadows, and it's always closed. There's something intriguing about the old city that seems appropriate to your own life. Perhaps it's the sense that you could learn how to be if only you were able to phrase the question suitably. Not knowing means you are reduced to blundering along, hoping to encounter an accident that will instruct you.

Yet it had seemed to me that the accident was more likely to happen in Kyoto than anywhere else. And I felt the old yearning again as I made my way toward the shrines and temples of the Eastern Hills.

At the Gion Yasaka Shrine, the city ends and the hills begin. I went up through the main gate. The cheerful tumult of mercantile Kyoto was replaced by the slightly more muted but still good-natured bustle of a busy shrine. Kyoto had plague problems in the ninth century, and the compound of gaudy orange torii gates and shrine buildings was established throughout the lower reaches of the forest to help keep the pest at bay. Once inside, a series of wide granite stairs and upward paths leads you to the main shrine plaza. An old Noh stage hung with banks of paper lanterns in the middle stands across from the central shrine building. The shrine's principal deity is encased in this large structure, but no one is ever allowed to see him . . . her . . . it—even the deity's gender seems ambiguous, and the only corporeal manifestation I've ever heard of is as a small, round mirror.

You address the deity with conventional prayers. Long, thick ropes hanging down in front of the facade of the building have hollow metal gongs mounted at the tops just under the overhanging eaves. Before praying, you swing the ropes to sound the gongs and rouse the deities. Then, after you've finished, you clap twice to let the gods know it's okay to go back to napping or whatever they were doing before you bothered them. On a busy day, the shrine plaza fills with petitioners, and the gong-rattling and terminative clapping become an incessant barrage that must keep the gods hopping.

Behind the shrine, the garden steepens and spreads out until it is large enough to be regarded as a park. Some of the "best" cherry trees are just behind the Yasaka Shrine, and during that brief, heady period in April when cherry blossoms stun the world with their pale pink light, the gardens spreading up the sides of the hills become filled with celebrants in an agreeable mixture of tourists and locals, rich and poor, young and old, aficionados of the poignant and common drunks, and until late in the evening, wherever you go, human contact is at its most unremitting.

But by May the blossoms have long been gone and the trees were swelling masses of bright green leaves glowing in the hazy sunlight. Gravel paths lead up past arbors of ancient wisteria branches heavy with pale mauve racemes of scented flowers hanging above the edge of a scummy pond of motionless water that was the bright milky green of Japanese *matcha* tea. The pond-side irises hadn't begun blooming yet, although an occasional wedge of dark purple could be seen, exposed like crumpled crepe de chine between the stiff lips of the yellow-green calyx, and the summer lotuses in the pond were still only tightly packed green balls lifted above the surface of the water on delicate stalks. I continued up toward the top of the garden, passing bank after bank of low shrubs crowded with the flame-orange blooms of wild Japanese quince, a flower I'd completely forgotten about, probably because it shares a season with the highly competitive cherry blossoms.

There's a cusp at the top of the garden that separates it from the wild mountains directly above. When I first lived in Kyoto, this was the kind of place I soon came to cherish. At the bottom of the garden, just behind the walls that close the shrine off from the city, even the dirt between the various sub-temples and stupas is neatly raked with long-handled bamboo brooms. But here, at the top of garden, little is done to improve things. Dead branches are cleared away, paths are maintained, and stepping-stones cross streams, but windblown leaves and flowers are left where they fall, and nothing is planted, nothing is pruned, no young branches are fitted with thick copper wires or bamboo splints to train them to grow into more "natural" shapes. The foothills of the Eastern Hills are lined with temples and shrines, each of which appropriates this wild mountain backdrop as an integral part of its beauty. Dark ancient stones carved with calligraphy long since rendered illegible by moss or lichens can still be found within the forest, but it is the bright new green of maples and somber old green of cedars and cypresses that set the tone up here. At this highest point of the garden, the mountains rear up so abruptly that walking turns into climbing, and nature organized as landscape garden abruptly becomes real nature, wild and tangled.

I turned south, working transversely across the steep hillside until I reached a temple cemetery, then began climbing again. Above me, the spring mountains rang with bird songs. Clouds of gnats lifted from weedy rills occasionally, and fallen camellia blossoms littered a shelf of bright moss, like slashes of vermilion on emerald velvet. Granite tombs were staircased up the slope of the hill and provided a magnificent view of the city spread out below. I continued higher on up through row after row of gray tombs fitted closely together like teeth in a skull. A breeze picked up. I met a calm snake sunning itself on an overturned stone lantern, and I found my first patch of wild Japanese fringed iris, blooming in the wet shadows at the edge of the cemetery, their furry lilac tongues exposed. I heard the spring breeze shifting in the cedars that formed a blank wall surrounding the tombs, and I smelled the incense made from crushed cedar boughs drifting up from somewhere below. This was where I had begun when I lived in Kyoto. The renewed sense of longing was undeniable. I wanted to *be* there. Even though I was.

There's a haiku by Basho that says it well: "Even when in Kyoto, nostalgic for Kyoto, at the song of the *hototogisu*." The *hototogisu* is a kind of Japanese cuckoo whose song, heard only in spring, strikes the Japanese as ineffably poignant. And poignancy, in Japan, is a prized validation.

I selected a convivial tomb at the very top of the old cemetery and spent an hour gazing out at the spring haze thrown over the old city like a gauzy shawl, softening the rectangular grids of buildings. Why had I cared so much about it? Why had I had to leave?

Of all searches, perhaps the most potentially fruitful is the search for something that doesn't exist. There's no possibility of the disappointments ensuing from success, for one thing. Failure, too, is impossible unless you lose faith in the process of searching itself. I am not being ironic. An artist is simply someone who is looking for something that can't be found, and the art is the record of the attempt, deployable—despite Aristotle's insistence upon the aesthetic necessity of "wholeness"—within the lineaments of the deficient, the incomplete, the fragmentary.

There are dangers to be avoided by the aficionado of the nonexistent, however. You have to be able to distinguish that which exists no longer from that which never existed. The former may very likely encumber you with traces: old bones, pottery shards, crude glass beads stitched to bits of ratty brocade, hieroglyphs carved on stone cenotaphs recording genealogies fat with begat after begat, ancient stone towers clutched by strangler figs or jungle banyans that when hacked away reveal . . . what? Just more towers? Is that *all?* Where's the higher wisdom? The purer being? Where's the *meaning?*

The mute regard of lost worlds begins to resemble the round silver sun-disk mirror hidden deep within the heart of a Shinto shrine, showing you, finally, only yourself.

I hiked back down through the shrine gardens, then turned south and took the old lane leading up to Kiyomizu Temple. The interior road passes temple residences and elegant old tea shops, all hidden behind clay walls topped with slate-colored roof tiles and with small wooden gates giving access to front gardens. There's a hut on the corner where the great Basho himself once stayed. The hills loom directly above the town here, and much of the original architecture has been preserved, maintaining a sense of old Kyoto.

I stopped at a tea shop that was situated along the edge of a narrow carp pond. The pond was squeezed so tightly between the long, overhanging eaves of the tea shop and the neighbor's garden wall that it appeared to be indoors. I sipped frothy green tea and watched orange and yellow and silver and calico fish cruise just beneath the surface of the brown pond water, leaving an imbrication of overlapping Vs whenever their dorsal fins touched into the air. Beyond the wall could be heard the televised mantra of mass chanting, the supplicants' tinny voices supported rhythmically by gongs and trumpets and tambourines as they repeated unceasingly their appeal for fortitude. Baseball season had begun. And from what I could tell, the Osaka team's leaky infield and well-known inability to solve Ham Fighter pitching seemed certain to doom them to ruin.

The road up to Kiyomizu Temple is lined on both sides with

shops. Mixed with traditional crafts galleries and antique stores are chintzy souvenir stalls vending the usual trinkets tourists still seem to buy. At the top of the hill where you turn left to go on up into the temple compound is a famous shop selling *shichimi,* a blend of seven spices that forms the most popular condiment for soba noodles. The predominant flavor is of red pepper, with flakes of dried citron peel and seaweed also identifiable. The spice mixtures are still packaged in single sections of bamboo with a hole drilled at one end, then stoppered with a bamboo plug. *Yatsuhashi* is another traditional food sold in the area, a kind of semisweet cracker with a tang and texture that seems equal parts of cinnamon and cardboard.

As you draw nearer to the temple, the uphill road narrows and the stalls become more tightly packed together so that the need to acquire a key ring or T-shirt or ashtray or long-handled shoe-horn with an image of the great temple displayed on it becomes irresistible for many.

Then, abruptly, the shops end and a series of massive, wide granite stairs like neatly aligned tectonic plates provides access to the outer temple gate hanging above you. Kiyomizu Temple itself was unchanged. But then it had been there in one form or another since the eighth century, burned down occasionally but promptly rebuilt each time, the most recent fire disaster being in 1629, so a certain continuity was to be expected. The temple is situated on the side of a steep hill. A dancing platform extends like an oversized balcony out over the wooded gorge far below, supported by an impressive superstructure of immense pillars formed out of whole trees. Like the narrow lanes of the Gion district, Kiyomizu *is* Kyoto through and through. It could not be anywhere else; there could be no Kyoto without it.

Kiyomizu Temple — the name means "pure water" — was established before Kyoto itself became the capital of Japan; and while other, newer temples and palaces have come and gone, leaving few traces, Kiyomizu endures, clinging to the side of its mountain. The main image enshrined here is of Kannon, the Bodhisattva of Compassion, an eleven-faced, thousand-armed ancient statue of the deity that is so sacred it can endure being looked at only once every thirty-three years. (The next possibility is in 1997, apparently; make your travel plans soon.) There is a sacred waterfall called the "sound of feathers" that figures in the establishment of Kiyomizu, and the temple itself belongs to a

Buddhist sect that was already settling into a dozy decline by the tenth century.

But what do you do with a place like Kiyomizu once you've poked into the various sub-temples and examined the various curious stones and stone lanterns and lion-dogs and faded paintings? More people visit Kyoto than any other Japanese city, and more Kyoto visitors go to Kiyomizu than any other single place. In a city with over a thousand major temples, why does this one so capture the imagination of visitors?

Everyone not being herded through in a relentlessly organized tour probably discovers the answer after being there for a half hour or so. What do you do there? You gaze at the hills. You ruminate. You view the fresh growth of spring foliage or the rich green of summer foliage or the brilliant autumn colors of maples and gingkos or the muted monotones of the winter landscape, and you become aware that for over a thousand years people have come here and done what you're doing and perhaps wondered what you're wondering and finally ended up just leaning on the worn railing of the outthrust dancing platform and watching the trees on the hills across the way toss and heave in the warm breeze, or darken in the rain, or disappear silently beneath an evening snowfall. Things haven't changed. The seasons roll through their patterns on the far hills, and as you stand watching birds lace together the emptiness between the old temple and the older hills beyond, you receive a powerful sense of the rightness of things as they are. Nothing's changed. Nothing changes.

But of course, the sheer longevity of the place is not really the point. Old as it is, Kiyomizu still earns its keep. It is a working temple, busy with purpose. Pilgrims still come here to pray; ascetics still stand under the sound-of-feathers waterfall and bellow promises of abnegation under the icy splatter of mountain water. Kiyomizu—and Kyoto, too, for that matter—could have ended up as a mere curiosity, an archive of attractions, fit only as a backdrop for self-photographing tourists. And although there is something of that tone of living museum to the place, beneath the endless rumble of tour buses can be found an unaltered reality. The past is not just what was made way back when; it's what was thought up then, too. A genuine continuity exists. And even in these dark days of Big Macs and MTV, there is still something of the non-manipulative, non-exploitative, non-false preserved in Kyoto.

Kiyomizu is a good place to start looking for it. Because as much as any other place I've ever seen, Kiyomizu situates itself within the true worth of the eternal.

Fine. But why can't I live there again?

Arthur Waley, the great British orientalist and translator of *The Tale of Genji*, never came to Asia. He claimed that he loved Japan too much to visit it.

Was he right?

Mountains have always been more than just a backdrop for Japanese and Chinese poets and painters. To leave the city and go into the mountains was to make a fundamental philosophical choice. It meant you had the will to abandon the petty concerns of humdrum reality and seek something higher, something deeper, something truer. This attitude was always a value judgment, and never merely an aesthetic choice. The idea that the mountains were "more beautiful" than the city was irrelevant, even if true enough. The choice was a philosophical matter. The question was never, What do you like? but always, How should you live? And the answer always involved selection, simplification, renunciation. You had to be able to make do with the sound of the wind in the pines and the silver glow of the moon at night. You had to be able to appreciate the coldness of mountain water and the bitter purity of fern tips or other wild fruits and vegetables you gathered yourself. You had to be able to be alone, or, at the most, make an occasional visit with a fellow hermit suffice.

The sputterings of "normal" human contact were to be avoided. The Chinese Taoist sage and the Zen practitioner in Japan accepted intuitively that retreating deep into the mountains was absolutely requisite for keeping your eye on the ball.

Chinese landscape painting makes this same fundamental point again and again. The tiny figure in the elongated landscape scroll is never just a tourist. He is an adept. The rich tradition of eremitic poetry provides the same message. The great Chinese recluse/poet/mystic Han Shan ("Cold Mountain") summed it up:

Climbing up the Cold Mountain road,
The Cold Mountain road seems endless.
The way's too long and the ground's too stony.
Streams are too broad and undergrowth too thick.
The moss is slippery even when it's not raining,
And pine trees sigh even if no wind blows.

Who can leave their links to the everyday world
And come sit with me up in the white clouds?

In the Peace Corps in Korea, I lived in the middle of Pusan, a huge, roiling, dusty city stuffed with petty concerns. Humdrum hardly covered the daily thump and blunder of the vol's life there. And the steep, ancient Korean mountains did beckon, albeit vaguely.

But it was only after I'd moved to Kyoto that the question came more sharply into focus. And it occurred to me then that the fundamental understandings of the Chinese sages were true. The basic premises of Taoism were true. The arguments of the Zen commentators were all true. There is a simple, clear, unavoidable argument that runs throughout two thousand years of Chinese and Japanese thought: live now. Don't wait. And don't let yourself become distracted by the accumulation of baubles.

This has always struck me as being as obvious and indisputable as it is rare.

And the question then becomes: what are you going to do about it?

But there's actually another question. It's all very well to believe that you have to become a recluse — or, more likely, some sort of quasi-recluse — in order to be free. But why can't you do that here? In New York or California or even Iowa?

If it is the eremitic life that's so attractive, why can't you find the same thing in the mountains of Utah or Tennessee? You don't have to link up with some cult of swaggering, loony ex-hippie survivalists who place their faith in crystals, weed, astrology, and semiautomatic weapons. You should be able to find whatever it is you want in the Alleghenies or the Adirondacks or the Sierras.

And yet it always seemed to me that it had to happen in Kyoto. Why?

If the only sensible undertaking is the search for that which never existed, then you might as well begin looking wherever your initial failure had seemed most expressive. At least then you'll have the pleasure of nostalgia. For me, that would mean going back to my house in the mountains north of the city. The structure itself, of course, might very well seem the same, excluding whatever minor modifications the present tenant might have inflicted. But what it had been like to *be* there would be irrecoverable. What I should actually find would be the entity that had replaced the house I had lived in, erasing it in every way except the literal. Would that be instructive?

It is, of course, a familiar cliche that one can't go back to the past.

So don't look for what you had? Look for what you looked for?

And wasn't this exactly what I wanted to remember, anyway? The sense of promise? The giddy spring and sparkle of those palmy days of non-compromise?

The Wizard of Oz was the first and most famous of a series of books about the Land of Oz. Oz was an alternate world peopled by astonishing, whimsical characters. Although there were malign forces afoot, goodness always triumphed easily. In one of the best stories, the evil Gnome King threatened to transform innocents into fanciful bric-a-brac to brighten the gloomy chambers of his underground palace. A clever hen thwarted his plans. Everything came out okay.

As adults, we transpose our childish fondness for fairy tales onto more mature subjects, such as TV shows like *Star Trek*, where L.A. actors wear boldly latex face makeup no L.A. actor has ever worn before, or envelope-pushing literary undertakings like *Sex*, celebrating the incomparable Madonna.

The classical eremitic impulse was always rooted in disenchantment with the indignities presented by "normal" life. The renunciation of the world would, of course, be securely placed within a positive frame—one went *toward* something, after all: a philosophically and/or aesthetically purer life. The tiny figure tucked down in one corner of the Chinese landscape painting must depict an aura of serenity. And the serenity is always presented in terms of the mountain landscape he inhabits. He is *at home there.* You have to leave home in order to find what he found: your real home.

The idea of renunciation seems alien to us in the modern world, even vaguely perverse. You are, after all, supposed to try to make the community you live in a better place. Yet to turn one's back and retreat into the simplified, subtle pleasures of seclusion proposed by the literati poet/painter was the ideal throughout much of the history of the greatest culture the world has yet seen. That that culture is currently reduced seems irrelevant. China has always revolved through immense dynastic cycles, the workings-out of which are imperceptible, particularly to the participants themselves. Even if those ideals developed by the T'ang and the Song and the Ming and the Ch'ing do fail to appear as integral to the next great Chinese empire, their argument in favor of simplicity will still seem valid precisely because it is not just escapism.

But is wanting to be "in nature" the way the tiny human figures are tucked away in odd corners of Chinese landscape scrolls truly any different from wanting to be confronted by Klingons or, even more numbingly banal, by the concupiscent shenanigans of a dubiously insatiable bimbo?

Is there ever any reason to leave home?

The floorboards of the old Eizan electric tram line are hardwood planks held in place by brass screws that have been worn smooth from generations of passenger feet. The interior trim is also crafted from wood and polished to a rich patina, too, and the shelf benches fitted against the inside walls of the car are covered with a velvet-napped material the color of fresh spinach. The conductor punches tickets with a nickel-plated device that he clicks agreeably as he makes his way up the listing, swaying car, walking with the wide-track gait of a sailor familiar with stormy seas.

The Eizan tram leaves northern Kyoto full of passengers, most of whom are bound for the suburbs above the city. By the time it finally begins climbing toward the villages in the steep northern mountains, only a few people are left. All the rings suspended from hard rubber loops sway in unison as the old tram rattles around corners. The track runs so closely to the mountain that branches brush against the side like the sound of a quick rain squall raking a tin roof. There were occasions when I lived in Kurama Village that I was the only passenger to go all the way to the end of the line, and I felt sometimes that I should stop on my way out of the car and personally thank the tram driver and the conductor for performing their duties so commendably. But doing that might have embarrassed them. It might have implied that any train line arriving at its terminus with only a single, goggle-eyed foreigner on board must amount to very small potatoes indeed. So they maintained the stiff dignity of transportation industry professionals and I maintained the stiff dignity of a service-dependent member of the paying public, and all of us stared straight ahead with politely held breaths as I, the foreigner, made my solitary way into the steep night beauty of the mountain village.

Kurama Village is a narrow spot on a narrow road, but it has a long history and a famous temple on the top of Kurama Mountain that attracts busloads of pilgrims in the summer. The temple was founded in the eighth century, and like much of Kyoto, it has been burned down and rebuilt at irregular intervals. The mountain itself is considered sacred, and to climb it is an act of devotion.

The little village exists only because of the sacred mountain. The valley is too steep for most agriculture. Rice, in particular, has always been impossible there. Farmers have carved out narrow plots curved to the contours of the mountainside. They grow squash or beans or cucumbers, but the efforts are half-hearted, and when I was there, the cucumbers, at least, required more effort to defend them against marauding monkeys than they were probably worth.

Near the train station was an inn for pilgrims come to worship at the mountain. A few souvenir shops sold geegaws nobody really wanted, and there was a ratty hot-springs spa that most people wisely ignored. A stonemason had a big yard in Kurama where he hewed the rough, orange-gray rock that came out of a

nearby quarry into crude stone lanterns that reflected the unso-
phisticated aesthetics of mountain life. The village itself was little
more than a few houses arranged on either side of the roadway,
and residents turned extra space into parking lots during the
brief summer tourist season. A tributary stream for the Kamo
River ran down the middle of the valley, and an enterprising
local family had set up a flume system that drove a waterwheel.
The waterwheel powered a set of pistons fitted to an archaic
wooden crankshaft. The pistons pounded into declivities formed
on the hard dirt floor of a shed, reducing cedar fronds to a fine
pulp that would be sold to incense manufacturers in the city.
This was the extent of Kurama's industry when I lived there. But
when I finally made it back out to Kurama, the waterwheel was
gone and the incense manufacturing business had been replaced
by something called the Kurama Spring Water Company.

A steeply pitched granite staircase leads up through a gate
enshrining a pair of fiercely grimacing guardians. You're immediately in the damp shade of a deep cedar forest. Moss and ferns
cover the ground, and patches of fringed iris catch the occasional
spears of filtered sunlight like tiny mauve faces displaying furry
tongues. The primeval forest on Kurama Mountain has never
been logged, so the ancient cedar trees grow to prodigious
heights. Holy trees are encircled by a kind of thick rice-straw
rope with dangling strips of pure white paper, and this marker
proclaims the apotheosis of the spirit of the tree. The path up the
mountain is a series of switchbacks, with an occasional shrine or
pavilion or gate offering an excuse to stop and catch your
breath. The oldest structures date from the tenth century, but
unlike the more business-minded Zen Buddhist centers in the
city, there are few improvements and things are left as they've
always been: beautiful old buildings in a beautiful old forest.
Birdcalls deepen the silence, a sudden toss of crashing escape in
a sunlit glade off to the side indicates the near miss of an
encounter with a monkey or fox or feral dog, or perhaps even a
wild boar, which are said still to be found in these mountains.

The famous fourteenth-century warrior Yoshitsune spent his
boyhood being trained in martial arts on this mountain, so many
of the stone cenotaphs and stupas are connected to his youthful
adventures. The temple mountain originally was part of the
Tendai sect, the earliest major Buddhist sect to flourish in
Japan. But it has since become the headquarters of its own self-

generated sect, which produces a small booklet explaining how slightly more than six million years ago a deity named Maô-son descended from Venus and landed on Kurama Mountain, bent on the salvation of humankind. Ever since then, a great spiritual force has been emanating from the mountain, flooding the world with "glorious light" and joining all people into one—much, I suppose, in the way the immense TV tower on Mount Sutro in San Francisco bound the pre-cable Bay Area together with *Cheers* and *Married with Children.*

When I lived in Kurama, I wasn't sure whether this explanation about Maô-son coming down from Venus was true or not. College composition teachers advised us to "be specific," but I always wondered if stipulating Venus wasn't asking too much. Nevertheless, that the mountain had a mystical aura about it seemed acceptable enough. Besides, the sense of holiness itself seemed less important than the ancientness of effort, the thousand years of unceasing human affection and endeavor that have made Kyoto—and Kurama in particular—so enthralling. And so demanding.

The main temple is just under the crest of the mountain, but at the very top is a shabby little shrine that marks the spot where the deity from Venus actually touched down. An immense cedar tree grew there, and that ancient tree became a Bodhisattva—a being that had achieved Buddhahood but, through compassion for suffering humanity, elected to forgo paradise in order to stay here and make a difference. I always liked that tree. A shrine surrounded it with a diminutive interior worship hall where you could make offerings and pray to it directly. That the tree probably wasn't really six million years old didn't bother me. The cedar had been struck by lighting sometime early in the nineteenth century and blasted down to its roots. It was like a huge hollowed stump, then, thrusting gnarled scarps toward the sky, with only a few living branches occurring here and there up its length. The inside seemed like a cavern, glistening black and polished with years of wind and rain and snow. The tree was so old that it had generated near-aerial roots, and new saplings had emerged from these, surrounding the old hulk like organ pipes, the largest of them now small trees on their own.

How could the old cedar's Buddha-nature be recognized? If you asked, you might be told that the tree was believed to be trying. And if you looked at the tree in those terms and didn't scoff too hard, you might actually see it.

Hiking down the backside of the mountain leads you eventually to Kibune, a village even smaller than Kurama, and even more tightly packed in between steep mountain cliffs. Kibune has a shrine but no real claim on the holy mountain, other than as a back door. Kibune also has a sparkling little stream with a row of inns perched precariously on its low banks. In late spring and summer the inns erect wide, low platforms that stretch out over the stream, and maids wearing the indigo kimonos typical of the region serve beer and sake and traditional mountain food. You come down hot and sweaty from your moment with the ancient Bodhisattva tree and dangle your feet in the icy mountain water and gaze back up at the heavy face of the mountain hanging high above you.

I sit beside the murmuring stream as evening quickly darkens on the western slope of the mountains, and it occurs to me that what I wanted from Kyoto was to be there. That is, I didn't want to *do* anything in particular there, I just wanted to *be* there. Surely something like this sums up the travel experience. The traveler is an observer, a voyeur, a creature clinging to the periphery who can leave after it is over. Although the traveler is engaged in little more than his or her own amusement, that amusement can certainly be sophisticated and instructive. Yet the traveler is always a tourist, and a tourist never commits to the country he or she is in. The country—the culture, the people—is something you take up and *use*, then put back when you're finished.

The goal for the Peace Corps Volunteer, then, was to somehow behave like a non-tourist while still clutching the second half of a round-trip plane ticket. That that would be very hard to do seems obvious now. (That vols actually *did* do good for the people they were meant to help is not at issue.) The act of living thoughtfully in a country not your own—the condition of faux nontourism—is not in itself reprehensible. You can learn, and you can teach. But the odd situation does seem to create dislocation within the faux nontourist's sense of self. In order to relieve the numbness of merely *being* there, you have to do something there. For young Americans who have spent their entire lives being educated, the natural inclination is to continue training yourself. Thus, the experience of living in a foreign country becomes as seductive as academic graduate school, with all the attendant joys and perks relished by those on an extended quest for a Ph.D. in literature or history or philosophy.

Perhaps the more practical among us were right, those who rushed back to tightly packed years of law school or business school, then launched themselves valiantly into the real world, empowered to rip out fistfuls of still faintly palpitating cash.

And yet, and yet, being there, just being there, is so coruscatingly beautiful. . . .

TO SPEND THE NIGHT LAUGHING

by Susan K. Lowerre

Susan Lowerre, who still can't decide if she wants to be a writer or a fisheries biologist, has decided she's glad she met her husband, Lula, one afternoon while she was cutting up dead fish.

"Lula's a lot of things I'm not, like patient, diplomatic, and neat, as well as dark, handsome, and Brazilian. And he travels well, extremely well."

Susan first wrote about Senegal, the country of her Peace Corps assignment, in *Under the Neem Tree*. A Volunteer in the late eighties, she returned to Senegal with her husband for this travel piece, taking time off from her doctoral studies in marine biology.

She tells of her first night in Senegal. At midnight it was hard to find a hotel. Their room had a bed, a light-bulb, and a cracked mirror on the wall. The sheets were brown but had once been white. Everything smelled of urine. They didn't care. They were in Africa. Until the bugs. Lula said alcohol might help. They put Scotch whisky on their arms and legs, as a goat bleated in the courtyard and the guardian snored. A woman's heels tapped down the hallway. It was three a.m. When the fight broke out between the whore and her customer, they decided alcohol would help. Unfortunately, the fight was in Wolof, a language Susan did not speak. It was a doozie. In the morning,

Susan said, they only laughed about it. "No complaints from Lula, no why-didn't-you-plan aheads, no guilt trips for bringing him to a whorehouse on his first night in Africa. Just laughter."

Abdoulaye came to stand by my window. He was dressed in his red fez and a blue and white striped *boubou*—which looked like two single-size sheets sewn together at the shoulders and sides and then left free to fall to his feet. They had almost finished loading the baggage on top of the public transport van. The man who had been up on the roof, tying things down, yelled to me to pull my arm inside and for Abdoulaye to stand back. He thrust his foot into the open window and jumped to the road. The clamor woke up a rooster packed in a box behind us and it began to crow.

Lula and I sat in the last row of seats and waved to a baby girl being held by her mother in the seat ahead of us. The baby was pretty with reddish-black skin, huge brown eyes, and little gold earrings. She tried to pull the headwrap off her mother's head, exposing intricate cornrows and what looked like little leather packages, *gris gris*—magic charms made from the words of the Koran—pinned to the top braid. Abdoulaye asked the woman if she was traveling all the way to Dakar. She said she was. He explained I could speak a little Pulaar, and we were family of his, would she please look after us? He spoke very fast, the way he does when he's not trying to make me understand. She said she would.

I looked past Abdoulaye at Torregi—a town consisting of a gas station, a restaurant, and a boutique that sells tea, powdered milk, plastic hair, shampoo, strange bottles of cheap perfume, and cold sodas. The boutique is run by a Frenchwoman who is married to the Senegalese owner of the gas station. Public transport stops here because it marks the split in the paved road— you can either turn north toward Podor or continue east on the main road to Saint-Louis on the coast. I looked at the reddish-tan sand dunes, dotted with tortured acacias. They always made me think of Dr. Seuss trees, their unreal shapes the only break in a landscape of sand.

A woman came to the side of the van and leaned into the window, trying to sell plastic bags of strange fruits and nuts for the passengers to eat during their journey. There were three other women sitting by the side of the road selling chew sticks—twigs the Senegalese use as toothbrushes—kola nuts, and watermelons. They all wore *pagnes*—strips of cloth wrapped around their waists like skirts—and *boubous* and headwraps of *lagos*—the ubiquitous African print material—with patterns of geometric conch shells and roosters and butterflies, diamonds and ovals in reds, greens, oranges, yellows, and bright blues, made brighter against the dark brown of their skin.

The driver came around to the front of the van, after checking the loading of the bags, and opened his door. I looked into Abdoulaye's face. It was so black. It was strange to see it unsplit by a grin. We had shared so much laughter. I told him we would write, that he was a good man. He said I was good. We shook hands. The driver started the engine and I turned to wave to Abdoulaye. He grew small—a black man in a red hat, with the wind tugging at the edges of his *boubou* and the flat, dusty land trying to swallow him.

We were on our way to Dakar, the capital. I stared out the window, watching Senegal pass—the mosques, with their moon and star outlined against the sky, huge herds of Brahma cattle interspersed with goats and small Pulaar herdsmen, thatched-roof villages matching the color of the desert. I thought of the West African guidebook I had bought and read on the flight over from the States. It said the Portuguese were the first to come to this area in 1444, but that by the 1600s the French had driven them out. Later the French competed with the English for the slave trade, which was why The Gambia existed—a skinny finger of a country, following the lines of the Gambia River, poking into Senegal's middle. The Gambia had been an English colony; Senegal was French. I had seen French soldiers' graves in Bakel by the fort. They were unkept and slanted at crazy angles, and I thought it must have been terrifyingly lonely to die in a corner of nowhere for nothing, in another people's land of strange beats, unbearable heat, and disease.

Senegal won its independence in 1960. It is the farthest west of the West African countries and about half the size of California. Different tribes make up the Senegalese people, like tributaries of a river: Wolof, Pulaar, Sérèr, Mandinka, Soninké, and Diola. Although they each have their own language, the national language is French and most people understand Wolof. The money is stable. It's tied to the French franc. So is their government, which is democratic. Most Senegalese cannot read or write, although they are beginning to learn. The Muslim faith is strong, seemingly having come with the desert. It's strongest in the north, which is flat and was once savanna but now is part of the Sahel, and weakens toward the south, where there are still jungles and rainbows and dark snakes hanging like thick ropes from the trees.

I had looked up these same facts in the library in 1985 when the Peace Corps told me I was coming to this country, armed myself with them, and then been utterly unprepared. It was like looking at a map of Africa, seeing the green splotch that represents Senegal and looks like a person's profile turned to the left—The Gambia making a great slash of a mouth and Dakar marking the nose. After I returned to the States, I would look at my map of Africa and wonder how a green spot could represent a country. I would remember the lepers in Dakar, begging with no hands; the beat of tamtams along the Fallemé River, where they still believe humans can turn into lions; the Mussulman calling people to prayer before the sun has risen; women pounding millet and children screaming *tubob*—white person.

I watched the flat, dry land pass my window. This is the forehead of Senegal's profile. It seemed strange I should know this road so well cutting through rural Africa, what the French call

"en brousse": the mosque just past Figo, the *marché* at Thilé
Boubacar, the turnoff to Dagana. This is the Fleuve, the north-
ernmost region of Senegal. It's named for the Senegal River,
which marks Senegal's northern border with Mauritania. It is a
harsh land of drought, filled with the dust of the Harmattan
winds blowing down from the Sahara. It is the land of the
Pulaars and Toucouleurs, originally of the Fulani tribe—tall,
thin people with high cheekbones and natural grace. Or it was.
Now dams have been built at the headwaters and at the mouth
of the Senegal River, and with the thirty-year-old irrigation project have come many Wolofs and people from more southern
tribes, even men from Guinea—development.

Five years ago I lived here. I tried to run an aquaculture program. People thought the completion of the dams would inter-
fere with the fishes' spawning cycles, changing the flood patterns
and closing the river's mouth to anadromous species. I lived in a
Pulaar village named Walli Jalla, which means "to spend the
night laughing." Abdoulaye and another man, Demba, worked
for me at the fish station, where we produced fingerlings and
tried to determine the best way to grow fish in the desert. The
Diengs, who lived next to me in Walli Jalla, asked me to take
their last name during my second year. I cried when I left them
and said I would come back in five years. I would come to see if
there was still a fish station, still ponds holding precious ovals of
water, still the heavy seine that Abdoulaye, Demba, and I had so
many times taken from its hooks in the warehouse, draping the
brails across our chests, to pull the net against the water, into the
bank, its black threads glittering with bright spots of fish, their
scales flashing in the sun. I would come to see my *tokoram*, my
namesake, Mbinté's daughter, whom I had held in my arms the
day she was born.

For those five years in the United States, I longed for Senegal:
the unfenced desert and the magical green-blue river cutting
through it, swift kingfishers collecting along its banks. I missed
the villagers' greetings, their warmth and easy laughter, the simple wisdom they possess—that life and death are in store for all
of us. A zillion times I dreamt of my return, until Senegal
became a mystical land of shifting sands and turbaned men, a

land where I once knew something, something I can't seem to remember in the United States, no matter how hard I try.

I made reservations on the New York–Dakar flight and everything changed. This was a Senegal I could go to. My dreams became nightmares. I remembered the inescapable heat, like some giant's sweaty hand pressing me to the ground; the millions of flies, delicately tickling as they endlessly crawled on my skin; the smell of raw sewage. I remembered a man who followed me screaming his hatred of white people, ending by spitting in my face. No matter how hard I tried, I couldn't forget being sick. I was medically evacuated twice from Senegal, once for parasites and once for something called relapsing fever. Senegal became for me a land of sickness—like some childhood food I was violently ill from and couldn't bring myself to eat again for the rest of my life.

My husband and I came because we had collected donations of clothes and medicine for the village—not because it was so important to me that I would overcome my fear, but because I couldn't face the donors. We had come and Senegal was neither my dreams nor my nightmares. It was something of its own, something it is impossible for me to understand when I lie in my comfortable bed at home listening to the whir of the refrigerator. Sitting on the hard bench of a public transport van, next to a man wrapped in a *kala*—a piece of cloth the men wrap around their heads and necks until there is only a mask of skin and eyes showing—while the never-ending, flat, brown land passes and a baby cries—this is real. I am tired and uncomfortably pinioned between Lula and the van's wall. The smell of sweat is very strong and I'm hoping the baby won't go to the bathroom and add urine to it. I waited five years to come here and now I can't wait to take a shower and eat a Western meal. But I know memory will change this. I am already changing the week we spent in the village.

When we were there time moved so slowly, as if it were made of something thick. In the States, time feels like water gushing through your fingers as you try to hold it back. In the village, it felt like a fly drowning in honey. Each day was a week and those first days were suffocating. But now they're gone and it seems they went too fast, and if I could I would call them back. They've become something precious I spent too carelessly.

❈   ❈   ❈

The Peace Corps provided us with a driver named Majoor, who took us to the village. We never would have gotten our bags of medicine and clothes to Walli Jalla without their help. Majoor met us at the airport and took our bags to the Peace Corps compound. Two days later he drove us up to the Fleuve. He said he hadn't been there since I was a volunteer. There were no volunteers there now because of the border war with Mauritania. There had been a regional travel ban until 1991.

I had read about the border war of 1989 in *The Washington Post,* buried near the end of the World Section. It started as an argument over land between Mauritanian herders and Senegalese farmers near Bakel, where the borders of Mauritania, Senegal, and Mali come together. It grew into terrible riots. It was strange to read of Mauritanians rising against their Senegalese neighbors and of Senegalese dragging Mauritanians—or Nars, as they call them—from their boutiques. I had thought of the Nar boutique in Podor, where we used to buy our Western treats: cold sodas, plastic packs of butter—half of which were usually rancid, sugar. The owner had tried to teach me how to say "Thank you" in Arabic.

Nar boutiques had been a part of Senegal, as common as the flies, and as much a part of the landscape as the acacias. I could not imagine Senegal without them. They were talented silver workers and I wondered what had happened to Nar Alley in Dakar, where you walked between stand after stand of silversmiths showing their wares of filigree earrings and necklaces, pewter teapots, and silver toe rings, calling to you to come see their work or to drink a glass of tea. I could not imagine Senegal without the Nars, their fine-worked silver, their camels— brought to Senegal to graze during the dry season—or their women in the Podor *marché*—their skins stained blue from *boubous* made of cloth dyed blue-black with indigo.

We didn't see any camels. I had never traveled this road without seeing small groups, or a single camel here and there, dust-colored against the dust, stretching their long necks to reach the tenderest leaves of the acacias. We saw instead, as we entered the Fleuve region, whole villages marked as refugee camps. I worried about Baa Baa, Mbinté's husband. He had lived and run a boutique in Rosso on the Mauritanian side of the river. Each year Mbinté had crossed the water to spend the month of Ramadan with him.

The sun was low and sending long rays of pale yellow light, which caught the dust and looked like paths to heaven by the time we drove between the Nianga rice fields toward the pumping station that marks the turn to Walli Jalla. We had been driving for nine hours. The rustling gold of rice fields spread out as far as the eye could see. Here and there were patches of brown stubble, the grain having been harvested. People were everywhere: standing in front of igloolike houses made out of rice straw, which families build so they can live in their fields for the harvest; in circles with long wooden poles beating a pile of cut rice; pouring the grain from a pan held high, letting the wind carry away the chaff; filling white plastic sacks with the season's harvest. The clothes of the people made bright spots of red and green and blue among the gold. Friends and neighbors called greetings to each other as *charrettes*—horse-drawn carts—drove by, taking a family to or from its field. A few lucky men rode bicycles, their heads wrapped in *kalas* and their *chias*—traditional pants that look like a full skirt sewn together at the bottom— billowing in the wind. As we turned a corner we saw a huge, green John Deere rice-harvesting machine in one of the fields, eating a season's grain with its flashing metal blades. Later I was told it could harvest in an hour what used to take ten men a day, bent double, their hands low to the ground, one clutching a bundle of grain as another cut it with a sickle.

We turned at the pumping station and drove down into Walli Jalla, a village of mud houses with thatched roofs. It sits on the edge of the Doué, a tributary of the Senegal River. In the mornings women pound millet in wooden mortars and little girls pull buckets of water from the river. Meals are cooked over open fires. The light of these fires, kerosene lamps, and occasional flashlights are all that break the darkness of the nights.

We drove past the makeshift soccer field, past my old compound with its three buildings and crumbling walls. I asked Majoor to stop in front of the Diengs' compound. It had been more than two years since I had heard from them. The last letter I received was from Tijon, Baa Baa's younger brother. He had someone write it for him in French and asked after my health and my parents' health. He said he was running a restaurant in

Podor and that everyone greeted me. He didn't say Samba was dead. Samba was my village father. He was very old when I left, a little stooped, leaning on a wooden cane to walk. Each year in the States I worried that Samba would die before I returned, that I would finally save the money to come back and he would be gone. Sometimes I thought I would know if he died, that even in the States I would feel it, something lost from my life. When we landed in Dakar I decided I would not think of him as alive. He had been so old and I had seen too many Walli Jalla funerals. But as we drove along the Fleuve I began to picture his smile, the warmth in his eyes when he called me daughter.

I had sent two letters the month before to say we were coming, one to Abdoulaye and one to Tijon, but I didn't know if they had gotten them. There wouldn't have been enough time for them to write back. Sometimes it took a month for a letter to get to Walli Jalla.

There was a second as the truck engine died and no one moved, and then Lula opened his door. Fatu, whose compound is across from the Diengs', looked up from the *haako* leaves she was preparing for dinner. She called "Mariyata," my Senegalese name. She began to chant "*Hayoo* Mariyata" in a high, excited voice, laughing and clapping and running to engulf me, twirling me around, chanting my name, laughing. Oumar and his wife, Fatiim, and Mbinté came next in a rush of "Mariyatas" and greetings and shakings of their heads as they said they couldn't believe it. They hugged me and joined the laughter. They had never hugged me before. I thought Muslim men didn't hug women. Baa Baa came and shook my hand and said I probably didn't remember him because he had been in Mauritania when I lived in Walli Jalla. He introduced me to another Baa Baa, a young man I didn't know, whom everyone else seemed to call El Hasan.

The village wrapped around me: the Diengs, Fatu, the family of Amadou Aan, who had been a little boy and now was a teenager. Fatiim kept asking if I remembered the people I was greeting: the old woman who cooked the wonderfully sweet, doughnutlike *beignets* and had had an affair with Samba; the fish woman, who walked from compound to compound with a plate of fish on her head to sell to the villagers—her son having pulled the fish from the river that morning, lifting his nets over the side of his dugout canoe in the pale dawn light; Fatiim's mother; Mbinté's aunt? I just laughed and continued shaking hands.

They pulled us into the compound and told Majoor to bring the truck. Through arms and smiles and snatches of Pulaar words I saw Samba slowly rise from his prayer mat in front of his house, where it seemed he had always sat, always would sit. I went to him. He has lived in this land for ninety years. The skin of his face seems polished by time, its passing having worn the skin thin and smooth until it appears almost translucent, like the red-black of the darkest garnet held before the sun. There are furrows above his eyebrows and lines slashed into his cheeks from a lifetime's worth of laughter. His face has great peace, like a calm, deep pool given a century's worth of secrets to hold. I held his hand and we laughed, and I thought maybe he knew how much I loved him. I told him Lula was my husband, and Lula came to shake his hand. I had brought my husband to meet my Senegalese father. It seemed during the two years I lived in Walli Jalla, Samba never stopped worrying about my lack of a husband. He could relax now.

I asked Mbinté if she didn't think my husband was cute, hadn't I gotten a good-looking man? raising my eyebrows and laughing as we threw our arms around each other. The women tried out Lula's name on their tongues in soft whispers and giggles, and I explained that he came from Brazil, a very big country south of the United States.

The children stayed on the edges of the circle around us, like wild things ready to jump free at the first sign of danger. Mbinté tried to coax Mariyata *tookosel* to come greet her white-woman godmother but she refused, pulling away from her mother's hand in wails of fear, her face contorted with horror. She had no memory of white people, couldn't know I had carried her wrapped against my back with a *pagne,* as the village women did, when she was only a month old. Mbinté's older daughters, Maimoun and Huley—whom I used to put on my knees for horsey rides during long, hot afternoons—came to us with shy smiles and shook our hands with just the barest touch of their fingertips; but Mbinté's sons, who had been born after I left, looked at our pale skin and ran away.

I kept mistaking Mariam for Aisata. Aisata had been sixteen when I left and Mariam a little girl. They told me Aisata was married and lived in Guia with her husband and a son. Mariam hadn't looked like Aisata, and now she looked exactly as I remembered her sister. Mariam was engaged. She showed me a black-and-white photo of her fiancé. She said he was more hand-some than Lula and I pretended to be mad, and we fought over who had caught the better man and held each other's hands.

It was dark by the time Majoor left to stay in Podor. Fatiim and Mbinté brought out millet-stalk mats for us to sit on and Oumar walked over to us holding two chickens upside down by their legs, saying they were ours. I had eaten chicken with the family only once, the night before Mbinté left to spend Ramadan with Baa Baa. Dinner was usually *leceeri e haako*—couscous and leaf sauce—or corn pudding, and lunch was rice and fish. They ate meat to celebrate Muslim holidays and special occasions.

The chickens squawked and flapped their wings, trying to break free. I wasn't sure what I was supposed to do. I said it would be better if they cooked them. Did they expect me to cook them over the open fire for my new husband? Two in one night was too much. Oumar said we owned them. We could kill them both and eat them or take them with us when we left. Maybe we could save the second one for another night. Oumar asked which I wanted killed and shone a flashlight on flapping wings and yellow, angry beaks. I picked the one with reddish-brown feathers. Later a woman asked if my family had killed meat for us, and when I answered yes, she asked where the heads were. This seemed to be a Pulaar joke. Everyone laughed, so Lula and I laughed with them, even though we didn't get it.

They brought pillows for us so we could lie back and stare up at the desert night while they killed and cooked the chicken. I had tried to tell Lula about the nights—how immense and very black they are, studded with more stars than you imagined exist-ed. The Milky Way looks like diamond dust, and falling stars cut the night with ribbons of fire. In Walli Jalla, the night sky is unmarred by man and its power makes humans seem very small. Under its arc you can imagine being drawn to a strange land by the power of a star.

I told Oumar the sky is not the same in Virginia; there aren't as many stars. It isn't nearly as beautiful. He pointed to where the moon was rising behind Fatu's compound, a huge red orb, and asked if we had a moon in Virginia.

The next day he asked about Bill Clinton. He pronounced it "Beel Clintone" so at first I didn't understand whom he meant. He said, "The new head of your country." He had seen him on TV in Guia. Guia is where Abdoulaye lives, one village over

from Walli Jalla on the paved road between Podor and Torregi.
The electric lines have grown out from Podor, and now the Guia
compounds that can afford it have electricity.

They served us a bowl of chicken. Tijon had asked if we wanted couscous or macaroni with it, and I had tried to say either,
but they understood neither. I explained to Lula that he should
eat with his right hand—the left being reserved for the bathroom—and invited the men to join us. Usually men eat around
one bowl and women and children at another. To have a white
woman guest always confuses things. They want to honor their
guest—which means eating with the men—but at the same time
men don't eat with women. At first they wouldn't join us, saying
we must eat our fill, but after we had each eaten a wing and a
drumstick, they came and dunked their right hands into the
washing bowl and helped us finish. They said Lula must eat a
lot. It was very important. Men needed to eat to keep up their
strength.

When dinner was over, Fatiim came to carry away the bowl
and bring clean water for us to wash our hands. As we spoke
with the men, the faces of the women and children came slowly
in ones and twos into the circle of light made by the kerosene
lamp, until the whole family sat around us, the planes of their
faces touched by the lantern's glow. Oumar told us Samba's wife,
old Maimoun, had gone blind from cataracts and that if they had
the money they would take her to Dakar for an operation. He
said his daughter, Jenaba, had died. She must have been born
after I left. They said they hadn't received my letter. They wanted to know how many children we would have. Two was not
enough. So many children died. I remembered reading somewhere that Senegal's population had almost tripled since the sixties.

I thought of Mbinté telling me, after she gave birth to
Mariyata, that she didn't want any more children. She had two
sons while I was gone and now the women teased her about the
sixth child in her womb. She is my age—thirty. Later I was
alone with the women, and they asked me if I had brought them
the pill. They needed something their husbands wouldn't notice.
I told them the pill was strong medicine, only a doctor could give
it, and Fatu said she knew how to cause an abortion.

They told us we must bring our children to visit so they would
know their Senegalese family and that when Mariyata was

grown and her wedding planned, they would write us and we must come to the celebration.

They asked after the white people they knew. Were they healthy? Had they found work? They asked about the volunteers who had lived in Walli Jalla before me — Steve and Dirk — and about the volunteers who had visited me — Cindi, Kevin, and K.T. They asked about Linda, who had come to work at the station but left because she was sick. They wanted to know about Andrea, who was one of the early fisheries volunteers and stayed on after her two years to be coordinator of the aquaculture program. I tried to explain how large the United States is and that we hadn't all come from the same village. I told them about the people I could. But it was Steve they wanted to hear about most, and I had no news of Steve. I had never met him.

Steve had built the fish station, hired Demba and Abdoulaye, and left before I came to Senegal. The Diengs loved him; the men at the station worshiped him. During my two years I had heard innumerable Steve stories. Whenever I did something at the station the men didn't like, they would tell me Steve never would have done that. He was the perfect ghost, like an older brother who had died in his youth. I could not compete with him.

Oumar looked up and said, "You are the only white person who ever came back. Even Steve never came back."

I tried to explain how difficult it is to come back: the money, the distance. They wanted to know which was farther from Walli Jalla, Mecca or Virginia. I wanted to make them understand the real distance between their village and my country — not the miles — but the food, the language, the luxury you learn to take for granted, the power of having enough money, a car, being thirty instead of twenty-four. I said everything is different in the States and after a year or two passes, that is what you know. You think you no longer know how to live in the village, how to greet your neighbors, asking after their tiredness, their children, their health. You do not speak Pulaar, no one speaks Pulaar, and your tongue becomes heavy. Senegal becomes a foreign land. You are afraid to return. I was afraid to return. I was afraid of getting sick.

Mbinté said they had been afraid, too. They had been afraid I might die when I had the fevers.

I told them the other volunteers had not forgotten them. They would never forget them. I knew because I spoke with Cindi and

Kevin and K.T., and we always spoke of Senegal, of our lives there, of the people we had known and of how we would like to go back. Except it was always next year or in a couple of years that we would go. Senegal didn't fit into our American lives. There was so little in common with the two worlds we had lived in.

I was unprepared for their memories. Demba brought from the wall of his room a faded Polaroid of me eating at the bowl with him. He had had it framed in bright red and someone had painted designs in the corners of the glass over the photo. Abdoulaye showed me an envelope filled with old photos and a card my mother had sent made out of cutout carousel animals. I had given it to him when he was teaching me the Pulaar words for "elephant" and "zebra" and "ostrich." He had a postcard from me in Paris that I didn't remember writing. It was in Pulaar and said Frenchmen were not nearly as macho as Senegalese, that they would never last at the fish station. Oumar had the string of gold stars I had hung on my neem tree for Christmas and Mbinté the earrings I had given Mariyata the day of her naming ceremony. They all had stories, as if I had been gone a month instead of five years.

It would have been the same with any of us, and I realized we hadn't known how they would remember us; what we had meant to them.

We were like celebrities or millionaires, a glimpse of opportunity in a life that offered little. White people came from countries paved with gold: where everyone has a job and a house lit with electricity, there are no fevers, people eat meat each day, and buildings are warm when it is cold and cold when it is hot.

It seemed everyone wanted to come to the United States: the woman who owned the restaurant across from our hotel in Dakar; Majoor, the Peace Corps driver; the Diengs; the people we spoke to in Podor while we waited to buy medicine for Oumar at the *dispensaire*. Collé sat with us when we ate dinner at her restaurant and told us we should bring her back to the States. She would take care of our children. I said we had no children and that her *poulet* Yassa was very good. As soon as we had children, she said, we must write her and she would come. She wrote her address on the back of a page ripped from a recipe book and told us to wait a minute as she ran back to the kitchen. She returned with a pair of fake gold earrings for me that she helped me put into my ears.

Majoor said he would like to live in Minnesota. Mbinté told us to take Mariyata. At the *dispensaire* a woman tried to give us her baby, and on the walk back from the *dispensaire* women called to us from mud doorways, telling us to take their children to France. We were white, we must be French. I said we couldn't; we didn't live in France. We lived in the United States. And so they called, "Take our babies to the United States."

The men of my family told me Senegal was bad; there was no work. Abdoulaye told me he hadn't received his salary at the fish station for two years. The station no longer had outside funding. Demba had taken me to see it. The big ponds were dry gashes in the clay, the little ponds overgrown with weeds, the warehouse a mess. Abdoulaye said it is better to work for a white man than a black man because white people are not corrupt. Tijon said white people do not lie. In the States, they told me there is much work and many machines—the John Deere harvester had convinced them of the power of machines.

That first night they asked if I could help them get to the States. I said it is true, the United States is rich, but it is a country where it is easy to lose your heart. Many Americans do not gather with their families around the bowl, take the time to greet their neighbors, or give to beggars. They have many things but they do not have the time to sit in the shade to talk with their friends.

El Hasan looked intently from my face to Lula's, as if he could find words there I hadn't spoken. He had lived in Mauritania with Baa Baa and knew something of living in someone else's country. He said hesitantly that he would not want to live somewhere at the price of his heart.

The next time they asked me, I told them no one spoke Pulaar in the United States. They would not be able to work if they could not speak the language. Each night after that was an English lesson, with Lula as their teacher. We would gather in the room Mbinté had given us to stay in, and someone would light the kerosene lamp Baa Baa loaned us. The men came armed with Bic pens and notebooks. Pulaar just recently became a written language and the men sounded out words with great difficulty, touching the letters with their index fingers as if they were reading braille.

Before we came, I went through the few Pulaar books I had, gathering words like a life-saving harvest, putting them on the computer with their English definitions, making another list of English words and Pulaar equivalents. I had hoped these lists would take the place of the Pulaar I had forgotten. But it was not I who studied them. The men hunched their backs, with their heads low and almost touching, staring at the magical words, trying out the strange feel of them in their mouths. The lists were alphabetical so they started with "abdomen," "abundance," and "acne," until I explained it would be better to learn the words they would use most, and we worked on greetings and how to say, "I do not understand." They could not believe Americans ask only, "How are you?" In Senegal, it is rude if you do not ask after a person's family, their children, their health, their children's health, their parents' health, their work, their tiredness, and how they are surviving the cold or the heat, depending on the season.

I could not convince them the United States is anything other than a land where dreams come true, so I told them it is very cold. On the Fleuve, a cool day is in the nineties, except during the cold season, from December to February, when temperatures drop to the seventies and eighties and sometimes at night even into the sixties. Each morning as we came from our rooms still muzzy with sleep to wash our faces and hands with water from the big teapot used for the bathroom, Mbinté or Oumar or Samba would ask how we had stood the cold and shake their heads with disbelief when I said this wasn't cold. I told them in the States it gets much colder and ice falls from the sky like rain. They would be terribly cold and become sick.

I didn't have the words to explain that if they were lucky they might find work at Kmart or McDonald's. They thought black Americans would treat them as family and speak Pulaar, or at least Wolof. They had never been black in a white man's land. They weren't poor in Walli Jalla.

They were nonplussed by my stories of extreme cold. They said white people have medicine for everything. They would take medicine against the cold. Oumar, who is Samba's oldest son, said he knew it would be hard and that the language and cold would tire him and that he would long for home. But it would be worth it because he would make money and send it back to the family.

Finally, in exasperation I said I realized no words of mine would show them the United States. I could use every Pulaar word I knew and all those on the lists and they would still not understand what I was trying to say. Oumar was made from the wind and the dust and the heat, the Koran, and *leceeri e haako*. I thought the States would kill him. The States would make it almost impossible for any of them to live again in the village.

I said I would try to find out the rules. There would be many rules. Whoever came would need a passport, like what Lula and I had used to come to their country—they would have to go to Dakar for that—and a visa to get into the United States. It is very difficult to get a visa. Oumar said they could bribe someone in Dakar, but El Hasan explained the visas came from Americans.

I thought of the customs official at the Dakar airport who had looked through our bags for a Walkman. He couldn't believe we didn't have one and asked us if we could mail him one, writing down his name with the address of the customs office underneath.

In the States, this is corruption. In Senegal, it is a way of life. People give gifts to those in power, even those with just a little power. Americans restrict it to really big things, like political campaigns. It's the same with bargaining. In Senegal, you bargain for everything; in the States, we bargain only for the most expensive items—our cars, our houses.

The day we walked with him to the rice fields, Baa Baa wanted to know if there were boutiques in the United States. He said he was very good at running a boutique and would like to have one there. I had never really talked to Baa Baa before. He made me nervous. He was so serious and religious, and I thought he might consider us infidels. He didn't gather with the rest of the family at night to tell stories and laugh and practice English.

As we walked up from the pumping station to the dirt road, we saw across from us a mosaic of cattle and goats and sheep, seemingly without end, eating the rice stubble of a harvested field. There were no herds like this five years ago. Some animals had been taken farther south, but many died from the drought. There were always carcasses by the side of the road.

Baa Baa said the rains the year before had been good, although this year they were not so strong. I had seen signs of more water everywhere, shimmering like mirages in deep *mari- gots* —natural low places that catch the water, holding it, as the sun steals back the moisture of the flat land. I wondered if this was why Senegal seemed so much richer. Collé said there were fewer thieves in Dakar now. You could feel the difference. You could even see *tubob* tourists in shorts, carrying shoulder bags made out of *lagos* —which cost a fortune at the *marché* Carmel— walking along the Dakar sidewalks without being followed by a pack of pickpockets.

Baa Baa said with the completion of the dams along the Senegal River they could now grow two seasons of rice. Before, the water had been too low during the dry season for the pumps to give it to the fields, and the fields had been left fallow for half the year.

As we walked, children and adults called out *tubob.* Everyone had something to say, a number of people asked for gifts, and Baa Baa looked annoyed. I said it was difficult to be a white person in his country and his expression changed to surprise. Most Senegalese thought white people came for the money. White people always have good jobs—the average Senegalese makes less than $500 a year—tubobs live in houses with electricity and toilets and running water. They don't wash in the river, eat with their hands, or squat over a hole.

But the white people thought they came to help these people, at great sacrifice to themselves. I thought of Abdoulaye's sister, who had told me next time to bring her gold earrings. We had spent our savings on the plane tickets.

That night Mbinté and I went to Baa Baa's boutique and sat with him on his prayer mat. Mbinté had told me Baa Baa knew how to make *gris gris* —the magic charms made of words from the Koran, woven together with intricate curlicues and scrolls, which were then sewn into little leather packets. Kevin was living in Washington, D.C., and asked if I could get him one against bullets. Cindi was getting married in July and I wanted to give her one so her husband would take no other wives, like the one Fatiim had. Lula and I wanted a *gris gris* to have children.

I was afraid to go alone to ask Baa Baa for the magic. He knew I didn't pray five times a day, my forehead touching the dust. What if he thought it was wrong to make the charms for a nonbeliever? Mbinté said she would go with me and held my hand as we entered the circle of light from his kerosene lamp. He told us to sit, as the lamp's flame danced with a sudden gust of wind, throwing strange shadows onto the mud walls. Mbinté and I looked at each other. I felt as if I were in the middle of church and had a terrible desire to giggle.

Mbinté explained to her husband what I wanted. Baa Baa said he could make the marriage *gris gris*, but that charms for bullets and children were very difficult. There wasn't enough time left in our stay for those. Mbinté suggested a general wellness *gris gris* for Kevin. I asked about a *gris gris* to help Lula and me find work. We were finishing Ph.D.s in marine science but had heard we might need a little magic to find jobs.

The next day Baa Baa asked me to come to his boutique again. He was sitting on his prayer mat surrounded by notes written in Arabic. He explained these were the teachings of the powerful *ceerno* — Muslim religious man — he had studied under. On the floor before him was a beautiful design of intricate scrolls and Arabic words forming an arch, drawn on heavy white paper in what looked like black fountain pen ink. He told me it was the marriage *gris gris* and that he was almost finished, but he needed to know the names of the couple. I said Rehana Ba, Cindi's Pulaar name, and Chris Williams. He looked perplexed at the name Chris Williams. What had happened to Samba Sarr? I explained Samba Sarr wanted the health *gris gris* but not to be Cindi's husband. I imagined the confusion: Cindi giving Chris back her engagement ring, the outraged families, star-struck Kevin. Baa Baa wrote Rehana Ba in Arabic and then looked thoughtful. He said, "Creeesss Weeleums" very slowly as he wrote from right to left.

I stood to go. Baa Baa told me to say nothing to the villagers of the things I had seen. He was dressed in a satin *boubou*, the pale green color of the ocean on a sunny day, sitting on his prayer rug. He leaned intently over the marriage *gris gris*, I suppose reading the magic that was already there, while the late afternoon light streamed through a window cut high into the wall behind him and fell softly onto the back of his shaved head and around his shoulders like a mantle.

Lula was giving a party for the Diengs, having explained this was a Brazilian custom for the groom to give a dinner in honor of the family of his bride. The men had nodded their heads at his words and asked us to let them plan the fête, since they knew more about goats and rice and tea. Baa Baa had gone to Thilé Boubacar's Thursday *marché* to buy the goat, explaining they were cheaper there than in Podor. He had brought back a ram and asked if it wasn't a fine animal, so we took a dozen photos of different people standing by the goat.

We had given the family 50,000 CFA ($200) for the fête and asked them to keep whatever was left for themselves. The family is really four families: Samba and Maimoun, Oumar and Fatiim and their seven children, Mbinté and Baa Baa with five children, El Hasan and Ciewlo—who were just married, so they have only one son—and Tijon. They had fed us for the week, insisting on killing a total of four chickens and cooking innumerable eggs, until I had thought to say all white people don't eat omelettes each morning; we would be happy with just bread.

Still, Baa Baa called me to his boutique to say the food for the party had cost only 25,000 CFA, pointing to the remaining 25,000 laid out in a careful pile of 5000 CFA notes on the boutique counter. He asked what I wanted to do with it. It was for the family. He said that was too much. It was expensive to travel to Dakar, did we have enough money for public transport? I thought of Maimoun's eyes. It was not too much. I hoped it was enough.

The night before the fête, the women of the compound— Fatiim, Mbinté, Ciewlo, Mariam, and I hennaed our feet. Pulaar women henna their hands and feet to beautify themselves for fêtes and ceremonies, making patterns of bandage tape and then covering the skin with a mixture of water and henna after it has been pounded to a fine green powder. Over this they wrap plastic bags, over which they wear socks to hold everything in place. When everything is removed the next morning, the skin and nails are stained rusty red. After several weeks the red fades from the skin, but you have to wait for the nails to grow out.

We patted the cool green henna onto the soles of our feet and drank glasses of hot Chinese tea. The tea is very strong and sweet and steeped in fat-bellied teapots over open coals. Always there are three rounds—*loowal, saane,* and *fartak*—drunk from shot glasses. The tea is poured back and forth between each of the glasses until a layer of foam, the color of old lace, is made in the bottom of each glass. Then the tea is poured back into the pot and sweetened with cubes and cubes of sugar before it is poured out into the three glasses. It is an honor to be served first and an insult if you do not drink all three rounds.

I had originally thought I would henna my hand, explaining that in the United States people wear shoes instead of flip-flops so no one sees your feet. But Oumar asked quietly, "Lula will see your feet, won't he?" Later that night he told stories of when I had lived there, teasing me about my Pulaar and my frustrations, imitating my voice in a high singsong. Lula mimicked me in the same voice and Oumar said he had given my husband a good joke, one he would remember. He looked at me with teasing eyes as we laughed and the light flickered and Mbinté and Fatiim helped me pat the henna onto my feet, while Oumar pointed out spots they had missed.

As he usually did, Abdoulaye came to spend the evening with us, sitting next to me, remembering how we had worked at the fish station. He told of the time I said the men should treat the brood stock like their women and we laughed and laughed. He insisted on helping me pull the sock over my plastic-encased foot, while the women clucked their tongues against the roofs of their mouths in mock disapproval, saying if the pattern was no good it wasn't their fault. Oumar said we should stay up all night talking and Mbinté said they didn't laugh like this when we weren't there.

The van stopped for an old Puloo standing by the side of the road leaning on a cane, carrying a few things tied in a piece of cloth. The driver got out, took the man's money, and slid open the side door. The man's joints seemed stiff with age and he had a hard time climbing into the van. His face was worked by the heat and the dust of the desert. He belonged to this land, seemed to have grown out of the dunes and the acacias. He looked around the van uncertainly, slowly unwrapping his *kala*. He seemed scared, and I wondered if he had ever ridden in a car before.

This man must have lived here when it wasn't desert, could remember it as savanna, covered with sweet-smelling, waist-high grass, when the elephants came each year during the cold season to drink at the riverbanks. Men like these fought and died for France in the Second World War, while others survived and returned to their villages. They were grown men when Senegal became independent. They had seen the road paved, the coming of cars, the pumps that can drink the water from the river and spit it back out onto the land.

The old men's faces are so different from those of the young men, who seem eaten by an insatiable hunger for all that is Western. They have stretched so hard to catch the promises of the West they have lost a foothold in their own land.

I thought of the young men who had come to our fête, invited by Tijon so he could show off his white friends. They were all dressed in Western clothes—one in shorts and a shirt made of *lagos*, another wearing swimming goggles on his forehead. Their eyes held resentment and dislike as they gathered on a mat around Tijon, making tea in a huge pot and offering us none. They demanded we take their picture.

I looked back at the old man and smiled. When Senegal lost these men it would be losing more than a generation. It would lose great chunks of history and much of its traditions.

So much has changed, just in the five years I have been gone. There are electric lines along the road between Thiès and Saint-Louis and little superman phone booths in front of thatched-hut villages. There are mud houses between Guia and Podor with blue plastic roofs. Aisata's new house, at her husband's compound in Guia, has fluorescent lights, a refrigerator, and a fan. Oumar said electricity would come to Walli Jalla soon and there are plans for running water. There are so many trucks and cars driving between the government post at the Cité and Podor that they make the night air noisy with their engines. Guia has a school, a small bank, and a maternity ward. The Diengs have learned to drink well water instead of river water. They have been told schistosomiasis will come with the dams. Between Thilé Boubacar and Saint-Louis there is a patch of land fenced off with barbed wire. A man from Guia died in the Gulf war.

Senegal sent troops to help the allies, while Saddam Hussein's family spent the war in Mauritania. Tijon and El Hasan told me they had wanted to go fight.

Still the land itself, the dunes and the trees, the herders and their goats seem timeless. There is patience in the heat and dust, the ritual of making tea, and the old people's eyes. The family survives it all, quietly burying its dead and bringing forth its children. Samba sits on his prayer mat in the shade and little Mariyata refuses to wear shoes. Baa Baa says he will move back to Rosso; many Nars have already come to Senegal. The family continues to gather around the bowl and to pass the night laughing.

SOUTH
OF GRINGOLANDIA

by Philip Damon

Philip Damon returned to the U.S. in 1965 after his Peace Corps tour in Ethiopia. He spent three years at the University of Iowa Writers' Workshop as a Teaching and Writing Fellow, and then joined the creative writing faculty at the University of Hawaii. Since then his short fiction has appeared in numerous literary magazines. "South of Gringolandia" is a travel piece about his attempt to discover Mexico.

He arrived there on New Year's Eve in 1979, with a band of "renegade yogis" by way of an ashram in the Laurentian Mountains of Quebec. He'd already been given the spiritual name Shiva, and was on his way toward renouncing all worldly, academic and literary ambitions, when the guru, "a wildly charismatic Indian swami with a flair for the melodramatic, revealed himself to be out of control, his moral authority having eroded to the point of mutiny in his own ashram."

Damon called himself Shiva until 1989, when it became clear that while the Deity would forever be a force in his inner life and practice, the name got in the way of others' perceptions of him. "But you can still catch me meditating on the Mahadeva," he says, "even on occasion doing the dance of Shiva."

SUMMER SOLSTICE

We left Cuernavaca by midmorning on the solstice, and at my urging were now running south on the trunk road about five kilometers to the west across the Amacuzac River from the main highway to Acapulco. Chucho and I sat in the back, and in the passenger's seat next to Eduardo sat his friend Hector. Chucho and Eduardo were amusing themselves and Hector by poking fun at my "gringomania"—a condition of sentimental excesses they defined as either dismissing Mexico as a land of drunks and bandits or else adoring it with a blind eye toward all its faults and weaknesses.

"Typical Shiva," chuckled Chucho, "to make us take this slower road so he can savor the ambience of rural Mexico as we go."

"It appeals to his romantic naïveté," agreed Eduardo.

I laughed and raised my hands in surrender. We had just passed through the lushly rustic villages of Temixco and Acatlipa, only a few kilometers apart, and I'd been musing as I often did on how idyllic it would be to return one day to some sleepy town such as these, find a room in one of the old tile-roofed houses with trees and flowers growing rampant in their yards, and do nothing but practice my Spanish, eat beans, rice, tortillas and salsa, and write. "You guys have certainly got my number," I told them.

Yet while my Mexican friends often took a cynical stance

toward my occasional exuberances over the charms and delights of Mexican culture, I trusted it was also what ingratiated me to them. I was no wide-eyed gringo tourist after all. I had lived here for nine out of the last fifteen months, and Chucho and Eduardo had gotten to know me pretty well: enough to know that what appealed to me about Mexico was what they themselves wished to preserve of their rapidly deteriorating society. Nonetheless, it would have been unrealistic of me to deny their smoldering, ongoing anger.

The political climate south of the border being what it was, there wasn't a whole lot a generation of angry young men could do in 1981 to change things for the better. Regardless of Mexico's "democratic constitution" only the PRI party ever won an election anywhere of any importance. Nor was it a secret that my friends' anger was as much directed at what they perceived to be an arrogant and manipulative nation of bullies to the north — the United States of Gringolandia — as at their own homegrown corruption in Mexico City and every provincial capital from here to the Río Grande. And finally, of course, what was I but a gringo, any way you cut it?

At the town of Alpuyeca we turned toward the northwest, and my anticipation mounted as we neared our destination: the ruins at the ancient ceremonial site of Xochicalco. The countryside had taken a drastic turn as well, more open now and drier, as we left the fertile river valley that ran another ten or fifteen kilometers south to Lake Tequesquitengo. We were in the foothills of the Occidental range of the Sierra Madres, which loomed in the distance to the west between us and the Pacific Ocean. It was a rush for me to be in this country and to be so near to Xochicalco once again.

Eduardo was recalling for Hector the story of our initial meeting, which took place precisely here, synchronously enough, a year ago to the day: "*Sí, en el solsticio también,*" he told Hector.

And as happened so often when my Mexican friends slipped naturally into their rapid-fire colloquial Spanish, my own thoughts drifted quickly away, also to the solstice of the previous summer.

I'd spent the day meditating and wandering the extensive, elevated grounds of the site. I was unable to discover, however, how the rays of the sun on that day of the year were supposed to cast their significant angular shadows on certain of the surviving structures — in particular, the intricately carved base of the Pyramid of Quetzalcoatl. Even so, it had been a rich and wonderful experience for me.

Among the ruins I was especially taken by the impressive slope-sided ball court. The presence of such a court, where games were played apparently to the death, was taken as much for granted at any of the ancient sites — Aztec, Olmec, Toltec, or Mayan — as the temples and pyramids themselves. But it was almost impossible to imagine such a blood-sport scenario there on the grassy court as I contemplated the breathtaking vistas in every direction around me.

Despite its size, beauty, and significance as a pre-Aztec center, Xochicalco was not on the main circuit of ruins, and I was especially gratified by the almost nonexistent visitor amenities. Besides the single, rustic, thatch-roofed *puesto* offering a few dusty bags of *doritos* and unrefrigerated *refrescos*, one was pretty much left to one's devices. There was no admission fee, no guide looming behind every crumbling structure, and hardly any other people around at all. I sat in lengthy meditation, almost believing that since the time when this place was alive with current events there had been nothing or no one to intervene. I felt totally immersed in an aura of sacred history.

That afternoon I hiked down the steep and winding road to the highway and waited for the bus to Cuernavaca, where I lived in the upland northern outskirts of the city in a renovated monastery with a group of renegade yogis from North America. It was a thrill to be standing here, with just a hint of the ruins in the hills above and the mountains in the distance beyond, wondering what this whole countryside must have once been like. The next thing I knew a car was pulling up beside me and there was Eduardo, a stranger to me at the time, in typical Mexican fashion offering me a ride.

It turned out he was on his way to Cuernavaca as well, and we had the hour-long drive to get acquainted. I told him I was a professor near the end of a two-year leave from the University of Hawaii, and he said he was a lawyer working mainly with native *obreros* and *campesinos* in rural areas of the state of Morelos, educating them in their rights and organizing them into workers' unions and farmers' cooperatives. His English was impeccable and he said he'd been to the States on several occasions. "But I am the most content when I am here, among *los indios en el campo.*"

When I told him where I was living he said he knew the monastery well. Did I know that Erich Fromm and Ivan Illich once brainstormed there? That it was closed by the church because the monks were undergoing psychoanalysis? He'd heard of our group's arrival, and the yoga classes and organic garden we'd started. It sounded to him as if we were the perfect group for the place, and he hoped he could come and visit us soon.

He inquired how I'd enjoyed Xochicalco, and I waxed enthusiastic over my day in the ruin but confessed I'd been unable to figure out the secret of the angles of the sun on the solstice. He nodded and smiled. "Yes, it is a bit esoteric."

Then he added, "But I have a friend named Hector, who is something of an expert on things Olmec and Toltec. Perhaps some future solstice we might return with him, and he could enlighten us both to the ancient mysteries of the sacred site."

"I'll look forward to that," I told him.

"Then shall we say it's a date for a year from now?" he suggested. "A day of meditation and ancient wisdom on the summer solstice?" He extended his hand and we shook on it.

Before driving me to the monastery he took me to see the Spanish colonial house on Humboldt Street, just down from the city's main *zócalo*, where he lived and had his office. We parked in the rundown courtyard out back and gazed at the tower crowning the near side of the several-story residence. "Since you're a writer," he said, "it might interest you that in that highest room was where Malcolm Lowry wrote *Under the Volcano*."

It interested me greatly, I said, and he smiled.

"I would take you up in person, but someone is living there and you'll have to imagine it as it once was." I assured him that was enough for me as we ascended the spiral stairs with the wrought-iron railing to his handsomely tiled arched doorway.

The large front room that served as his office contained a pair of desks littered with documents, several bookcases full of books and magazines on Mexican history, culture, and social issues, a sofa and two chairs, and on various shelves and tables plus every available inch of wall space were numerous Indian artifacts — pottery, paintings, masks, and shields. It was impossible for me to drink it all in, and I sank down onto the sofa overwhelmed by the effort. Eduardo laughed as he handed me a cold beer. "Don't try to make sense of it all at once," he advised me. "You can only hope to comprehend Mexico a single step at a time."

But now my awareness was snapped abruptly back to the rapidly decelerating car, and as I looked out the windshield I saw we were at the turnoff to Xochicalco, and the area was crawling with soldiers and policeman. "*¿Qué pasa?*" exclaimed Chucho.

Almost immediately we were being waved to the side of the road and then were approached by an army officer who'd been leaning against his Jeep. Parked up in front of us at the turnoff was a deuce and a half with a bunch of soldiers in a file with their rifles at port arms. I made every effort to be attentive as Eduardo asked the officer what the trouble was, but once again the exchange was too rapid and colloquial for me to understand fully, and all I could get was something about President López Portillo. Eduardo asked several urgent questions, each of which the officer curtly dismissed with negative utterances, then he turned abruptly away from us and strode back to his jeep.

"*Pinche* Portillo," growled Chucho at the officer's back.

"*Chingada su madre*," joined in Hector.

"What's going on?" I asked Eduardo. "Did something happen to President López Portillo?"

The three of them burst out laughing. "Shiva thinks maybe there was an assassination or something," said Chucho.

"If only that was the case," remarked Hector.

"No, Shiva," said Eduardo, "nothing has happened to him. On the contrary, he has decided to have Xochicalco all to himself on the solstice. The ruins are closed to everyone but him."

"No kidding?" I was having a hard time grasping the idea of it. "All day?"

"I'm afraid so. Our president can do that, you see."

The four of us sat there and stared at the scene before us. It was as if martial law had come to this remote outpost almost two hours south of the Federal District. I could see that my three companions were very upset. "Why couldn't he have picked somewhere closer to *Méjico*," snarled Hector, "like Teotihuacán?

"But there is something rather admirable about it," I was moved to say. "Don't you think? I mean, the president of a whole country? Meditating at an ancient ruin on the summer solstice?"

And suddenly the three of them were laughing once again. "*Pinche* Shiva," said Chucho.

Eduardo turned and faced me with sudden sobriety over the back of the seat. "It sounds like you're suffering from another attack of gringomania, amigo."

"It's a chronic condition for him," said Chucho.

"Well, how many presidents *would* do something like that?" I challenged them back. "I can't imagine Ronald Reagan making a pilgrimage like this. He probably doesn't know what the solstice even is, much less its significance at a sacred place like this."

"If López Portillo was as tuned in as you would like to believe," said Eduardo, "he would share the ruin with all citizens who wished to pay their respects and experience the energy of the solstice. That he insists on having it to himself, I'm afraid, betrays his priorities and the priorities of his government."

It occurred to me that perhaps it had been an unavoidable security measure and nothing more. Wasn't it possibly *not* the president's desire to exclude everyone else from the ruin? Except, of course, the result had been the exclusion of everyone else, regardless of Portillo's personal motives. And my companions obviously saw it as just another example of the perks of privilege in their economically and socially imbalanced country.

But, of course, I saw their suffering nation from a different perspective. I saw it as a place where there still existed a more or less universal sentiment of good will, where a crowd of people could queue up in a compressed crush and maintain unbelievable patience and courtesy, where people were notoriously inclined to give faulty directions rather than disappoint a total stranger, where to save water last summer electricity in the city of Cuernavaca was turned off every evening between eight and nine and everyone made do with butane lamps and cheerfully endured in shadowy stores and streets. I often wondered how that would have gone over for a month in the middle of the summer in the States.

The people here treated one another and strangers alike in the kindest manner I had seen since the early sixties in Africa, where my first wife and I hitchhiked over two thousand miles during our time there in the Peace Corps.

But now as I regarded my three amigos I understood the absurdity of arguing the merits of Mexico with them. How could I hope to understand what they were feeling? What did I know about how it had been for them to live all their lives in this culture so full of contradictions? I'd spent eight months here a year ago and been back only since the end of my semester in May. Not that I didn't feel that next to a lot of gringos—most of my brothers and sisters at the monastery included—I could call myself a friend of Mexico, perhaps even one who showed a propensity for genuine appreciation. But what did that count for in the long run?

In Africa and the Middle East, I had shown a similar propensity for appreciating Ethiopia and the other countries I visited and worked in. But then, as now, to claim a true knowledge of a land where one couldn't even comprehend the idiom when spoken in a colloquial manner? Presumptuous, to say the least.

On our way back to Cuernavaca I felt the sting of alienation even more acutely as the conversation around me slipped, as if punitively, into incomprehensibly rapid Spanish, and next to Chucho there in the backseat I felt suddenly alone. For a bitter moment it occurred to me that I, too, had been deprived by the events of the morning: of something I'd looked to for a year. I'd expected, after all, to learn some things from Hector today that would have enhanced my appreciation of Mexico by leaps and bounds. I'd also expected to enhance the connection between me and my Mexican friends in a kind of experience of ritual that would leave us bonded at levels beyond our cultural and racial differences. Now here we were, all of us turned away from the ceremonial site, yet with them taking it a whole lot more personally than I had.

My thoughts, still habitually in English, drifted from my amigos to the nettlesome question of what in the world I expected to find in this country—which beckoned so compellingly while beyond almost every other turn seemed to lurk a rude reminder of how impossible it was for a *norteamericano* ever to feel truly at home within its borders. What was it I was looking for here? I wondered with self-disgust. Having thought of myself as a nomadic outsider since boyhood, I could identify with Mexico's ambivalent cravings for recognition and respect but also freedom from the machinations of its self-absorbed gringo neighbor to the north.

Then we were entering the familiar southern outskirts of Cuernavaca, and as though he could read the look of distress in my eyes, Eduardo addressed me in the rearview mirror: "*Oye,* Shiva, in just three days we'll be in Yecapixtla celebrating the Day of the Baptist, and our disappointment of today will be nothing but a fading memory."

And as I looked into his sympathetic gaze and then the smiling faces of Hector and Chucho, I felt a sudden renewal of that wonderful acceptance I'd experienced almost nowhere in the world so wholeheartedly as I did among friends and acquaintances, even total strangers, in this marvelous country. Only moments ago I'd heard the three of them laughing and talking on the periphery of my own thoughts with a certainty I was being ridiculed as a linguistically hopeless intruder among them. Now I understood they'd merely been allowing me my own space, ever polite in their Mexican way, and that any alienation I was feeling had been entirely self-imposed. But what else was new?

I smiled into the mirror and nodded. *El día de San Juan Bautista:* after *La Navidad de Jesucristo* the second most celebrated holy day in the Mexican year. It was also an auspicious day on the widely worshiped Aztec calendar, thus serving to fuse Spanish and native traditions that often seemed to be operating at such cross-purposes. There was a definite reassurance in this coincidence of dates for my friends—modern Mexicans with a sense of loss toward pre-Hispanic values and rituals. To me it also seemed to encapsulate the challenge of Mexico's future: Would its marvelous diversity be allowed to survive with a continuing good will among all? Or would the disparities in wealth and privilege widen to the point of social calamity—even another revolution? And how did a sympathetic gringo like me figure into the mix?

DAY OF THE BAPTIST

I had learned about Yecapixtla and the Day of the Baptist from Eduardo the year before on the solstice, as we were saying goodbye in front of the monastery. I already knew of his interest in Indian culture, of course, and his work in remote rural areas with peasant farmers and workers, and during that first visit to his place I'd also learned of his membership in the nationally known dance troupe called Las Danzas Aztecas. I was not prepared, however, to hear him say, "*Oye,* Shiva. Tuesday is the Day of Saint John the Baptist, and each year we travel to a village east of here called Yecapixtla and dance in the square before the cathedral. I thought you might like to make the trip with us if you're free."

When I told him I'd love to go I neglected to add that I'd have broken out of prison to be free for an event such as that. I'd been fascinated for months by the strange, historically tense marriage binding pre-Hispanic religious traditions and those imposed on the region by *los conquistadores*. Virtually every monument to Catholicism had been erected on the ruins of an Indian temple, as often as not from the stones that had been knocked down to make room for it in the first place. This outrageous fact was a source of emotional distress among the Mexicans I knew, most of whom were part-Indian, part-Spanish and torn between feelings of anger and feelings of guilt. Yet for me there was something about it that was not so easily written off as colonial arrogance and abuse.

I had gotten my first hint of it in January and February, after I arrived in Mexico with the eccentric busful of meditation freaks who'd broken away from their Indian guru under traumatic circumstances and were setting out to establish an ecumenical spiritual refuge committed to democratic values and processes.

Our first two months in the country we lived in the ancient valley town of Tepoztlán in the shadow of the remains of the pyramid known as Tepozteco. I'd made the five-hundred-meter climb to the lofty ruin on numerous occasions, but I only had to glance upward toward the vertical north wall of the valley to feel its presence—or, strangely enough, to step inside the sixteenth-century cathedral. Was there any difference, I often wondered, between one spirituality and another? And was it so surprising that holy ground, however bloodily acquired, remained holy ground?

So now here was I, on the morning of the Day of the Baptist, in a GM van at the eastern extremity of the rural state of Morelos, watching this bunch of modern-day Mexicans change into elaborate costumes that transformed them before my eyes into the very Aztecs, perhaps, who over four hundred sixty years earlier might have greeted—first with trust and later with venom in their hearts—another redhead of European descent named Hernando Cortés.

Yecapixtla was nearly at the end of the road that led up onto the southern slopes of the great Popocatépetl, geological inspiration for Lowry's *Under the Volcano*—which was literally where we were now—and my mind was aswim with the ancient Aztec culture asserting itself around me. It wasn't just Eduardo and the half dozen other *danzantes* in the van with us. There were a good hundred of them, men and women, ranging in age from seven or eight to seventy or eighty, all of them dressed in costumes of their own making—brilliantly colored feathered headdresses, hand-tooled leather chest and shoulder ornaments, feathered skirts, and wristlets and anklets of a multitude of tiny marine shells, which when each dancer moved created infectious waves of musical rhythm.

Like a storybook army they climbed out of cars and vans and descended, in a growing mass, on the *zócalo* fronting the cathedral, where townspeople and peasants from outlying villages and hamlets had already begun to gather.

It was obviously a major regional happening, and I felt privileged to be here as a guest of the dancers. Once again, the cathedral had been raised from sacred ancient ruins, and it was oddly uplifting for me to join Eduardo and his fellow dancers inside the old colonial structure as they gathered for an Aztec prayer before the icons of Catholicism and then a final review of their repertoire for the day. No one among them appeared to find anything contradictory in their actions.

As in an army, or a closely knit tribal band, there was a clear-cut hierarchy of respect and deference which radiated upward from the youngest to the oldest among them. It fascinated me to study the different age groups. There were the taciturn white-haired elders, still lean and limber despite their many years; the calmly assertive middle-aged leaders, clearly the carriers of moral authority; the confidently forceful ones in their physical prime, among whom stood the statuesque Eduardo; the stripling youths of recent maturity, showing signs of restless impatience despite their well-schooled sense of discipline; and the children, ranging in size up to adolescence, awed by their place among the rest yet also impressed by their own appearance. Together, they were nothing short of spectacular as they soberly emerged from the cathedral and entered the *zócalo* in order of generational rank.

I found a place to sit on a low wall among the onlookers and noticed immediately that they were speaking not in Spanish, but Nahuatl. It was a relief, I realized, not to feel for a while quite so inadequate in my ability to comprehend anything spoken colloquially in any tongue but English. How could I be expected to understand anything in Nahuatl, after all? Hearing its ancient American syllables uttered in conversation added to my sensa-

tion of going back in time, to a half millennium ago when everyone from here to Mayan Yucatán spoke some variation of this
native language.

Yet I was not so naive in my gringomania to be ignorant of the
violence that had also been a part of Mexico before the
Conquest. Who could swear these humble souls around me
now—in clean straw sombreros, their wives modestly shawled in
dark gray linen *rebozos*—were not a lot better off than their forebears in those pre-Columbian times of enthusiastic blood-letting
and -taking? It must have been terrible back then. All I knew
now was that as the dancers began their first number it was as
though the best of *all* traditions was suddenly asserting itself
among us, and that we were all being transported to a better
place and time—perhaps better than any that ever existed.

The dancers had arranged themselves in several concentric
circles, and the sound of hundreds of thousands of tiny shells
being shaken in unison was almost immediately hypnotizing.
Eduardo had been joined by a striking woman introduced to me
earlier as Maria, which seemed an appropriate name for this
day—or not, depending on how you looked at it—and along
with several of their contemporaries they soon emerged as the
performing, if not quite ceremonial, leaders of the company. He
was strumming a mandolin and she had another stringed instru-
ment that was slightly smaller. They danced and strummed to
the unrelenting beat of several drums, adding a melody that was
almost minimal in its repetitiveness and served to deepen the
mesmerizing effect of the multitude of shells. I went into a kind
of foot-tapping trance and was shocked to discover when the
dance was over that half an hour had passed.

And that was the way the day went. After every couple of
dances the troupe took a break to guzzle down bottles of cold
Coke, and I took the chance to explore a bit of the town. There
was a mysterious compound not far away about the size of a city
block, surrounded entirely by a high stone wall bearing a plaque
that proclaimed the area a *monumento colonial.* On the outskirts of
town in the opposite direction I found a quiet spot where I sat
and gazed in wonder at the volcano hovering in the high alti-
tudes north of us. Later I spent more time inside the cathedral,
contemplating the statue of Our Lady of Guadalupe as the
sound of the dancers just outside the door echoed against the
vaulted ceiling above me.

It added up to a strange blend of enthralling effects, down to the six-piece brass band that set itself up in competition to the dancers a little before lunchtime, at the arbored edge of the *zóca-lo,* creating a crazy counterpoint that, surprisingly, was never more than a minor annoyance the rest of the day.

At lunch I joined the troupe as a guest of the mayor under a large tent and feasted on *chile relleno,* beans, rice, tortillas, salsa, and cold beer. The *alcalde* spoke no English, but I could sufficiently understand his Spanish to get that he was especially honored to have a *norteamericano* among his guests on this *día sagrado.* I told him on the contrary it was I who was honored, and we toasted each other with *cerveza.*

By the end of the day I was both energized and exhausted, not to mention disbelieving that the dancers were still standing. They had displayed a wide array of movements, pairing off at times with counterparts in opposing circles, while at other times spotlighting individuals or even various age groups. Eduardo, Maria, and the other thirty-something dancers carried on their leathered and feathered shoulders the responsibility of keeping the whole thing going, from the instrumental accompaniment to the lead in the various dances, yet everyone participated and contributed greatly. It was an unforgettable experience for me to be here, and I was already wistful as the van pulled out of town for Cuernavaca with the last rays of the sun glowing gloriously on the snowcapped peaks of Popocatépetl. Echoing in my ears were the strumming of stringed instruments and the hypnotic rhythm of shells and beating drums.

It was well after dark when they dropped me off at the monastery, and Eduardo got out of the van and walked with me to the large wooden double doors. "I was glad you could come with us today, Shiva," he told me. It seemed strange to see him dressed now as a modern Mexican barrister on holiday.

Impulsively I reached out and took him by the sleeve of his jacket. "Eduardo," I told him, "you must have some idea how important this day has been for me."

We shared a friendly gaze for a long moment before he finally answered: "It's a shame more North Americans don't find the opportunity to know our country as it is."

I nodded in agreement as I shrugged away the implied distinction between me and the majority of my countrymen. Overseas in the sixties it was almost a badge of honor to be singled out from a generation of Ugly Americans, even to be mistaken for a *non*-American, but how could it be any more honorable to feel morally superior to one's own countrymen than to citizens of foreign lands?

So now it was the following June, and along with my anticipated return to Xochicalco on the solstice I had another Day of the Baptist in Yecapixtla to look forward to. I'd been looking forward to both returns, in fact, since before I left Hawaii for my second summer at the monastery. They seemed to symbolize for me my reasons for returning to Mexico.

Not to say I wasn't looking forward to being back in the monastery, among my brothers and sisters with whom I'd undertaken this remarkable cultural experiment in the first place. Or to seeing all the work that had been done on the place in my nine-month absence — particularly the Findhorn-inspired garden for which I'd created a compost system the previous spring. But the thought had begun to haunt my mind that my unlikely membership in this leaderless cult had more importantly been the universe's way of getting me to Mexico in the first place.

It wasn't long after that first Day of the Baptist, in fact, that I'd introduced my first Mexican friend to Eduardo and the Aztec Dancers. Chucho and I had been amigos since the end of March, when our group took up residence in the vacant monastery. A mystically inclined accountant at the state capital in Cuernavaca, he lived with his wife and two daughters a five-minute walk away from us. In his spare time he looked after the nearby weekend *casita* of his mother and her two cows, dozen or so chickens, and newly planted orchard of fruit trees. Chucho's mom, a widowed Mexico City artist, had designed, supervised, and participated in the construction of the charming *casita*, whose tiled roof and shuttered windows gave the look of a miniature hacienda. It was often a relief for me to spend a few hours here away from the metaphysical wool-gathering of my tightly strung brethren.

When I told Chucho about the dancers he was immediately intrigued, and in late July, not long before I returned to the Islands, he and I and two other Mexican friends caught another appearance of the troupe in Ocotepec — a dusty village just a few kilometers east, on the Tepoztlán road, of the landmark *glorieta* featuring the charging statue of Emiliano Zapata at full gallop which marked the northern gateway to Cuernavaca and breathtakingly greeted all visitors arriving from the Federal District.

While lacking the overall spectacle of the earlier event, the performance in Ocotepec was sufficiently impressive to capture Chucho's interest. It was wonderful to watch him become lost in the troupe's rhythms, and I expected at any moment to have to restrain him from joining them. This was a different experience for me from Yecapixtla—more vicarious—yet it was a rush to think I'd played a role in bringing Chucho back into the vicinity of his own ritual heritage. Soon after, we agreed to journey together to the slopes of Popocatépetl the following Day of the Baptist.

During my August-to-May school year back in Hawaii, while I was visited occasionally by sweet reveries of anticipation on my own account, I had begun looking forward to our upcoming excursions almost more on Chucho's behalf than my own. His addition to the plan seemed to hold a significance I was yet to comprehend, but that had something to do with my amigo getting in touch with his, well, "roots." There was a chronic unhappiness about Chucho, and it seemed to have a lot to do with being born and raised in Mexico City and being alienated from his own native sources. Thus I saw our excursions to Xochicalco and Yecapixtla as having almost more to offer him in the long run than me.

Yet my premonitions notwithstanding, I was unprepared for a first glimpse into what that might be all about only a couple of days after I returned the following May. Chucho had waited until then to tell me his news—until after the evening meditation in the monastery temple, which he'd attended, and while I was walking him home on the unpaved road with the lights of the city glowing below us several kilometers to the south.

I was still flush with my recent arrival, basking in the glow of being back in this place that was both so exotic and so wonderfully familiar. I was curious about what seemed to be troubling his mind, but also distracted by my current raptures, and was glad when he invited me into his mother's *casita*, where we sat cross-legged on the tile living room floor and gazed out the floor-to-ceiling leaded windows onto the orchard. The moon was only a night from full and we turned on none of the lights, simply sitting together in silent appreciation of the play of the shadows from the larger trees on the thriving saplings of the *huerta.*

Here was the setting in which he gave me the news: short but far from sweet. Since I was gone, he'd been obliged to resign his position at the state capital, and by so doing had entered the burgeoning ranks across the country of jobless *desempleados.*

I was encouraged that he seemed to be approaching it in a positive and constructive light. He had more time now to devote to his mother's charming property, he said. And this would give him some precious time to explore his options for the future. I'd been amazed a year ago at the extent of his workday, which ran from eight-thirty or so till two, when he took a three-hour lunch break as a kind of last vestige of the traditional Mexican siesta, and then he'd be back at his desk from five till eight in the evening. A miserable, demeaning schedule, from my point of view, all the more so for my sensitive friend who'd have preferred the life of a scholar or a religious contemplative.

Though he never complained, it used to amaze me that he could stand it, toiling in a cavernous plaster-walled chamber with a couple of dozen other public servants tabulating the finances of the sputtering state machine. During the week he'd seemed to live under a terrible burden, which was lifted for only brief periods of time—when he was feeding his mother's cows and chickens, when he was playing with his dog or at moments with his daughters, when he joined our evening meditations, or when he and I hiked together in the wooded highlands behind the monastery. A quarter Indian, when he was footloose in the wild he was a panther released from its cage. Following him uphill in the heavy forest always presented an invigorating challenge, and I often wondered what life would be like for him if he was freed from his desk in the bureaucracy.

But now, despite his show of optimism, he appeared more heavily burdened than I remembered, and rather than a liberated soul I felt I was looking at a condemned man. It was alarming to consider what the consequences might be of a long-term unemployment.

Restlessly he rose to his feet and went to the kitchen, and I noticed again the weight he'd put on in a year. In the light of the moon I could see his two favorite books on the table next to his mother's reading chair: *Los Agotados* by Rius, and *In Search of the Miraculous* by P. D. Ouspensky. Rius was a brilliant leftist cartoonist whose books ridiculed every level of the Mexican social establishment—one of them aimed at doctors was called *No Consulte a Su Médico*—and the subject matter of this one, the title of which translated to mean *The Worn-out* or *The Used-up* or *The Exhausted*, dealt scathingly with the widening gap in the country between the privileged few and the increasingly disenfranchised many. Despite their deliciously irreverent humor I found Rius's books to be godlessly pessimistic, although one of them on natural diet and health I might have wished Chucho would give closer attention.

It had always interested me, on the other hand, that my friend preferred to read Ouspensky in English that was translated from the original Russian. Not that his command of the gringo tongue wasn't up to it. For two years as an illegal alien in the late sixties he'd cultivated cannabis at a commune in the Arkansas Ozarks, both for smoking and the many other uses he insisted the hemp plant—*el cáñamo*—could be put to in a rational human world.

It was this theme, in fact, that he found so compelling in the writings of Ouspensky, whom he referred to as Pedro and found more to his liking than the mystic/scientist's own teacher, G. I. Gurdjieff. This was the search, as Chucho put it, for a "rational miraculous." At times I was afraid he'd invested his mental and emotional well-being in a personal discovery of this elusive ideal—and worse, it seemed to stand for him as the only hope for a healthy and happy future Mexico.

During my wildest raptures of gringomania I'd have argued there was no country more capable of effecting a harmony between the spiritual and the secular than Mexico. Wasn't that the significance of the serpent in the grasp of the eagle on their national banner? Yet the more jaded side of my nature wondered what hope there could be for the enlightened ideas of Gurdjieff and Ouspensky—or whatever philosopher you could name—to become the official policy of any nation, much less the ineptly corrupt apparatus that called itself the government of Mexico.

Chucho returned from the kitchen with a bottle of rum and a quart of Coke by the necks in one hand and a couple of large glasses in the other. He seemed so unusually vulnerable as he sat back down that I lacked the heart to remind him I ordinarily drank neither of these beverages. As I watched him fill our tumblers I winced at the proportions. "So what are your plans?" I asked him.

He leaned his head back and almost drained his drink, then we sat silently together for several minutes before he emptied his glass and answered me: "No particular plans at the moment."

I watched as he mixed himself another drink and this time knocked it about halfway down. He gazed for a while at the moon. "I plan to be *bery* careful not to make the same mistakes all o*ber* again," he said, and I almost laughed as I recalled that when he drank any distinctions between *v* and *b* were all but abandoned.

I nodded, took a sip of my drink, and disguised a shudder with another question. "I guess that leaves out the government."

He laughed. "*No más el yobierno,*" he said.

When I raised my glass again I merely moistened my lips, watching him as he finished his second drink and cleared his throat to say, "I don't know, Chiba, what I'm going to do."

I remembered that he lost the use of the un-Spanish *sh* sound as well. It was all I could do not to smile. "And what does your mother say?"

He frowned and shook his head. "She says six months is long enough to find myself and it's time to go back to work."

I could imagine Matilde's attitude, proud and productive Mexico City matron that she was. A sophisticated woman who spoke English fluently, she had raised both her sons to be sensitive, intelligent, even artistic, but the loss of her husband with neither Chucho nor his brother yet in their teens had put the responsibility of their practical training on her shoulders as well. That may have been her weak spot. "And Blanca?" I asked.

"She seems . . . *más favorablemente dispuesta,* but I'm afraid she is torn between wifely loyalty and her own personal preference. Even my little girls would probably prefer me to return to work."

We both laughed. Chucho's wife spoke no English, and her shyness pretty much ruled out any possibilities of a conversation between us in Spanish. She was wonderfully hospitable to me and had fed me some savory meals, but I never knew what was on her mind.

"What would you prefer to do?" I asked him now.

"I am thinking of returning to school. Perhaps here in Cuernavaca at the University of Morelos, or else in Mexico City at UNAM. I regret never finishing my degree at UNAM when I had the chance."

I nodded. "Going back to school sounds like a great idea. It's never too late to do it either."

He shook his head dubiously. "But I don't know, Chiba. It has been such a long time. I would have lost all my . . . how do you say, *créditos?* And what does this sad country have to offer a man with a university degree? A post in another office somewhere, if one is lucky? I would rather remain here, on the edge of nature, or else somewhere like Yecapixtla, under the volcano."

And suddenly I recalled the awesome sight of Popocatépetl looming above me. Several times I'd dreamt of it while back in Hawaii. I'd even reread much of Lowry's novel—cynically devoid of hope as I found it most of the time to be—in my impulse to recapture my feeling that day of proximity to its elemental power.

"That is something to look forward to, isn't it?" I said.

"Very much."

And together we allowed the conversation to drift to our mutual anticipation of the Day of the Baptist, only a month away.

I left him a while later still drinking rum and Coke on the floor of his mother's *casita,* full of mixed emotions as I walked back to the monastery in the light of the moon. My own glass remained half full on the floor beside his.

So there I'd been, wondering how all of this was tied in to Chucho, and now here comes the news of his transitional crisis—which was clearly testing his most fundamental capacities to pass on through to the other side, and, at least as it applied to him, have a better handle on life. In the meantime here I was, still wondering, what kind of test lay in store for me.

But from tonight on it always came back to Chucho. Just as I'd often suspected that my underlying purpose for being a part of this Family of Light was simply to bring me to Mexico, I could now almost imagine that my purpose for falling in love with Yecapixtla on the Day of the Baptist had been to introduce Chucho to the same transcendent experience. He'd passed through the town only once or twice in his life, and had certainly never been there on a Day of the Baptist with the Aztec Dancers creating a kind of reunion of the gods out of the mysteries of their rhythm. Who knew what insights he might come away with? Or with what kind of healings he might be blessed?

Would he manage, I wondered, to emerge from his personal depression even as his country plunged ever more inevitably toward its own? The editorialists in Mexico City's daily *Excelsior* were already anticipating it as *La Crisis*, on the threshold of the eighties, and there were inflationary concerns everywhere one went over the future of the peso. Certainly the answer for Chucho did not lie merely in getting another job, as much as his wife and mother might have preferred him to do so. Wasn't it rather in finding what he'd hoped for years to unravel from the secondhand, anglicized prose of "Pedro" Ouspensky? A "rational miraculous." Or what seemed to translate to: a credible meaning to life amid the reality of cultural prejudice, social injustice, and racial violence.

It had struck me the year before that we were looking forward to the Day of the Baptist and his Christian name happened to be Jesús. I'd called him that, in fact, the first month or so I knew him, until I learned that everyone but Blanca and his mother called him Chucho—the universal nickname for the multitude of Jesúses in the Spanish-speaking world. So now here was my friend Jesús, on schedule to immerse himself for a day in the rhythmic rituals of his ancestral heritage and that day just happened to be named for John the Baptist. How auspicious was that?

I imagined some kind of epiphany or initiation on the horizon for Chucho, waiting for him under the volcano. And I could also imagine a moment of mutual realization between Chucho and me, perhaps, as we stood there together entranced by the drumming and dancing of the reborn ancient Aztecs. I'd dreamt one night in Hawaii that the two of us had discovered a magical bridge across a yawning gap that seemed to span culture and history, somehow connecting the urges of reason and miracle, uniting the two of us over space and time. A bit on the sublime side, one might scoff, but who could say? There seemed to be limitless possibilities.

Then came the disappointment of the solstice and the burden of additional importance it brought to the Day of the Baptist. Fittingly, a new concern had arisen over the condition of Chucho's car, a ten-year-old VW that lately had been showing the effects of the Cuernavaca roads, in particular the cobblestone *camino* he painstakingly descended several times each day on the way to town. He was nervous, he told me, about driving the seventy or so kilometers up into the rarefied air around Popo. But oddly enough he seemed increasingly nervous about the experience itself, and I almost suspected he was using the car as a possible excuse to cancel.

Taking him at his word I checked with Eduardo, who said they could possibly fit the two of us in the van, but I could tell it would be an inconvenience. There was always the ubiquitous provincial bus, which would mean a circuitous, un-air-conditioned tour of eastern Morelos with a stopover in Cuautla; this wouldn't have bothered me except for the question of time, but Chucho had no stomach for that anyway. "You are used to taking buses, Shiva," he told me, "but I am not. In order to travel by bus in comfort one must either live in a house with a dirt floor or else suffer from acute gringomania. It is safe to say I qualify on neither count."

Meanwhile I monitored a deterioration in the quality of my morning and evening meditations, to where they were spent almost entirely in a fret: would my expectations be satisfactorily realized, or would all be thwarted by conditions beyond my control?

The year before, I had approached both the solstice and the Day of the Baptist without expectations or preferences, and each time the result had been immense personal satisfaction. Now, however, I seemed to be set up for nothing but frustration. I began to wonder with a trace of irritation why things in Mexico—people, events—couldn't be more predictable and dependable.

On the evening of the twenty-third, the day before the Day of the Baptist, I still had no idea how, when, or if Chucho and/or I would make it to Yecapixtla. It was too late to get a ride in the van for myself in the event Chucho neither drove nor chose to go at all, yet I wrote on the board by the monastery door that I'd be gone for the day, figuring if it came to it I'd take the bus. But then between dinner and meditation the neighborhood *mensajero* showed up with a handwritten message from Chucho: "*El coche parece funcionar bastante bien andar a Yecapixtla. Hasta mañana. Jesús.*"

Suddenly my concerns appeared stupid and wasteful. Hadn't I urged myself to "let go and let God"? To "be here now"? I went to sleep that night with a host of delightful recollections from the year before, anticipating a day that could only be fuller with unexpected events, encounters, and revelations.

Chucho seemed to share my anticipation as we set out the next morning, and both of us beamed in appreciation of the holiday atmosphere that dominated downtown Cuernavaca. Flowers graced every corner and the people were dressed as if it were Sunday, with many of them obviously on their way to church. "Look, Shiva, they're celebrating just being alive," admiringly observed my friend as we pulled out of town and onto the highway that ran eastward to Yautepec and the volcano beyond. Reminded of Chucho's dilemma, I could feel how he might be envying these simple people their simple reassurances.

Much of the way we had Popo directly in our sights, the purity of its gleaming, snowcapped peaks oblivious even in June to the rays of the sun rising steadily above it. It was almost as though its magnetic force and not the VW's laboring engine behind the seat provided the means for our approach. Once we'd passed through the noisy municipality of Yautepec, also festively done up for the Day of the Baptist, it loomed even more unavoidably before us. I was moved to remark on how drawn I was to its presence.

Chucho nodded. "You know, Shiva, when I was a *chico* growing up in *Méjico*, before the air became so *sucio* you could not see more than a mile away, we had the volcano in view all of the time, and it was very much an everyday part of our lives."

We drove the remaining ten or so kilometers in silence. I could only imagine the sense of loss my friend must feel for the magnificent city of his boyhood. Even now I loved to spend time there, polluted and decadent as it inescapably was—marveling over the architecture, the art, the parks, the incredible *mestizo* culture that thrived despite its own runaway chaos and the almost total aloofness of a self-absorbed Gringolandia to the north. Just as did most of my Mexican friends, however, I preferred conditions out here in *el campo*, where strangers still greeted one another like old friends and you could breathe clean air and hear yourself think.

Not that it was at all quiet when we arrived in little Yecapixtla. As soon as we parked the car and got out in a rising state of exhilaration we could hear the sounds of the dancers, who hadn't even started their performance, yet had already set the rhythmic tone of the day just by their presence in the town and the uncountable numbers of shells that marked their every movement. If they *had* been an Aztec army, they would have stirred the hearts of the regional peasants merely by their auditory presence. With both of us smiling from ear to ear, Chucho and I followed the beckoning sounds in the direction of the *zócalo*.

And the morning went much the same as the year before. Now, however, it was the two of us in an almost trancelike state: rising from our seats on the low wall among the peasant audience only the couple of times Chucho went to purchase paper cones of fresh papaya and mango from the *puesto* at the edge of the square, and when the two of us slipped just before lunchtime behind a nearby house to empty our bladders. And then, when it was time to eat, I was faced with the first major change from the year before.

Apparently the mayor was no longer in office, and his successor was not so comfortable with the politics of Eduardo and some of his fellow dancers. "*Pinche politicastros,*" snarled Chucho when Eduardo informed us of the situation.

The troupe was splitting up for lunch among the homes of several more hospitable members of the community, he explained, and unfortunately he didn't feel he could invite us to join them as I'd done beneath the mayor's tent. These would be smaller gatherings, and to a degree they'd be imposing already. "There are one or two *restaurantes*," he assured us apologetically. "I'm sure any of them would provide an acceptable lunch."

Guiltily Eduardo hurried away, leaving us standing there outside the cathedral. I looked at Chucho. "Well, shall we find a clean, well-lighted place and have some beans and rice?"

Rubbing his hands over his amplified waistline, he said, "*Posiblemente.* But I'm not so sure about the restaurants in this town. *Espera aquí.* I'll be right back."

I watched as he went in the opposite direction from Eduardo, then I turned, first toward the volcano looming mutely in the lofty near distance and then to the scene immediately around me. In the rapidly emptying *zócalo* I felt uncomfortably alone, and almost for the first time that day I was listening consciously to the brass band, vying for attention as it had the year before at the woodsy fringe of the park adjoining the cathedral. Ironically, now that it was only them playing there was hardly anyone left to hear them but me. I recalled a year ago thinking they ought to listen to some Herb Alpert albums. They were dressed entirely in white and weren't half bad actually.

Apparently the band was here on this day of tribute to Saint John to assert the Hispanic side of the national identity, and I fell once more to pondering the challenge of reconciling cultural and religious disagreements. Why must tribes and traditions be so intolerant and adversarial? Can any of us be anything, ultimately, but enriched and enhanced by a diversity of influences? And didn't the greatest of all thrills have to be the discovery of the unities and harmonies within each successive appearance of difference?

I was reminded of the spring of 1964, when my first wife and I had flown from Addis Ababa to Jerusalem, then in Jordan, on an Easter charter excursion. During our nine-day stay in the Holy Land we and another Peace Corps couple had rented a car and driven north for several days in Syria and Lebanon. We were blown away by the bazaars of Damascus, as well as by the breathtaking mountainous countryside with its soaring raptors and nimble-footed goats gazing down at us from rocky perches. But what captivated my imagination beyond anything else during those few days was Beirut.

Nestled on the eastern shore of the Mediterranean and protected by a lofty range of mountains, it was a jewel of a city that seemed in its architecture and its style of life to be the perfect blend of race, religion, and culture. European and Middle Eastern, Christian and Muslim, it seemed the closest thing to an ideal place I had so far visited in my brief twenty-seven years, and I made an immediate vow to return, perhaps as a professor one day at the picturesque American University with the coastline campus. What a shock it was a few years later to watch on the news as the denominations and factions that gave Beirut its rainbow of flavors turned against one another and proceeded in the process to destroy their magnificent city.

But then my attention was drawn back to Yecapixtla, the brass band, and Chucho, who had found us a place to eat. "It's a kind of party," he told me, "and we've been invited to join it."

I followed him away from the zócalo, and together we walked a couple of short blocks in the direction of the huge compound with the plaque proclaiming the area a colonial monument. I was about to ask him if he knew what was inside its high wall when he announced, "Here we are."

We were standing before a large open metal gate, staring into a paved area about the size of a volleyball court, which was probably where the residents of the compound within ordinarily parked their cars. Today, however, the area was dominated by a long table, covered by a plastic cloth and an abundance of food, and two rows of benches at which sat thirty or forty men. Most of the food seemed to be meat, and in front of every other man or so stood a bottle of what appeared to be tequila, drowned worm and all. The only women in view were a half dozen or so harried-looking matrons in soiled aprons, who were busily serving the men. From the doorways of two of the houses several small children studied the boisterous gathering. It was not, all in all, a promising scene, and I remained outside the open gate, reluctant to enter.

Chucho was alert to my feelings and asked with concern, "Do you have any problems with this place, Shiva?"

"Well," I confessed, "it's probably not the one I'd have picked myself."

He laughed. "If you wish to get to know a country, my friend, you have to experience a wide range of places."

I nodded, then shook my head. I wondered where we'd sit. I wondered what I'd be able to eat. The rapid Spanish phrases coming to us from the reveling men at the table sounded vulgar and guttural. They held fatty pieces of *carne asado* in their hands and tore at them with their teeth in a way that was almost brutal to behold. Each undermasticated mouthful was washed down with a long gulp of tequila. This was definitely not the kind of meal I had in mind.

But before I'd found the words to amplify my misgivings, one of the men at the table had spotted us in the entranceway and was rising to greet us. He was dressed in a soiled undershirt and his belly hung over his baggy, unbelted trousers. "*Hola*," he said, wiping a greasy palm and fingers on his pants before reaching out to shake Chucho's hand and then mine. He gave me a brief but polite appraisal as Chucho thanked him in Spanish for inviting us to join the table, dismissing the idea with a magnanimous wave of his glistening left hand and motioning for us to sit.

There was a narrow parting along the bench across from our host and together we squeezed into the space. Immediately a glass of tequila was placed before each of us, and Chucho drank half of his down in a single swallow. Then someone put a grimy-looking plate of meat in front of each of us, and I stared at mine with rising alarm until Chucho came to my rescue: *"No come carne."*

Then someone was asking me, *"¿Pues, que quiere comer?"*

I shrugged. *"¿Tal vez, arroz y frijoles, por favor?"*

Platters of rice and beans were quickly passed toward us from the end of the table, and Chucho, his mouth already full of meat, helped himself. As I spooned some for myself onto another questionable-looking plate the men around us nodded and smiled, and I felt a pang of guilt for my earlier feelings. Weren't these Mexicans, after all? Why shouldn't they be agreeable? And what had my earlier feelings been all about anyway? Had I been judging them as whiskey-drinking carnivores? I knew what my fellows at the monastery would think if they saw me now in this scene, but didn't I pride myself on my ability to get along in almost any situation?

I realized that since Eduardo's news I'd been expecting us to go somewhere quiet for lunch, somewhere we could share with each other our impressions of the morning, somewhere we could talk about the "rational miraculous." I'd expected to have him to myself.

Now I watched Chucho empty his glass, then pour himself another from the nearest unlabeled bottle. I took a sip from my own, blinking involuntarily as my throat constricted and my eyes began to water. Not only was it potent, it was also vile. Everyone around me, in the meantime, was drinking it down like water.

Actually several turned out to be drinking beer, and it wasn't long before I was, too: Superior, in weathered bottles. Despite the undercurrent of aggression bristling among them, they seemed friendly enough. Yet as was often the case with minimally educated Mexicans, none knew how to adjust their discourse sufficiently for me to understand them, and I quickly realized I was not going to be a part of the conversation. Nor was I able to make much sense of it, rapid and colloquial as it was. I caught some cynical political and sexual innuendoes, but after that I was content to listen to the music of the language and get what little I could. It gratified me to see how comfortably Chucho had settled in among these strangers, and even though I'd still have preferred to be alone with him elsewhere, it was easy for me to sip my beer and smile whenever they laughed over something one of them said.

Soon I'd had my fill of beans, rice, and tortillas, and it wasn't long before Chucho had wolfed down enough to be pushing away his plate as he belched and loosened his belt. In the meantime the tequila continued to flow, and the staccato chatter and laughter became increasingly laced with *pinche* this and *chingada* that.

I was beginning to recall my initial misgivings as we'd stood in the open gateway, and my suspicion of something more than a little bit brutal lurking beneath the surface. These were common men, yet to a degree urbanized common men who'd lost the natural dignity of the simple peasants in the *zócalo*. Great waves of dissatisfaction seemed to radiate from these men, striking me as a little bit dangerous, and I felt I could almost understand the attraction they held for Chucho. And then one of them handed me another beer and I drank it down almost as fast as I had the first.

I'd never seen Chucho in this vulgar mode. He seemed perfectly at home, matching these strangers drink for drink and coarse joke after coarse joke. During a brief lull, while Chucho was chuckling over something someone had said but wasn't paying attention to anyone in particular, I spoke into his ear: "The dancers are just about due to get started again. I guess we ought to be getting back pretty soon."

His eyes were alarmingly bloodshot as he turned and fixed me in his gaze. "But how would it look to just get up and go? After accepting all their hospitality?"

I shrugged and looked around us. A manic enjoyment was evident on the faces of the men, but it seemed the smiles of the women serving them were far from genuine. And the eyes of the children watching from the doorways suggested a hint of fear along with childish curiosity. Or was it my own fear I was monitoring? But fear of what? These men? That seemed remote, even paranoid, despite the rising aura of aggressiveness in their drinking and laughter. Of disappointed expectations?

I turned to Chucho once more. "Well, how long do you think it'll take before we can leave without offending anyone?"

This time I'd interrupted him, and he regarded me for several seconds before saying, "There is no obligation on your part, Chiba. You are not obligated to remain. Why don't you find out how soon the dancers will be starting again? Come and let me know and perhaps I'll be ready to leave by then."

I was scarcely noticed as I left, muttering, "*Voy a regresar,*" several times to no one in particular. At the table I'd gone back and forth between seeing myself as an invisible nonentity or as the butt of an endless run of colloquially uttered racial jokes and epithets. Either way, they were all too polite to be anything but courteous in their aloofness, and I hadn't heard the word *gringo* pass anyone's lips so far.

For all I knew their failure to acknowledge my departure was simply their shy embarrassment on my behalf for ungratefully leaving the party, however temporary my absence might be. Or who knows? Perhaps for disdaining the meat they so generously offered. It wouldn't have been the first time, or the last, I'd partaken of generously offered flesh food. But never anything like this meat.

I couldn't help wondering if I might have been able to establish a degree of communication with at least a few of the men had I remained there drinking with them. It was unlikely. There was no way I could have conversed with any of them, and what would we have conversed about anyway? It had been easier to be ignored by them, whether out of politeness or because I was a contemptible gringo. But if that was the case, what did it say about Chucho?

It was almost the first time I'd been among Mexicans and not had a bit of a fuss made over me—for being *el gringo simpático,* and I was reminded how increasingly alone I'd felt since Chucho left me in the *zócalo* to find us somewhere to eat. It occurred to me that a year ago I'd been alone without ever feeling that way while today I was with Chucho and felt more alone than I'd felt anywhere in a long time.

When I got there the dancers were already assembling outside the cathedral for their afternoon performance, and the brass band was taking advantage of the last few moments when the crowd was back and they were still the only entertainment. Most of their songs made me think of bullfights. When I approached Eduardo he seemed preoccupied and showed little interest when I told him we'd been invited to eat at the house of someone in the community.

As they began their first dance I found a seat on the wall to sit and watch, but after my three quick bottles of Superior I was less a master of my thoughts than I'd been all day. I could not take my mind off the unsavory gathering I'd just left. Those men obviously held a powerful force over Chucho's awareness, and wasn't it safe to say that it was not an appeal to his nobler faculties? As I looked around me now I couldn't help remarking once more the contrast between them and these humbly sober country people, who seemed so much more wholesome in the quality of their lives. I wondered if any of them had been organized into a union or a co-op somewhere by the reformist lawyer dancing for them today.

It seemed increasingly clear to my agitated mind that Chucho would be better off as far away from that gang in the garage as I could possibly get him. But how could I justify rushing in and rescuing him from his own reality? How could I even do it? My mind was becoming so restless I could scarcely concentrate on the rhythm of the dancers, and soon I was rushing off to tell Chucho they'd begun their afternoon performance.

But he still wasn't ready to go. I could hear his voice even before I'd entered the open gateway, laughing in a way that made my blood run cold. In the open gate I could see the number of men at the table had diminished—at least some of them had felt free to leave—but when my friend and I made eye contact he simply arched an eyebrow and shrugged. What could he do? his look seemed to say, and he raised his glass to me and drained it.

Back at the *zócalo* I did my best to enjoy the dancers as I had the year before. I understood it had everything to do with quieting the mind of expectations. I had only to release mine and it was all here for me, just as it once had been. Easier said than done, however. I gazed at the brass band, whose horns made a kind of irrelevant counterpoint to the rhythms of the dancers' shells, drums, and strumming strings, and I understood just how irrelevant I was, too. Irrelevant and a little inebriated.

Here was the band, vying for attention in their almost foolish way, and here was I, somehow doing the same damn thing. Didn't I know better? Didn't I know in my yogi's heart that the purpose of it all was to let it all go? Hadn't I learned as far back as the Peace Corps not to expect anything or anybody to change but myself?

But I couldn't surrender my concerns to the rhythm of the dancers, and after an uncertain period of inner torment I knew I had to go back and try it with Chucho one more time. I told myself I needed to save him from that pathetic celebration of mediocrity. Hadn't our purpose for the day been to uncover a treasure of insightful realizations that would carry us both into our next stage of awareness? And hadn't the plan been for us to do it together? The Mexican and the gringo in transnational synergy?

This time I heard him laughing and joking halfway up the street, and the raucous sound of it almost turned me back before I reached the compound. But I walked straight to the table and sat back down next to him on the bench. A dozen or so remained, and nobody was eating. The women and children were nowhere in sight.

"Chiba!" he greeted me. "Welcome, amigo, to the company of hopeless *borrachos!*"

Despite the beer someone had placed in my hand and which I was now thirstily drinking, I still felt the urge to get him out of here. "Don't you think it's time for you to stop all this?" I demanded. "Don't you think you've repaid your welcome enough?"

He laughed pathetically and hung his head, then looked at me sideways with a wicked leer that made me think of a couple of dozen Tex-Mex westerns I'd seen in my life. "You don't get it, do you, hombre? You just can't understand what's going on here, can you? It's a macho thing, man. I can't leave here now. What would these Mexicans think of me if I did?"

I stared back at him, trying to find the Chucho I thought I knew. Even as he waited for an answer from me he joked with the two guys across the table from us — their eyes as bloodshot as his — and suddenly I realized what was happening here. These were *los agotados* we were among: the worn-out, the used-up, the exhausted. And here was where Chucho was making his statement, his last stand. Drowning his sorrows in the oblivion of macho drunkenness.

But I still refused to accept it. "Look at Eduardo out there!" I wanted to shout at him. "Look at what he's making of his life — in his mastery of traditional dances and with the workers and the farmers in the fields. Doesn't what Eduardo's doing make you not want to give up?"

Instead I turned to him and said, "But what do you care what these guys think of you?" I was talking out loud now, knowing no one else could understand me anyway. "Who are they to you? What do you care about them? What do they care about you?"

He straightened his head and met my gaze with reddened eyes. "You just don't understand, Chiba. Here is where I belong."

I nodded at him as I rose back up to my feet, and then at the other men still sitting at the table who'd been politely but amusedly silent as the two of us conversed in the gringo lingo. "I guess you're right," I told him. "I'll see you later."

"Enjoy yourself, *hermano!*" he called after me.

And I could still hear his voice above all the others in the randy conversation halfway back up the block from the squalid compound, as I returned once again toward the echoing sounds of the brass band and the relentless rhythm of the dancers' shells.

PIQUING THE SPIRITS

by Mary-Ann Tirone Smith

In Mary-Ann Tirone Smith's second novel, *Lament for a Silver-Eyed Woman*, the narrator says, "President John F. Kennedy went and gave us free tickets to the Federal Republic of Cameroon." Smith says that he gave *her* something to write about along with a ticket: "If I hadn't been a Peace Corps Volunteer in the mid-sixties, I wouldn't have been a writer since I have no interest in writing about the walls of the living room closing in and the resulting internal musings."

Smith's novels contain large events: D day, a terrorist bombing in Paris, the invasion of Shatila refugee camp, the sinking of the *Normandie*, the 1944 Hartford circus fire. Her walk-on characters include Ernest Hemingway, Adolf Hitler, Zelda Fitzgerald, Emmett Kelly, and Sargent Shriver.

She is the author of four novels, many reviews, several movie scripts and plays, and hundreds of op-ed pieces on a variety of topics that reflect on her personal philosophy: if I'm not outraged at least once a week, I'm dead.

Nestled upon a low ledge on the side of Mount Cameroon, an active volcano rising 13,000 feet above the equatorial sea, is the village of Buea, where I was a Peace Corps Volunteer. Conversely to the rationale for climbing Mount Everest, I hadn't climbed Mount Cameroon because I was there. It was home.

Home on the mountain meant cozy living in a two-room cement-block house where I'd read each night by the blue light of my Coleman lamp. And it meant taking long mist-filled walks, eating sweet mangoes picked from the tree in my yard, drinking warm Beaufort beer and listening to High Life at the Tip Top Bar, nibbling roasted corn on a stick that I'd buy from children in front of the post office a hundred yards down the mountain. The trek from the post office back to my house was mountain climbing enough. I chose to gain the looming summit vicariously, through the eyes and pen of Sir Richard Burton, who chronicled his ascent in 1862.

I marveled at Burton's descriptions of silver wildflowers, dry riverbeds lined with crystal quartz, whistling night winds that seemed to come from the center of the earth. But at the same time, I was vexed at his boast upon achieving the summit: "To be first in such matters is everything; to be second nothing." Never mind that African honey harvesters had been climbing the mountain during a time when Sir Richard's forebears were charging the Roman legions with peashooters.

In addition to Burton's tale, I enjoyed the colorful descriptions supplied by various houseguests who stopped to visit after climbing the mountain. Their accounts were not unlike Burton's and included vivid depictions of the crash site of a TWA commercial airliner.

In April, toward the end of my second year in Cameroon, I faced up to the fact that if I wanted to climb the mountain, I couldn't put it off any longer. I would be going home soon. April is a sparkling month in Cameroon, a short window of clear, balmy weather seated between the dry season of Ramadan, when the air is filled with Sahara grit, and a rainy season of relentless deluge. And so it was in a timely fashion that I ran into a fellow named Warren. Warren something, or something Warren, I didn't know. He was a location scout hired by a film company to find a "pristine corner of Africa" for a remake of *Tarzan*. He intended to climb Mount Cameroon and asked me if I'd like to be his research assistant. I said no to research assistant and all its secretarial/carnal implications, but said I'd like to go along for the ride. That was fine with him, though he still treated me like a research assistant, trusting me to "arrange things." What things? Things like "carriers."

I asked him if he was planning on bringing a lot of stuff up there. He said, "The usual," having forgotten already that I was no mind-reading research assistant. But climbing Mount Cameroon is not a matter of scaling sheer cliffs. It is a long steep hike. You go up one day, you come down the next. I figured a sleeping roll and two Cadbury bars were all anyone would require. One quickly learns in Cameroon not to make a production of things or else people think you're a masochist. Best to just drift along with the Cameroon philosophy of why do today what you can put off till tomorrow. I didn't say all this to the movie man. I just said something like, "Okay, Warren."

We would meet the next Saturday morning at six a.m. The starting point for the climb up Mount Cameroon is the Buea Prison Farm, situated on a fertile ledge above Buea. The prisoners who work the farm are all guilty of the same crime—their noses are bent out of shape. They'd been involved in boundary disputes or inheritance squabbles or fusses over crop rights. They went to jail to cool off. Real crimes were handled by tribal secret societies.

The prisoners always came out to greet prospective climbers, to size them up in order to make wagers as to who would make it, who would be back in an hour, and who would need a stretcher. If a climber wasn't back in five days, four prisoners would be selected to race up the mountain and rescue him. None of the prisoners saw such an emergency situation as an opportunity to escape. They could do that anytime they felt like it.

When the TWA jet crashed, the entire population of the prison farm headed up the mountain, where they found just one survivor, the military attaché to the American embassy in Yaoundé. He was clutching the diplomatic pouch. The man died shortly after rescue, but as the prisoners were quick to boast, "Owing to us, the mail is going through!" (Cameroonians speak in the present progressive, as do people from all over the world who have been oppressed by the Raj.)

The prisoners knew me well because I bought milk from them once a week. Their milk isn't homogenized, so when I'd get back home I'd spoon the cream off the top and eat it. I pretended I was eating a little bowl of the newest flavor of designer ice cream — African vanilla cream.

"Good morning, Miss Mary," the prisoners sang out as I prodded my motor scooter up the last of the treacherous "paved" road. The chunks of asphalt that once made up the pavement stuck up through the dirt in jagged points.

"Good morning, Mr. Prisoners," I called back.

They laughed at me. I have failed to get everyone to stop calling me Miss Mary. So I call them Miss or Mister, too, and they think this is hilarious.

They offered me bread and butter, but I graciously accepted just the bread, explaining that I was on a diet, a curious American custom where you try to lose weight. In Cameroon, to be fat is a goal overshadowing all others. They laughed at me some more. Actually, I refused the butter because it didn't taste anything like butter, it tasted like moosefat. I decided "moosefat" was apt when I first saw the cows. They didn't look anything like cows, they looked like moose.

The prisoners kept me company while I awaited our guide, Ngoundu. Ngoundu was a fourteen-year-old boy who sold odds and ends in the market to help with his school tuition. I bought a beaded Givenchy bag from him once, discarded by the local mission after they'd gone through the donations sent from a church in Paris. He borrowed my books all the time. He'd read all my books within three months, but he kept on borrowing them and reading them over again. He was a real smart kid.

I sat down on my sleeping roll and backpack stuffed with a sweatshirt, which I would need against the nighttime chill, and my poncho, which went everywhere since solid sheets of rain will come spilling out of the sky without warning to remind everyone that April would not last forever. Also, a can of Danish ham my dad had sent me on my birthday, and finally, a dozen peanut butter cookies wrapped up in the *Cameroon Times*. I made them from peanuts I'd bought in the market. The recipe: Crush the peanuts and set aside. Stir together one big spoonful of Lyle's Golden Syrup and a box of Nestlé's Quik sent to you by your mother. When you have a heavy paste, mush in the peanuts. Roll into balls. Eat. I think my cookies qualified as cookies though they weren't cooked. Baking cookies in a wood-fed stove is a production.

Ngoundu arrived. He brought along some company, his little sister Plebiscite, named after the 1960 vote of the Bamileke tribe, which decided to throw in their fate with Cameroon rather than Nigeria. The bump on the border of Cameroon where people speak English instead of French is made up of a most beautiful mountain range. Nigeria's loss was a heavy one. In Cameroon, Plebiscite is pronounced *Plebby-SEAT.* The little girl was about five years old, and I had seen her with Ngoundu often in the market. It is common practice in Cameroon for pubescent boys to be put in charge of small brothers and sisters. Babies go from being tied on their mothers' backs to tagging along behind big brother. Though both children were barefoot, Ngoundu carried in his bundle a supply of sweaters, ski hats, and mittens. It gets down into the low fifties on the mountain, and to Cameroonians, fifty degrees is frigid not chilly.

Ngoundu greeted me, Plebiscite gave me a hug, then the two did the same with the prisoners who sorely missed their own children. I brought out a couple of my cookies for them, and the prisoners gave them each a cup of milk to wash them down. Washing down my cookies required a fairly substantial gush of liquid. Ngoundu said, "Miss Mary, the gentleman is not arriving."

In Cameroon, not only are the verbs in the present progressive, questions are asked in the affirmative.

"Yes, Mr. Ngoundu. But I'm sure he'll be here soon."

"And so, he is here."

In Cameroon time, "soon" is the same as "now." There is one more intriguing language thing of theirs: they do not deal with the concept of either/or questions. So if you ask, I'm going to the post office—do I turn right or left? the answer will be yes. (Unless the post office is straight ahead; then the answer will be no.)

Ngoundu and I chitchatted for a while about the outstanding mountain-climbing weather until a Jeep rumbled into the yard. Warren emerged from the backseat wearing some sort of safari suit, the kind Dan Rather wears when he does the news from a third-world war zone. (Dan doesn't know that the third worlders are all wondering if his suits and ties were lost in transit. It is racist to come to Africa dressed like a great white hunter, but I don't really object to Dan doing it since I so enjoy the sight of his chest hair sticking up from the top of his shirt with the first three buttons left undone.) Warren also had on one of those cowboy hats with one side stapled up. (Unlike the movie man, Dan Rather knows where to draw the line.)

Warren also had a complicated Leica around his neck, along with a light meter and a pair of binoculars. His hiking boots looked as if they weighed a ton each. I had on my old sneakers with cockroach holes. Cameroonian cockroaches are six inches long and friendly, sort of like gerbils. I was using twine for laces as cockroaches go for laces first. My first morning in Cameroon I awoke to find these two little plastic tubes lying next to my sneakers. I'd kept my other pair of sneakers in Tupperware ever since.

I said hello to Warren and he said hello to me, then he noticed Ngoundu and Plebiscite smiling at him, so he said, "Hiya, kids." I introduced them, and the prisoners, too, and they all shook hands. He whispered to me to repeat the little girl's name. I did and explained its derivation, but he'd never heard of a plebiscite. He reached into his pocket and held out two Kennedy half dollars. "Little souvenir from America, kids."

Ngoundu and Plebiscite were so thrilled that they couldn't stop rubbing their coins against their cheeks and holding them up to the sky to gaze upon. The prisoners all exclaimed. Warren whispered, "If those are prisoners, where's the jail?"

I explained that this was a prison farm; the inmates lived in yonder farmhouse and were free to wander.

"They are?"

"They're not dangerous, Warren."

"So why are they prisoners?"

"Long story."

Still whispering, he said, "The children are putting the coins in their mouths."

"I know."

"Are they going to eat them?"

"Of course not. They're carrying them."

"Oh. Who are they, anyway?"

"The guide and the carrier. Now the carrier has something to carry."

He just stared at me. He was about to say something else, but I was already calling out, "Okay, everybody, onward." Then I started singing "Onward Christian Soldiers," a favorite hymn at the Baptist mission. The prisoners joined in, meanwhile eyeing Warren and giving one another "he'll-be-back-by-nightfall" nudges. I thought their assessment was probably accurate.

Ngoundu led the way with Plebiscite behind him, though she moved forward in a series of diverse lateral movements. She intended to dance up the mountain, apparently. Warren stood rooted to the spot.

"Where's our stuff?" he called out to me.

I turned. "Which stuff?"

"The tent, for starters."

"Tent? Oh, we don't need a tent. The Germans built three little, uh, lodges along the trail. Hut One, Hut Two, and Hut Three, just like football. We rest at Hut One and sleep at Hut Two, and tomorrow we reach the summit and you'll be back down the mountain in time for the cocktail hour at the hotel."

First he snorted at the cocktail reference, then he said, "What about Hut Three?"

"Hut Three is for wimps."

He trudged up to me. "Where's my sleeping bag?"

"Didn't you bring one?"

"You told me you'd arrange things." He rerooted. The muscle under his left eye began to twitch.

I said, "You can get in with me."

"Now you're talking!"

"But you have to carry it." I tossed it to him.

He said, "Best damn deal I made since I got here. I thought you didn't want to be my research assistant."

I didn't tell him I doubted he'd reach the first hut.

The start of the Mount Cameroon trail is a path winding through the prisoners' vegetable gardens. Warren thought the entire trail would be like that. "Why do we need the kids anyway?" he asked.

"They're guides. The rain forest has lots of trails."

"Oh. Is the girl going to cook for us?"

I told him child labor is a crime in Cameroon. Plebiscite was like me, just tagging along. I told him I would cook.

He said, "All right!"

All right, indeed.

Twenty minutes into the rain forest that skinned Mount Cameroon up to 9000 feet where the tree line ended, Warren and I were already huffing and puffing. Ngoundu was whistling another hymn, and Plebiscite was skipping, still taking ten steps sideways for every one forward. Warren said, "I need to stop and rest."

Ngoundu said, "No need to worry, sir. You are soon experiencing second wind."

Warren said, "I are?"

I hissed, "Be polite."

We trudged. The rain forest encased us. We couldn't talk, we could only huff and puff because the real trail is a lot steeper than the garden path. Though the sun was rising in the sky, we couldn't know it. The canopy high over our heads was so dense that the light was the equivalent of predawn. Warren struggled to comment. "How the hell, *huff-puff*, are we going to, *huff-puff*, film a movie in here?" Then he gasped for extra air.

Since it wasn't a question but rather an observation, I didn't give my opinion. Also, I had no opinion because I was concentrating on experiencing second wind. I was sweating, and my thigh muscles were being stretched to a point beyond where they'd never been stretched before. Though concentrating, I never noticed second wind. That's because second wind is the slow dissipation of the manifestations of body shock. Second wind is not an epiphany. I just kind of realized that I was no longer wallowing in regret, but rather enjoying the sights.

The Mount Cameroon rain forest made me feel like the incredible shrinking woman. The centuries-old, black, dank trunks of mahogany and ebony, bereft of branches, soared like pillars hundreds of feet up to the canopy so far above and so thick that it did not look like the entanglement of foliage I'd imagined; it looked like the night sky with just a few stars that twinkled on and off. The stars were pinpricks of sunlight that managed to peek through. No green, and no blue sky—only black. When you fly above the rain forest, you see brilliant emerald billows.

I was in a cavern, not a jungle, filled with cloned evil columns demonstrating that only the strong survive. Not a single little sapling anywhere. Only at the edge of the foot-wide trail did some sort of mutant vine make an attempt at headway. We came upon a huge fallen trunk, easily six feet around, long and rotten. Sprouting all over it were cartoonlike fungi, big nodules of yellow and orange and red; sponge balls were devouring the tree.

I said, no longer huffing and puffing, "Mr. Ngoundu, how long before the fungi polishes off that tree?"

He was used to my colloquialisms. "It is depending on the age of the tree."

"If you bring someone up here next month, how much will be left?"

"Nothing, Miss."

Warren's second wind must have kicked in because we had to stop so that he could put the Leica to work. A few background shots, I guessed. Ngoundu said, "Please, sir, you are not stepping off the trail."

"I aren't?"

I said, "Warren, knock it off."

Offended, he said, "I'm not doing it on purpose, you know!"

Ngoundu said, "The forest floor is soft. It is made of leaf mold and spores." Then Ngoundu dug a rock up out of the trail and dropkicked it with the inside edge of his bare foot. The rock made no sound when it fell amidst the pillars. It just sank out of sight.

Warren said, "Holy shit."

He got going with his zoom lens. Except for unseen insects living in the leaf mold (and wondering where the rock had come from), there was no life visible in the forest—no animals, no parrots screeching, no vines to swing on. You go to the jungles of Africa and all your childhood myths die hard. The silence began to get to me. The clunk of Warren's boots, the padding of my sneakers, and the silence of the children's footfalls kept getting louder. I said, "I feel the need to whistle 'Dixie.'"

Warren said, "Please don't."

Ngoundu said, "What is Dixie?" Warren lost out.

After a few choruses Ngoundu reassured me. "Do not be worrying, Miss Mary. At the Hut One clearing there is living for many years a colony of monkeys. They are making much noise."

Warren said, "Is there any light at the clearing?"

"Oh, yes sir. Much light."

We could hear the monkeys before we saw the light. Whoever decided to call a group of monkeys a troop was right on the money. Troops of fighting soldiers is what they were. As soon as we were in range, not only did they hoot and holler, they also began peppering us with coconuts that grew on the coconut palms planted by the Germans when they built the hut. Though it was no fun dodging coconuts, the light combined with the dodging invigorated us. And before we got to the clearing itself, we smelled it. The Germans had also planted roses, and the roses, reverting back to their prehybrid forms, practically enveloped the hut. Roses, untended in a rain-forest clearing, are too tough even for a mahogany tree. The sight that met us was not unlike the one that met Dorothy when she stepped out of black-and-white Kansas into the Technicolor Oz. We were welcomed not only by monkeys, but also by masses of fat pink polka dots.

Upon reaching Hut One, the first job climbers must attend to, according to Ngoundu, is to prune the roses and expose the steps of the porch and the door of the hut. Ngoundu took a machete from his pack and began hacking, getting rid of the canes that had made their way into the hut, where they'd withered in frustration at not having enough light to climb all over the inside walls, too. When we stood on the porch a million pink petals floated onto us, and we held our faces to the sun. Ah, sun.

We sat down on the two steps of the rose-bowered porch and drank coconut water from the punctured nuts Ngoundu passed around. Then we broke the nuts open and chewed on the sweet cool meat. The monkeys began to quiet down and just sit up in their palm trees sulking, enabling us to hear the birds calling back and forth—still no parrots screeching—and also something that sounded like croaking frogs.

"What's that croaking sound, Ngoundu?"

"Frogs, Miss." Then he said, "We are resting for twenty minutes only. Then we will be picking up speed as the trail is not so harsh once out of the rain forest."

I wondered why I wasn't famished, why a few bites of coconut satisfied me. Back in the States, you work out for half an hour and then you go eat everything in the refrigerator that isn't nailed down. Climbing Mount Cameroon was using up all my appetite. I was full. Of the mountain. I went into the musty hut to look around. It was just a big empty room. I sat on the floor under a window, panes long gone, roses pouring through. I took out my little notebook and pen, and wrote some stuff that might turn out to be the beginnings of a novel. But my writing was disrupted by a presence—Warren's. He was standing in the doorway. He cleared his throat.

"Is it twenty minutes already?" I asked.

He said, "Almost. You writing a letter?"

I didn't answer with No, I'm writing literary mainstream fiction, an explanation I'd developed when asked for the millionth time: You're writing a novel? What is it, a romance? Instead, I said to Warren, "Yes."

He wasn't listening anyway. He said, "Ya know, this isn't what I had in mind."

"What did you have in mind?"

"Mount Kilimanjaro. A safari. A line of carriers all calling me Bwana. The boys breaking out the table and linen and silver candlesticks and serving lunch. Turns out I'm getting some kind of Boy Scout experience."

I said, "Ernest Hemingway wasn't writing travel documentaries for public television, Warren. He made it all up."

"He did not."

I sighed. "People take cute little steam trains up Kilimanjaro. Mount Cameroon is the real thing."

I stood up and brushed off my backside. Someone was always disturbing my writing space no matter how remote. A room of one's own, Virginia, is not a viable choice. Not even in Cameroon. But then, neither are the rest of the choices.

"Listen, I think I saw a vine hanging in this clearing. The potential for great Tarzan scenes is why you're here. So what's the problem?"

"Movie people will want little steam trains."

"I thought you said they wanted pristine Africa."

"They'll need steam trains to get to the pristine parts."

"You want to go back?"

"No. I'm just depressed. I don't know what I'm doing with my life."

That was the research assistant's cue to say, C'mere, honey, and let's just make the big bad world go away. Instead I said, "Life is one preparation after another. You never really do life. Whoever thinks this isn't a dress rehearsal doesn't get it." He rolled his eyes. I said, "You started it."

He said, "You think we can get that Pebbly-seat to quit smiling?"

"Nope. But I'll bet Plebiscite will make a great Boy."

"She'll make a great what?"

"Tarzan's son. Or Jane's. Or whoever he was."

He mumbled something. I'm pretty sure it was, "Fuck Tarzan."

Above Hut One the tree trunks grew thinner, spindly. We could see rocky outcroppings on the forest floor. The smell changed from moldy to familiar. We passed a pine tree, more pine trees. That's what I smelled! Christmas in Connecticut! I felt a stab of homesickness, but I knew that my homesickness for Connecticut would be nothing compared to the homesickness I'd soon be feeling for Cameroon. Like an astronaut who's cavorted on the shores of the Sea of Tranquillity, who knows he won't cavort there ever again, I didn't think I'd ever get a chance to come back.

Warren said, "This is just like the Alps." He began taking pictures. I was going to tell him that his movie would have to be retitled "Tarzan of the Alps," but I had a feeling that he'd say, Fuck Tarzan, louder than the last time and there were children to consider.

The belt of fir trees was just a mile-wide swath, and soon they began looking puny, too, and we could see clumps of long grasses. The clumps grew thicker, and then there were no trees, just a vast plateau stretched out before us—a meadow filled with Sir Richard's silver wildflowers, and yellow ones, too, and purple ones, all daisylike and blowing in a nice breeze. I found I could not resist becoming Julie Andrews. I ran into the meadow, put my arms out, and twirled. I sang, "The hills are alive with the sound of music, with songs they have sung for a thousand years. . . ."

Peals of laughter rather than abbey bells rang out from

Ngoundu and Plebiscite, who didn't know this hymn though they did know how to twirl. And Warren discovered what he wanted to do with his life, I'd have to say. He began shooting with a fury, the clicking and whirring of the Leica not quite drowned out by "Do, a Deer," my next number. Warren was laughing from behind the camera. I asked him what was so funny. He said, "It's not a *teenage* deer, it's a *female* deer." Then he got on his stomach and took close-ups of Plebiscite's smile and Ngoundu's leaping about, and the wildflowers, then he turned over and was taking pictures of the massive ledge that lay ahead, hiding the summit of the mountain. I chose not to dwell on the knowledge that we'd have to climb that ledge. Then I got stung by a bee. I had picked a flower and a bee draining pollen did what bees do.

Everyone came running, but I could see the stinger and I pulled it out. Warren said, "Do you have bee allergies?" I didn't. Ngoundu and Plebiscite offered me no sympathy either. They just looked at each other, shouted, "Bees!" and bolted, heading out to hunt the dead tree where the bees might live. I sucked on my hand. Warren sat down next to me.

"You okay?"

"Yeah."

I changed the subject to Warren's favorite topic. "You're feeling better, right?"

"A little."

I said, "Listen, Warren, you've got a nice wife somewhere, probably a great family, and you've got this nifty job where you get to travel all over the world scouting movie locations . . . think of all the people back home sitting behind desks who really know the meaning of bored."

He said, "I'm bored to death."

I said, "Well, then, do you like honey?"

"I'm sorry?"

I could hear Plebiscite calling out to us, her voice mixed in with the sound of birds. Ngoundu shouted, "We are finding a bonanza!"

Running toward us, the children were holding out great chunks of honeycomb with the honey oozing out and stuck all over with dead bees. Ngoundu's and Plebiscite's faces were covered with honey, too, and also stuck all over with dead bees.

Warren and I demurely accepted the children's treasure, but

we picked the bees off our share before we dug in. The honey was so warm and rich and sweet that my fillings began to tingle. Such a nice change from Lyle's. We ate in a kind of bent-over position the way you eat Popsicles, but honey fresh in the honey-comb doesn't drip, it runs, and no position could keep the honey from trailing down our arms. Warren was masterly, though, at keeping honey from his camera.

Ngoundu said we would have a cleanup at a stream that was near Elephant Rock, a short side trip. Warren perked right up. "Are there elephants there?"

Plebiscite laughed. "Oh, no sir. The rock is *looking* like an elephant."

Ngoundu said, "It is the site of the airplane crash."

Plebiscite said, "And our uncle was turning into a leopard there."

I had to look away from Warren's puzzled face. He whispered, "Did she say her uncle turned into a leopard?"

"Yes. Their tribe is animist."

"What's that?"

"Look it up in an encyclopedia when you get home. C'mon."

We washed off at Ngoundu's stream and headed to the great outcropping ahead. Warren said, "It does look like an elephant." He brought out his camera and asked Ngoundu to climb the rock so he could have perspective.

Plebiscite said, "I am climbing the rock too, sir."

Warren said, "I wouldn't want you to get hurt, Sweetie."

She jingled with laughter. "The rock does not hurt."

I said, "But will it turn us into leopards?"

She jingled some more. "Oh, no, Miss Mary, for we are not piquing the spirits as did our uncle."

Warren asked, "What did he do to pique the spirits?"

"He was implanting a water-measuring gauge."

Ngoundu said, "Our uncle is a meteorologist."

I whispered, "*Was* a meteorologist."

Warren whispered, "I don't believe this."

"Of course you don't. You're not an animist."

I followed the children, who had scrambled up the rock in a minute; it took me several. They struck all kinds of poses for Warren, but I turned into a wooden Indian. The view from the rock was appalling.

Fifty feet beyond Elephant Rock was the tail end of the TWA

jet sticking out of the mountainside just like the half-Cadillac at the New York Hard Rock Café. While Ngoundu and Plebiscite posed for Warren, I gawked. The sight was so incorrect. I kept thinking, what happened to the people in the front three quarters of the plane?

Warren, of course, was wondering what suddenly made me so shy, and when he joined us he started clicking away again. Ngoundu, demonstrating his ability to read the tourist mind once more, said, "We are not going closer to the plane than this, Mr. Warren."

Warren said, "The hell we're not."

Ngoundu said, "A government regulation is preventing us, and also it is dangerous."

I said, "What if you go over there, Warren, and the plane falls off?"

He said, "It's fused. It ain't falling off." Then he seemed to think for a moment. He said, "Quite a cemetery, isn't it?" and he gazed respectfully, actually, and then put his lens cap back on. He said, "I wonder if anyone said kaddish."

In the next three hours, as we climbed to make Hut Two by nightfall, my thoughts and obviously Warren's stayed with the cemetery. I obsessed on immortality while I climbed. Neither Warren nor I exclaimed on the new wonders of landscape: bottomless fissures amidst endless fields of heather, large lumps of black lava that had oozed up during the last eruption. The lumps looked like clots of gore, hardened abscesses that would not hold back the insides of the earth too much longer. There were little creamy-barked, blue-leaved shrubs attached to the mountainside by threads. There was no trail anymore; Ngoundu followed a zigzag route of natural bare spots. Our preoccupation in the light of the fused TWA tail section finally was intruded upon by Sir Richard's dry riverbed filled with loose crystals, a ten-yard-wide valley of glitter. As we approached this dazzling mirage, I thought it was too bad Warren didn't work for Disney. I scooped up a handful of crystals and put them in my pocket. Ngoundu said, "Best not to take any, Miss Mary."

"How come, Mr. Ngoundu?"

"The spirits will be piqued."

I tossed back all but three. Warren said, "Chicken." He didn't know I'd kept three. I didn't tell him because Ngoundu would be offended.

Ngoundu took his dress shoes—plastic sandals made in Czechoslovakia—out of his bundle and carefully put them on. No socks. He carried Plebiscite across the riverbed piggyback. I could feel the points of the crystals pressing into the bottom of my sneakers. It was like walking with a lot of stones in your shoes, and the discomfort brought out all the other discomfort I had numbed out of my mind—my aching ankles, my aching calves, my aching lower back, my aching whole body. Worst of all, I could no longer numb out the sight that lay ahead.

Beyond the crystal-filled riverbed, between the heather and the moss-covered ledges surrounding the summit, the mountain was at its most steep, a sharp incline of crumbled rock and loose gravelly stones. Ngoundu had warned us that the last yards before Hut Two would be the toughest, and we would perhaps be forced to crawl. I believe I could have made it upright if not for the cruel fact of the pain I'd repressed for so many hours. So I crawled, and Warren crawled, too. But Ngoundu was very encouraging. He and his sister, who had scaled the incline with no trouble, now stood high above us calling out things like, "If you were fresh, you would be having no trouble." And, "Although you are not seeing it, Hut Two is lying just in the distance."

Warren yelled up, "Can *you* see it?"

"Oh, yes sir."

Warren said to me, "Notice I didn't say, Are you seeing it?"

"You're catching on."

We crawled faster.

Ngoundu had things timed perfectly. We would reach Hut Two as dusk fell. At the top of the incline we stood and we could see the hut, bundled in a hollow, situated by the clever Germans in a mossy green bowl to protect climbers from the winds, just now beginning to blow. And as the winds came up, the hut vanished into blackness. Dusk on the mountain lasted seven seconds. The sunlight was there, and then it was gone. I turned, thinking I'd see pink streaks in the western sky. Nothing. Blackness.

The hut had two rooms, one with sleeping ledges, the other— built for servants—without. I wondered why the Germans didn't have the guides and carriers just sleep outside in the dirt.

The Cameroonians were right: fifty degrees was freezing. I thought that a fireplace would have been real cozy. I dug out my sweatshirt and put it on. Warren thought better of asking me where his was. Ngoundu and his sister put on their ski togs, including homemade masks knit with designs of horrifying faces. Warren said, "Boy, those masks are scary. Can I get some made for my kids?"

Ngoundu asked, "Your children are needing to ward off spirits."

Warren said, "Nope. They'll wear them on Halloween."

Warren explained Halloween. Ngoundu and Plebiscite looked to each other. Warren may not have known of the universal need to ward off spirits, but they did. Ngoundu said his Mami would make some for Warren's children. Then Ngoundu took some sticks out of one of his pant legs and started a fire outside by the door. He threw on chunks of dried moss. The light of the fire revealed little rock ledges to sit on, and Warren and I collapsed into our seats and enjoyed the glow of the flames. We smiled at each other. We'd accomplished a day's climb up Mount Cameroon.

Ngoundu said, "We are eating."

I eyed Warren before he could say, We are? He laughed. I did, too. So did Ngoundu and Plebiscite behind their hideous masks because it took so little to make them laugh. I broke out the food I'd brought and Ngoundu broke out his. The little key attached to my can of ham had come loose and I couldn't find it. Ngoundu told me not to worry as he had a Swiss army knife, which he used to slit the outer edge. He lifted out the two-pound ham and placed it on an oft-used piece of aluminum foil that he'd peeled from a crumpled ball. All Cameroonian children have a foil collection scrunched into a ball. He put the ham onto the fire. Ngoundu's contribution was a stack of yam patties his mother had made, and he put those on the fire, too. I said to Warren, "Yams."

He said, "Yamburgers."

I decided that maybe I was beginning to like Warren.

The smell of frying ham and yams filled the hollow. We leaned back on our elbows and listened to the sizzling and the winds all around us whistling more and more loudly. We salivated heavily. And then we ate the most delicious meal I've ever had before or since. The ham was juicy with a taste of foreign smoke; the yams were smooth and sweet. Then Ngoundu went into the hut and came out with a pot and four tin cups. He filled the pot with water from his canteen and made us each a cup of Nescafé. I passed around my cookies, which really were tasty if you could get by the texture. Warren gave his share to Ngoundu and Plebiscite. He said to me, "No offense."

I said, "No offense taken," but the words came out in a garble as my tongue was cleaved to the roof of my mouth.

By seven-thirty, the little fire was no longer making a dent on the chill, and we all went to bed. The children refused to share the sleeping platform as they didn't think it appropriate. I was too tired to argue. Warren and I snuggled together in my sleeping bag with all our clothes on. I fell asleep between "good" and "night."

Warren woke me up around two a.m. He was sweating profusely and moaning in my ear. He did not desire me. He had a raging fever and I felt as if I were lying against a furnace. I got him out of the sleeping bag. He was delirious. He looked right into my eyes and said, "Gretchen! Batman is coming out of the exhaust pipe in the ceiling." In a conspiratorial voice he explained that Batman, there to rescue us, had apparently become stuck in the pipe. I actually looked up, Warren was so convincing. My first thought was to wake the children to help us, but I remembered that they were our guides not our nursemaids.

I don't go anywhere without my aspirin. I dug out the little bottle of Bayer. There were five left. I thought the odd number was strange. Maybe the leopard-uncle had snuck in and stolen one. I dissolved two into a cup of water and got Warren to drink it down. At first he fought me, but I told him to do as Gretchen said, and he obeyed. I gave him more water. Fifteen minutes later his fever still raged but he was no longer delirious. As soon as Batman was gone, Warren said, "Shit. I'm sick."

I told him how fevers could come and go in these parts—some could be explained, some could not. From my perspective, having lived almost two years among people who lost half their children to fevers, a healthy white man with an elevated temperature was no big deal. I said, "In the morning I'll send Ngoundu and Plebiscite down to get help. The prisoners will all be fighting over who gets to come up and carry you down the mountain. Or maybe you'll be feeling better by morning."

He said, "Shit."

I said, "Try to get back to sleep, Warren."

He said, "Shit."

I said, "Who's Gretchen?"

But he was asleep. Fitfully. I was in a rocklike coma in a second.

The next thing that disturbed me was the smell of Nescafé and dim light. Above my head the hand-hewn ebony rafters loomed heavily. I thought of the Cameroonians forced to lug the lumber up the mountain to build the hut for the Germans. I thought of Batman. I slipped out of the sleeping bag and went outside. Mists filled the mossy hollow. The moss looked like a mat of furry little green stars, but the stars were as hard as the rock beneath them. Ngoundu and his sister were squatted by a new fire.

"Good morning, Miss Mary."

And once again, I tried. "Good morning, Mr. Ngoundu and Miss Plebiscite."

Laugh, laugh, laugh. Then I said, "I'm afraid Warren is sick."

They said, "*Ashiya-o.*"

Ashiya is an all-purpose Cameroonian word much like aloha. Expressed with cheer, it is a greeting; with passion, it means "I love you"; with sadness, "sympathy." If you're feeling especially sympathetic you add the *o* for emphasis.

"He is too sick to go back down the mountain," Ngoundu asked.

"Yes, too sick."

We made the necessary arrangements. It would take the children four hours to get back to Buea. That's because you run down Mount Cameroon. I had not paid too much attention to people who gave me that info because I have this trick knee that goes out if I race down a flight of stairs.

Ngoundu said, "The prisoners will be back by two this afternoon, and Mr. Warren will be to the hotel by nightfall."

"Will they run down the mountain even if they're carrying Warren?"

"Oh yes, Miss."

I asked, "How long to climb to the summit from here?"

"A trip of four hours, Miss Mary."

I calculated.

Ngoundu asked, "You are leaving Mr. Warren to climb the mountain."

I nodded. "I'm not going to get another chance."

He looked at his feet. "Yes, Miss."

"I'm giving him aspirin, Mr. Ngoundu. He'll be fine."

He didn't laugh. He kept his head down. "Yes, Miss."

"He's not *that* sick."

He looked up. "Miss Mary, I am never questioning your loyalty. But perhaps the mountain is not wanting anyone today. Perhaps the spirits . . ."

Warren appeared in the doorway. His arms and face were covered with pink ovals. They were not rose petals. They were a rash. He had dengue fever. I said, "Shit." I said that instead of *ashiya-o* because I'd just spent the night being breathed on by someone with a highly contagious disease.

He said, "What is this?" He was holding out his arm.

Ngoundu said, "Dengue fever, sir. From which you will be recovering." Warren would have one unhappy week of fever, joint pain, and such an itch he'd go a little cuckoo. Batman would be back.

"What the hell is dingy fever?"

"Den-gee," I said. "Named after Dr. Dengue, who discovered it. Now go lie down. It lasts only, uh, five days."

"Five days! Shit."

"*Ashiya-o*," we all three said.

A piteous look came over his face. He said, "Will you come lie down with me?"

Jesus.

I walked him back inside the hut and tucked him into the sleeping bag. I said, "Once upon a time there was a little girl named Goldilocks, so named because of her beautiful . . ."

"Shut up. Now where did Dr. Dengue discover this disease?"

"In a mosquito's mouth. Right next to the malaria germs."

"I meant, which country."

"Need you ask?"

"No. You ever get it?"

"Not yet. But I will."

"*Ashiya-o*."

"Thanks. Listen, Warren, I'm going to climb to the summit. Ngoundu says I'll be back by two." He had a fit. I told him what I'd explained unnecessarily to Ngoundu. I said that if he just sipped water and took two more aspirins he'd be fine.

"Will you be back in time to go down the mountain with me?"

"Sure."

"I don't want to go back down with just the prisoners."

Jesus.

I told him I had a sleeping pill for him.

"Halcion?"

"Yeah."

"Good."

I gave him the fifth aspirin.

Before I left, he asked if I would take his camera and get a lot of shots. I asked him if that meant I'd have to fiddle with all his lenses and things. He said, "I didn't think to bring an Instamatic." He showed me how to work all the controls. Then he said, "What about my bottle?"

He took an empty Heineken bottle out of one of his camera satchels. I was surprised he'd remembered it. There is a tradition on Mount Cameroon—begun by Sir Richard. Upon reaching the summit, a climber leaves a bottle containing a piece of paper with his name and the date. It seems Sir Richard left graffiti wherever he went, and since there were no mosques or tombs to deface on the top of Mount Cameroon, he decided on the name in the bottle. Though it would be cheating I agreed to take Warren's bottle. So I shook hands with Ngoundu and hugged Plebiscite, and up the mountain I went laden with the Leica and the light meters and other lenses around my neck, plus the Heineken and my own Cameroonian bottle—Beaufort Lager. Supposedly, Sir Richard also put a few pages from Punch in his bottle, so not one to break tradition, I had stuck in the cover of the most recent *New Yorker* sent to me by a friend who was worried I'd come home with a plate in my lower lip and earplugs in my lobes. When I turned back to call out one last goodbye, the children were not smiling.

It was very cold and damp. The cold was not refreshing, though I was sweating with the effort of a second day's trudging. As soon as I left the hollow there was nothing to see but the path ahead winding through the mosses. The mist was so thick that visibility was just a few feet. I'd thrown my poncho on at the last minute, but I still felt as if I were in a cold steam bath. I reminded myself that this was the reason Englishwomen had beautiful skin. Not worth it. I trudged forward and up a rise.

At the top of the rise was a long mild incline and then another steep rise. I plodded on and on, up one rise after another, each steeper than the last, trying to convince myself that once I reached the top of the rise ahead I'd see the summit. It didn't happen. I got to the point where I made a threat: if the summit wasn't visible after the next six rises, I would turn back. Take that, spirits.

By the sixth rise, the mists had parted, the moss was gone, and the trail was just a wearing on the rock. No summit. I decided I'd had enough. My clothes were saturated with mist, and they weighed a ton. I turned my back on the nonsummit, sat down on a ledge, and looked into the murky round dot that was the sun. The mist was just about burned off. I sat for a good half hour and watched the mountainside beneath me become more and more defined. In the far distance, the pale jagged line that marked the coast became visible. The ocean was as gray as the air. And then the peak of Fernando Po emerged far out to sea. The island was the last of the Cameroon chain, half the height of Mount Cameroon. It still looked very big. I couldn't imagine climbing it.

I got up and said to the mountain, "Okay, I'm still coming."

Now just little drifts of mist materialized then vanished. They had turned yellowish. My body no longer ached, it hurt. I gave the mountain one hour to show its crater. I put my head down and concentrated solely on moving forward. The only thing I looked at was my watch. At the end of the hour I reached a plateau of solid lava. A rugged, bleak black table. There was no summit beyond. Again, I turned my back and sat down. I'd failed. And here I was surrounded by nothing. I felt alone. Alone is worse than lonely. I began to feel the way I did when I was a little child lying in the dark in the middle of the night. I was afraid of the dark but I wasn't allowed a night-light because people concerned themselves with the price of electricity back then.

I heard something. It was my heart. It seemed to me as if the whole mountain was pulsing along with it. My palms began to feel sticky, my stomach queasy. I was a child again. As a child, when I was too terrified to bear the dark any longer, I'd squeeze my eyes shut, will myself to take the covers from over my head, slither out of bed, and run to the wall switch. (I wasn't allowed a bedside lamp because I read too much.) I shut my eyes, but there was no switch to turn off the mountain and put me back in my little house in Buea. I'd taken Psych 101. Afraid of the dark meant afraid of death. Someone was about to kill me. I was going to die.

My mother's advice on fear of the dark was that I should say the rosary. But the last line of a Hail Mary is ". . . now and at the hour of our death."

My throat was constricting.

Fortunately, I also knew about panic attacks. I breathed deeply, told myself to get a grip on the reins, and stood up.

I couldn't see. My eyes were still squeezed shut. I opened them. I turned to face the adversary. I said aloud, "I'm coming, you motherfucker." I was all better. A variation on the F-word will get you past fear of the dark when a Hail Mary won't cut it.

I smelled rotten eggs. Sulphur. The yellow mists I'd seen wafting past me earlier was not mist at all. They were fumes rising from the earth. I took six steps and there was the crater opened before me, a broad ugly maw. I had been sitting on the summit during my panic attack. I'd conquered the mountain without knowing it.

The crater was a gaping ugly wound in the earth, its floor a web of red cracks burping up foul gases. I was looking at something that didn't appreciate having a voyeur about. I stepped closer, right up to the edge of the crater. A wind blew up from behind me. My poncho billowed out. It became a sail. I tilted forward. Vertigo enveloped me. This was not a panic attack. This was the hour of my death.

The same sheer force of will that had once enabled me to run for my wall switch now allowed me to hold my balance and not get sucked into the cauldron at the summit of Mount Cameroon. The wind subsided. I stepped back and hugged the poncho to me. I reached in my pocket and tossed the crystals back to the spirits that lived in the mountain. I said, "Sorry." I looked at my hand. It was still a hand, not a leopard's paw. I said, "Thank you."

I skirted the crater. On the other side was the pile of bottles, the ones on top sparkling, and each layer below etched with deeper and deeper patinas by the sands of countless dry seasons. I put Warren's on top of the pile. I did not put mine. The spirit in the mountain was an African version of Madame Defarge and I wasn't about to leave my name with her.

I got the hell out of there.

I skipped down the path in the style of Plebiscite. Take advantage of being alone, you fool, is what I told myself. I began writing out loud with my voice. Another "The Snows of Kilimanjaro." "The Mists of Cameroon." I wrote and wrote and didn't stop until my skin felt the absence of wetness. The mists were entirely gone, the early afternoon sun was strong, and I was hot. I stopped and looked up to see Hut Two sitting in its little bowl just a few hundred yards away. I took off my poncho. Underneath, I noticed the Leica nestled against my chest. I took twenty pictures of the ground.

At Hut Two, Warren was still sleeping. I sat outside waiting for the prisoners. It was a gorgeous day. I would have no trouble running down the mountain. But when the prisoners arrived, I couldn't stand up from my sitting position. My muscles had decided the job was over. The prisoners had to pull me up. Me and my muscles cried out. During the trip down the mountain my knee gave out every ten minutes. Warren, though in terrible condition, kept offering me the stretcher. The prisoners kept saying, "Aʃhiya-o." I kept saying, "I'm all right, I'm all right." That's because I wasn't dead.

Dengue fever is a real bitch. Warren came for a quick visit to say goodbye. He was all better and I was aching and scratching. But as soon as I got over it, I jotted down an outline of "The Mists of Cameroon" (a novel about a woman who falls in love with a leopard), read it, and threw it out.

A month later a big envelope arrived for me at the post office. Inside were poignant closeups of Ngoundu and Plebiscite. They would be overjoyed. Also, for their Mami, were shots of two American kids wearing her masks. And there was a photo of me, hair atangle, ratty clothes and holey sneakers, doing an imitation of the novice Maria in her Alpine meadow. There was also a blurred shot of the tips of my feet. The note from Warren said: I guess I forgot to show you how to aim. Thanks for the good time, Miss Mary. I'll invite you to the opening.

But by the time the movie opened, I was back in the United States; where, he didn't know. There was a Warren in the credits. That was his first name. The movie was filmed in the Cameroonian seaside resort town of Kribi, where the spirits are more tolerant.

BEAUTY
AND THE BEACH

by Bob Shacochis

Bob Shacochis was a Volunteer in St. Vincent and St. Kitts, in the mid-seventies. The Caribbean is the focus of the short stories in his American Book Award–winning collection, *Easy in the Islands*. A second collection of stories, *The Next New World*, is set mostly in Pennsylvania and Virginia, where he was born and raised.

Shacochis, a columnist for *GQ* magazine and a contributing editor for both *Outside* and *Harper's* magazines, is also the author of *Swimming in the Volcano*, a novel set in the Caribbean.

These books, he stated, "are very Peace Corpsish. White faces in dark places. Twenty-five years of American foreign policy from an intimate, and finally disillusioned, perspective. Are we helping or hurting people? —those sorts of themes ride atop a familiar narrative of love and ambition and family and pain and endurance and hope." This piece, "Beauty and the Beach," is Shacochis's description of what has happened to the islands of the Caribbean, a territory that has become his literary landscape, much in the way that Ernest Hemingway claimed Key West, Florida, and Cuba.

The first European explorers of the West Indies weren't an especially beach-oriented club of fellows. Their tongues loosened by the virgin marvels of discovery, they cataloged superb anchorages and felicitous shelters from storm, and prattled on about fruits and hardwood trees, savages and fertility, mountains, plains, rivers, and their most cherished of topics, gold, the breakfast of empires (the morality of stealing it, the pleasures of owning it). Sometimes they annotated their journals, as the pirate/surgeon John Esquemeling did in the seventeenth century, with a bland acknowledgment: "The sea coasts and shore are also very pleasant." Nothing suitably purple, alas, to endure through the ages for rebirth in tourist promotions.

Language is never as oversweetened as it is when used to enlist colonists or seduce customers in the nuclear age of tourism. Reading a brochure about a West Indian beach, those golden metaphors of paradise, has the nauseating impact of a dozen piña coladas. The beaches of the Caribbean, though, are more or less what they were to begin with: splendid places to build or careen a boat, launch or land it, smuggle whatever contraband is in vogue—whiskey, cigarettes, drugs, munitions—or unload an invading army. But unless you comb or guard them, beaches anywhere rate right up there with tundra for their intrinsic lack of productivity, their empty wallet of opportunity—which is perhaps why so many urbanites are beguiled by the daydream of a hot barren slope of sand, the tropism of benign nothingness.

Beaches are part of the imagery of retirement, a universal reward for drudgery, an emblem for the masquerades' enticement, illusions that achieve their meridian of success in our imaginations. Yet any fantasist' worth of weight in dreams they spin will tell you: beautiful beaches, like beautiful people, need something more to recommend them than their appearance alone.

"No one knows what causes an outer landscape to become an inner one," the novelist Margaret Atwood wrote in an essay about the island of Bequia in the Grenadines. Perhaps in the Caribbean the mystery is better approached by reversing the logic of her proposition. The beaches of the West Indies first exist for us northerners as states of mind, as paradisiacal figments in our collective consciousness. They are sought out with the same hot mixture of need and desire as lovers are—to give substance to the sublime vision and flesh to the unspoken wish of feelings, and to admire ourselves in a narcissistic sprawl of abandonment and sensual fulfillment. They can be tonic for hedonism, and a sanctuary for bums, brooders, and malingerers. The metaphysics of a beach, however, are never frivolous. Beaches are the welcome mats for interiors, jump-offs for exteriors. Geographically, they are the bruised lips of continents and islands, swelling or thinning in response to the moods of the sea and its endless kissing. Until modern times, beaches in the West Indies were not widely accepted as fine places to throw yourself down in some measure of undress to read a book, bake the body, and stew the senses. What are beaches supposed to be anyway? How do they fit into our quotidian lives? Are they like orgasms, luring us toward participation in something we might not otherwise do, such as slow down the speed at which we take nature for granted?

Maybe the instinct of the early adventurers to waste few words on the glories of the tropic strands was correct in its assumption about beaches. What, after all, is there to say about them beyond the obvious? The beaches can be, in one's attainment of them, as banal as Mercedes-Benzes, as tiresome or boring as a beautiful young Parisian glamour girl compelled to express the sadness she has begun to experience over the maladies of the third world. Haiti, for instance, she says between bits of *langouste*, is *très triste*. Modeling swimwear on the beach in

Jacmel has made her feel uncomfortable, pricked by the guilt of privilege. Oh well, what to do? In contemporary life, the fashion model and the tropical beach share a fundamental trait — both are creations of picture-taking and image-making, products of a system for the body, confirmation for the spirit, and guava jelly for the bread of our myths. On the other hand, West Indian beaches, the less democratic ones, can be no more meaningful than expensive sets for the cinematic inventions of people who require as many props as they can find to sugarcoat reality. And few good beaches come without an indigenous culture appended to them, a fact that is a source of chagrin for some visitors who insist on thinking they are beauty's elite guests rather than merely the source of income for impoverished locals.

Oh my, balmy lusts and gritty inscrutability — suddenly something so damn simple as a beach becomes ridden with complications. That, cynics may cluck, is how vacations go: the horror of leisure time inflamed by exotic temptations and airline deregulation. Still, no matter how we categorize or idealize the beaches of the Leeward and Windward Islands, their magnificence, never elusive, is one of the planet's most persuasive arguments for celebrating, even when hardships abound and infest, the rich extravagance of the surface of creation.

Composing a list of the Caribbean's most beautiful beaches is an arbitrary exercise and, as I see it, pointless, like counting movie stars. There is an overabundance of specimens, a proliferation of dazzlers, as plentiful as the jewels a young lady might expect to have at her disposal if she weds a crown prince. A beach with only beauty to offer our appetites usually confines our response to it to a sort of satiated idleness, or passive parasitic nourishment, a line of oiled tourists attached to the view like ticks dug into the scented hide of a pedigreed show dog. This circumstance is okay, I suppose, for benumbed victims of faraway turmoil, their vitality diminished by winter, pallidness, and office politics. Narcosis is the time-honored therapy of escape; like psychoactive drugs or the novels of Virginia Woolf, these sun-hammered beauties, at the apex of their heat and glare, have a hallucinatory quality: the prostrated beachgoer is flooded by the conviction there is nowhere else to be but here, now, stupefied by grains of sand and the relentless gelatin pulse of the ocean under sedation, stabled in a lagoon as blue as the sheets on God's own waterbed.

The beaches where idleness can be advocated more soberly are the ones that are too extreme for any behavior *but* a low profile and a meditative detachment. They leave you no choice. These are the beaches that openly declare themselves as border country—a frontier, a provocative edge, the perimeter of stability. Mortgaged to both land and sea, they are not truly one or the other but are exposed to the more recalcitrant struggles of both, the volatile and perpetual competition between elements. The battle resonates in your bones, and you are suspended, a neutral observer, between two kingdoms, two realities, and two habits of thought. Out on such beaches, a walker can scavenge a vivid experience of the desolation of limbo, a pause in eternity. These beaches most claim our interest by what lies before and behind them, so the most radical beaches of the West Indies have a tendency to indoctrinate disciples to the cosmic frictions. They are the beaches of solemn wanderers, and the sight of a lone figure out on the water's edge always earns our sympathy. Only the evangelists of apocalypse could have fun on one of these strands. The rest of us simply probe the perilous solitude and try not to be afraid of our own destiny.

There are numerous beaches like this in the Antilles, candidates to test our footing on *terra spiritus*, but the one I have in mind is called Argyle, on the island of St. Vincent. People do not swim at Argyle, fools do—and they drown. You could no more frolic with its treacherous brutish waves than you could with a herd of buffalo. The swells detonate with the force of dynamite, uplifting the cobbled bottom of the coast and rattling it in the swash. A first-rate boomer will throw stones that resemble cannonballs into the air, with a submarine gnashing and cracking like the deep noise that must have woken Rip Van Winkle. Here at Argyle your most intimate contact with the sea is respiratory, breathing the molecules of spray that fatten the air. The unbroken northeast trades, the incessant thunder of boat-shattering waves, the banged-up flotsam on the beach, the salt that crystallizes on your skin—Argyle's intense theatrics form a message for any human audience that can't be dismissed, yet I'm not sure I can tell you what it is. Vulnerability? The fragility of the ego? Yes, but there is also a call to defiance on this stage where progress will fail its audition forever and out of mockery will be given bit roles to perform: a smear of rust in the black wet cleft of boulders, the worm-eaten splinters of a sailing vessel, the mysterious barnacled lumber that seems to have been milled only to be set adrift for a century before coming home to land, the oxidized crumbs of something once so precious that perhaps men murdered for it, the baubles of colored glass given an opaque frosting by the surf.

God has a house on Argyle where He lives alone and unvisited, a recluse who keeps a small flock of black-bellied sheep. The old church is a poor abode for conventional worship. A cut-stone shell mounted at the north end of Argyle's littoral atop a green knoll wandered by goats, roofless from a long-forgotten hurricane, it has been adumbrated by negligence to the point where its impression on the polychromatic landscape is that of a misplaced charcoal sketch. Its facade, indented with an arched portico, is an eroding expression of Gothic Victorian piety, humbled from the day its foundations were laid by the decline of its colonial parish and the severe majesty of the shoreline. Surely, though, the church has achieved its greatest power of inspiration as a ruin.

The first time I walked the beach at Argyle, a Peace Corps Volunteer looking for a respite from my job at the Ministry of Agriculture in the capital, I felt assaulted by Argyle's misanthropic anger and its pervasive, violent godforsakenness. After an hour's taunting and bellowing by the ocean, and inspecting the piecemeal wreckage it had spit out on the coast, I turned inland with a sense of mutual rejection and hiked up through the salty pasture laden with the shards of Carib Indian pottery to explore the derelict church.

The seaward vestry, where I entered, was still roofed by beams and mortar, and its darkness contained a pair of wonders. First, an arched window, empty of glass or frame, faced the sea and created an indigo tablet radiating in a plane of blackness. The architect who designed this window had a knowledge of how geometry could shape and subdue and even glorify the apprehension of a place like Argyle Beach. As I gazed out this ecclesiastic hole, I realized that the church was not without its congregation. Scores of bats hung upside down from the vestry's ceiling, waiting until dusk, when they would swarm out of the church to feed on insects. They adjusted to my presence with a velvetlike rustling and mousey peeps.

Opposite the window, a chisel-edged shaft of afternoon sunlight had begun to enter the room from the west, falling through an entranceway that led into the former chapel, now a box of weather-stained walls opened to the firmament. I stood in the shadowed vestry, intrigued by the view of the church's gutted interior: its paving stones, some fractured or tipped out of alignment by the shift of earth beneath them (St. Vincent has an active volcano on its northern end), were free of weeds or the vines and creepers you expect to overrun an abandoned structure in the tropics. If there was a source for this sign of respect for once consecrated ground, I decided it must be the hunger of goats and sheep that, judging from the green pebbles of their manure, used the church as a manger.

It is not irrelevant to point out that there is no such thing as a deserted beach on the populated isles of the Caribbean. Someone's always nearby, tending to livestock, engaged in obscure labor, or simply spying, even if you aren't aware of them, but Argyle and its ruin of a church reeked of desertion. That is why, as I stood in the skeleton of the old church and invisible children began a hymn pianissimo, their voices serene, as if they sang not to proclaim their faith but to comfort the dusty souls still housed in the rubble of the church, I believed in the miracle of the moment—not that I was being serenaded by celestial lambs, but that the music of children was such a potent counterpoint to the harshness of the location, a triumph of endurance. I stuck my head through the passage and peered around the corner. Seated on footstool-size rocks that had tumbled out of the masonry, a half dozen youngsters, coached by a nun whose face I never saw, practiced the gentle harmonies of veneration. The children took no notice of me, and I withdrew to the sculpted hole in the wall of the vestry, uplifted by their chorus, which now blended with the susurration of the beach. Without a single thought entering my head, I studied the sea until twilight, and when I left the church was finally as empty as I originally expected it to be. Even the bats had departed without a sound, vanishing, like the choir, in an instant.

West Indian beaches are frequently the sites for a range of religious expression, impromptu devotion or primal rituals sensational to an outsider. I remember, on a ministry excursion to register farmers, docking at the harbor in Union Island in the Grenadines chain and being fascinated, farther down the beach, by the blink of candles and the muffled sounds of some weird conflict. I went to investigate and came upon an assembly of Holy Rollers, dressed in ghostly white, their heads, hands, arms, and feet indistinguishable from the moonless night, blue-white shapes that I first mistook as transparent, flying around the sand like great egrets and occasionally erupting in tongues.

On an island where obeah retains its ancient authority, an old crone had buried her husband's underwear below the tide line on the beach in front of their shanty. She was a sorceress, a practitioner of magic, and the spell she cast on her husband would activate with tidal shifts. When the tide was fully in, her errant spouse became possessed by a strange eloquence. He would take to the streets, reciting verbatim extensive passages of scripture and scenes from Shakespeare's plays—and do a damn fine job of it. Imperious and commanding, he was transformed by his wife's curse from a rum-sodden ne'er-do-well to an admiral of the Queen's English, laughed at as an imbecile and cuckolded by the supernatural.

I have witnessed on the island beaches baptisms that had all the energy of water polo matches, Rastafarians drumming day and night on their goatskin *tambus* in a hypnotic marathon of Jah-love, and a crowd of hopeful people wearing only rags kneel in prayer as they launched a new trading schooner into the precarious currents. But it is along the Caribbean's roughest beaches, beaches like Argyle that are the antithesis of user-friendly, where abstract passions seem to have their own natural zone, where they suddenly encounter an objective form, and here the sea is genuinely bottomless.

Beaches have been a traditional venue for outcasts and rebels, an ecology where you could pantomime the rites of manhood and yet go right ahead and reject the implications in favor of a higher order of meaning, if you happened to know of one. At the age of seventeen, against my father's injunction, which I considered evidence that I was on the right track, I was tantalized off the North American continent by a photograph of a beach I had seen in the pages of *Surfer* magazine, the ultimate beach publication. I was, that summer of 1969, as beachy as a kid could get who lived three hours away from the Maryland and Virginia shores. Right after high school graduation, I hopped on a plane headed for the Virgin Islands, two hundred bucks in my pocket from mowing lawns and my head full of half-cooked romanticism. Three months later I was back home, ready to start college, but my higher education had already begun.

There were no waves to ride in St. Thomas, where the pretty picture in the magazine had been snapped. Instead, there was the world-famous Magens Bay, one of *National Geographic*'s champion beaches, which you had to pay to sit on. It was the type of beach where pudgy Babbitts wore jock straps under their bathing *trunks*, women wore anachronistic one-piece suits with a skirted fringe and never seemed to tan, or burned so badly they required hospitalization, and both sexes trudged across the sand in street shoes. A beach hardly worth the trouble of getting to, plus I had received my first good slap of racism on my white middle-class self in Charlotte Amalie and needed to retreat from its sting and figure out what that was all about. So, I hitched a ride in a motorboat across the channel to the island of St. John and its national park at Trunk Bay, where I camped for a month.

Back then, Trunk and Cinnamon bays seemed to me like a summer repertory theater for apprentice machos and neophyte bwanas to cut their teeth on. The air was musky with a heavy emission of pheromones. We entered the innocuous bays with mask and snorkel and fins, convinced we were Neptunes, and swam around the point to waters where it was legal to spearfish, trying to harpoon whatever moved—mostly out of fear, I think, more than bloodlust, since none of us fellows in the campground really seemed to know what we were doing. We became barracudas ourselves when a girls' youth group from New Jersey moved into a row of unoccupied tents. One day I came out of the water howling in pain, my back sliced and peppered with sea urchin spines from swimming upside down into a reef in twenty feet of water, spying on a bikinied female floating on the surface. And in the evenings, we bad boys guzzled rum, on sale to any kid whose voice didn't squeak, and inevitably we closed the night down by crawling one by one into the bush, mindless jungle critters, to gag and retch and have our flesh bitten by bugs.

It is in the natural order of things that boys make asses out of themselves as they try to be the heroes of their own lives — though they have no monopoly on the behavior—and beaches are perfect backdrops for such posturing. No one could have been more impressed with his own manliness than I was on the beach that July in St. John—which means I was ripe for a turn-about in the way I had always looked at myself and the world.

You meet all manner of eccentrics on the shores and summits of the Caribbean, and in some ways they are the true treasure of the islands. In the tent down the path from mine camped a lone mid-dle-aged man, a shoe designer from Atlanta, and I thought of him as a guy with no ability to exploit the available resources. He would climb out on the iron rock at one end of the beach, pole and tackle box in hand, dressed as if he hated the sun, and catch fish too little for any purpose I could determine but humiliation. He was peculiar but by no means contemptible, and even by my style-conscious standards he deserved peripheral curiosity.

One night I strolled over to his campsite, attracted by his radio—the only artificially created sound to be heard issuing from the darkness—and the excitement of its broadcast: momen-tarily, men were going to land on the moon, a lemony wafer ascending through the palms.

The shoe designer invited me to sit down at his picnic table and share the dinner he had fixed for himself—those puny fish, sautéed in olive oil and garlic over an open fire. As I took a polite bite, I realized that while I had been living on hotdogs and junk he had been feasting discreetly on the gastronomic essence of the beach. We stared at the radio as the lunar module began its descent, and the voice of a woman shouted out of the night from a campsite nearby: "Turn that goddamn thing off!" I yelled back that men were about to set foot on the moon and suggested a place she herself should go. "Moon, schmoon," she com-plained. "Turn off that noise." Against my protest, the man from Atlanta smiled wistfully and shrugged, obeyed her command and blew out the candle burning between us as well. "She's got a point," he said. Moonlight and moonshadow filtered down around us through the black lace of vegetation over our heads. I asked him to explain the point he had just conceded. "Aesthetics before information," he said, "or you'll never have any good use for information." "Aesthetics," I repeated noncommittally, not familiar enough with the word to be certain of its meaning. He responded with the puzzling candor I have come to expect from strangers on tropical beaches. "Unless you plan on being Tarzan when you grow up," he said, "aesthetics are what you came here to develop, even if you don't know it." Then he left me without another word to walk out from under the canopy of trees and eyeball the silent violation of the moon. Four years later, after an asphyxiating university education crammed with sterile facts and figures, I returned to the Caribbean to spend a year with native fishermen, relearning how to learn. The gentleman from Atlanta had risen in my opinion to the stature of a Yaqui *brujo*. Considering who I was at the time, it's probably for the best that I received this wisdom not from an Indian shaman, but from a fellow who designed footwear and lived in the suburbs.

Almost twenty years later, though, I still like the overt manliness that some of the beaches in the Lesser Antilles seem to demand. Bathsheba, on the windward coast of Barbados, and Hope Beach, at the end of a long footpath on the backside of Mount Pleasant on the island of Bequia, are two of my favorites. The village of Bathsheba is the most picturesque and authentic on the island; its coastline is primordial, fanged with monolithic rocks. The surf is bullish, no place for anyone but seasoned watermen, who in this case happen to be young Rastafarians and rogues from Florida, out there surfing the rolling muscles of the Atlantic with the cut-throat grace of ospreys. Spectators line the beach, absorbed by this marriage of power and beauty, water and man. The tourist beaches on the leeward coast, like their mirror images in Antigua, are cornbread by comparison, Ma and pa beaches. Beaches as an incentive inducement for out-of-shape conventioneers. Perks for pursuing a life of complacency. Because of the twenty-minute hike it takes to get there, you're likely to have Hope Beach all to yourself, and if you swim out to test your courage in its tall waves, woman or man, you already know that the best beaches resist advertisement.

A few months ago I spent a suicidal afternoon of bodysurfing on the island of St. Barthélemy, out with a local friend at a spot called the Washing Machine. A more appropriate name for this cove of liquid thunder might be Paraplegic Bay. Monster waves hump out of the sea, ten feet high, and jam themselves between unforgiving walls of rock to slam on a shallow sandy bottom forty yards across. The role of a human here is aggressive surrender. Adrenaline gooses your heart and your mind is overcome by piscine instinct as you enter the barrel of a cresting wave and are consumed by the fury of its vortex. The singular pounding and tossing produces a sensation of being mauled by divine caprice, followed by the exhilaration of survival after you have kicked your way out of the ferocity of its embrace. I leave it to others to assign a value to such moments.

After a while a third bodysurfer arrived, appearing on the bare cliff above us. He climbed down the rugged footpath to the patch of beach where he stripped, hesitated for a second of savage appreciation of the building waves, and plunged into the water milky with swirls of agitated sand. He was a European teenager whose parents owned a hideaway on the island. With fluorescent orange zinc oxide, he had painted stripes on his face and circles on his penis, creating himself, I suppose, into a Carib warrior. He swam into the most lethal waves, whooping as he disappeared into the boiling cataclysm. Flamboyance is easily satirized, more so when it is a vestigial trait of one's own personality, and this guy was the 1980s version of a performance I once thought beaches begged for, years before in St. John. His showmanship amused me, true, and I wouldn't have minded seeing him humbled by the indifference of the dynamo we were all flirting with, but I also have to add that I admired the spirit of this guy, the hubris and brave stance, the wild rash and blood heat of the final days of boyhood. Next year, or the year after, he would disdain the jungle hype of ornamentation, and ten years from now, or fifteen, his body would begin its long dialogue with his desire, advising caution and compromise.

"I'm not interested in any beach unless it has the potential to kill me," I say facetiously to people whom I suspect don't want to hear anything about a beach that they can't find for themselves in a Fodor's guide or a four-color mailout. This painted-up kid, though, would probably nod his head, crack a smile of misunderstood fellowship, and agree that in the islands anything less than risk is not good enough. I will only admit that a beach shouldn't be perceived as the environmental equivalent of a nursing home, no more than racehorses should be hitched to plows.

As the citizens of industrialized nations experiment, in greater numbers, with turning the third world into their playground, they can expect to occasionally encounter playground shenanigans, bullying and petty extortion. The juxtapositions of culture and class are often too pressurized for a day to pass in utter peace. "Unspoiled" tranquillity is an aristocratic commodity and still costs a bundle, or requires the temperament, stamina, and flexibility of a pioneer. Few West Indian islands are spared socioeconomic flashpoints. St. Barts (St. Barthélemy), a tiny island in the French Antilles populated by Caucasians and sanitized by affluence, has purchased entry into what we refer to as the developed world with a gush of tourist dollars, thereby freeing itself from the insecurities that thrive on many of the other islands, and it has become the destination of choice for well-heeled pilgrims of the cult of ultraviolet rays who expect the Caribbean to be a New World facsimile of Saint-Tropez.

St. Barts' traditional culture, blanketed by the influence of outsiders, is too sublimated to have any clear impact on a vacationer, but the opposite is not true. Consider, as an example, the issue of nudity. The road that leads from St. Jean Bay, locally known as Tourist City, over the spine of mountain and down toward the exquisite Anse de Grande Saline, levels out onto a rock-strewn coastal plain, salt-plagued and arid, with no beach in sight and the land degenerating into an expanse of defunct salt ponds remarkable for their ugliness. The road is heavily traveled by mini-mokes and motor scooters that must pass an oddly placed billboard on their route to the shore, warning beachgoers, in paint faded to its last shade before oblivion, that nudism is prohibited in St. Barts. The sign sits out in the middle of a sun-dried, cactus-dotted field where no one would conceive of disrobing except as a form of penance, so its message seems ironic, especially when you are told that what is being upheld is a law of France, legislated in Paris. Since nudism is taboo throughout the Caribbean, and on the more conservative Commonwealth isles, where puritanical immigration officials will remove a *Playboy* magazine from your luggage and toss it in the wastecan, and nakedness on the beach fast leads to moral outrage, sexual presumptions, and serious trouble, the prohibition on St. Barts should come as no surprise.

But it is, it is. A mile farther, you park where the road ends at a range of dunes and start walking. Gee, your companion might still be muttering about the billboard, I really wanted to sun my butt. If you're a step in front and mount the top of the dunes first for a view of the beach, you can report the heartening news: No problem, honey—we are among lawbreakers. (Think of elephants, giggles a middle-aged tax lawyer from Tallahassee, publicly nude for the first time in his life. He lapses into a silly swoon of erotic free association and hobbles into the water to cool off.)

Grande Saline is the best beach in the Lesser Antilles to contemplate the details of the body's design, a quintessential beachly pursuit, and to ponder how the motif of a beach can check the manners of a society and challenge its moral structure. At the beginning of the era of tourism at the end of the 1960s until less than a decade ago, the merchants of St. Barts didn't want people in bathing suits in their shops. It showed disrespect, they thought, and made a very tasteless impression. Now they are accustomed to the ubiquitousness of swimwear, but the traditional islanders continue to think it is *bas-class* to peel in public. They are offended by the immodesty of tourists, they will tell you, and at the sight of a flagrant buttock will rally the gendarmes who will commiserate with both points of view. Predictably, the higher standard is economic, and rather than be constantly riled by displays of nakedness, a native predisposed to censorship will avoid the beaches where infractions are de rigueur.

The island is clearly confused by the issue of pubes versus profit. Its own tourist literature is spiced with glossies of topless females. One handout contains, next to a photograph of pink fish with gaping mouths, a shot of topless mother and pubescent daughter getting tips on windsurfing from a male instructor, a scene that would burst into flame before the eyes of a smut-crazed fanatic like Ed Meese. I stopped at the tourist board, operated by a young woman who lives with her parents in a typically pious fishing village, for clarification. "Breasts are different," she said. I immediately agreed. Breasts, it so happens, are not legislated against; the other stuff is. If you will permit me to describe her, this woman is attractive and very cosmopolitan, educated in France. Toplessness is omnipresent on the beaches of St. Barts, and I ask her, in the name of a writer's objective concerns, you can be sure, about the status of her own bosom. Was she relieved to have her breasts liberated by the advent of tourism? "Are you kidding?" she answered. Her mother and sister would never speak to her again if she went out on the beach with her breasts deliberately bared.

Anse de Grande Saline is an entertaining beach, not simply because of its buffet in the buff, the comical sight of swimmers flashing balls and buttonholes as they dive under waves, or the initially alarming tableau of a squatting mother, bare-assed and arrogant, distributing pâté sandwiches to her sun-browned children. Unlike the more pedestrian beach at St. Jean, Grande Saline has a conspiratorial insularity to it that encourages intimacy, a beauty that chides your inhibitions, and a level of wave action accessible to beginners yet lively enough to placate athletes. On an island imbued with imported pretensions, it is a beach where shedding has egalitarian overtones, and a sunburned tush is a flag for progress on an agenda that is out of control, but nonetheless irresistible.

It's December, a week before the rates go up and the travel industry starts shuttling a fleet of charters into the islands. The rainy season, which has been dragging on, has given me an opportunity to spend the morning sipping thick Grenadian coffee on the veranda of my cottage, an ideal place to contemplate the panorama of the most dialectically interesting beach in the Caribbean today. The Russian embassy was up here on the flowered hillside at the southeast end of Grand Anse Beach, the radio towers farther up were, ten years ago, an important military objective for the 82nd Airborne Division. The secretary of the woman in the cottage behind me, head of Grenada Tour and Travel, was gunned down with her friends Jacqueline Creft and Prime Minister Maurice Bishop, trapped at their side by turncoat People's Revolutionary Army soldiers as she delivered a basket of food to Fort Rupert, across the bay from where I sit. Yesterday, high above the capital of St. George's in the prison at Richmond Hill, I had watched fourteen people sentenced to death for their role in the coup that toppled Bishop's government and filled the island's sky with American fighter jets and assault helicopters, so today I am thankful for the relative harmlessness of the meteorological conditions and let the rain fall without complaint.

Out across the bay, rising behind the muted pastel pigments of St. George's, vast gardens are on flameless fire. Smoky, smoldering clouds mantle the island, releasing columns of rain that gradually marshal together and obliterate the mountainous landscape by degrees and gradations of hue until even the bay disappears, shut off by wet curtains of wind, impenetrable; then the immaculate two-mile-long rind of sand below me goes too, first drained of color and finally content, and the beach becomes a place to dread this morning, not only because of the squalls, but also because of a more formidable mood, a sudden intolerance of affection that echoes the misfortune of island politics. The emptiness of Grand Anse intensifies to a level of alienation; its purpose dilutes to the point of futility, a dream awash in disappointment.

As far as I know, no artist has ever painted this scene successfully in any style, its grayish greens and grayish blues, the available light rapidly aging except for an incandescence out on the shallows, where the sandy bottom bounces the weak photons back up through three fathoms of turquoise water and yet won't allow them to escape through the surface. The light within stays gathered and captured and strangely purified, like the light behind a translucent glass panel, gemlike, or the light of cobalt-glazed tiles. And everywhere in the atmosphere there is a unique ectoplasmic overlight of colorless infinity informed by a blazing source that is incapable of revealing itself. This is the weather sailors lose their way in, blown and blinded, and the beach is a place to huddle, chilled and dripping, under the shag of palms or the canopy of an almond tree. For Grand Anse, it is never so private as it is under storm.

The rain subsides, the view and the spectrum are restored. Beyond the populated hillsides that surround the careenage of St. George's, the mountains remain cloud-smothered, their ruggedness tempting you to imagine a heart of darkness beating in the hidden valleys. That vision, presumably, is why we're down here on the coast waiting for the sun to spotlight the beach rather than up hiking through waist-high begonias and bamboo forests in the interior. Cruise ships steam in from a horizon once dominated by the U.S.S. *Guam;* trading schooners take the northeast breeze downwind, full sail out of port. If you bother to know the history of the land spread before you, blood will seep, fires will burst skyward, cannons will boom, heads will roll in your imagination as they have off and on (mostly on) during three centuries of colonization, a decade of independence, and the aborted years of revolution. This vague sense of participation is what you've come for, isn't it? Cultural voyeurism and historical enlightenment are the essence and payoff of travel (though others might argue loudly for the themes of bargain shopping and creature discomforts).

As a paradigm of West Indian beachliness, Grand Anse excels. It has a texture of events, an aura of history, that is readi-

ly accessible, and the most spontaneous and sophisticated conversations about economics and power to be joined in this part
of the world. What could be better, really, than a beach where
tans come with a range of insights into the foreign policy of that
superpower you call home? More significantly, the beach has a
part to play in the indigenous culture. Local fishermen haul up
on it, get a fire going and a pot aboil with sea robin and plantain.
Native musclemen lope up and down the strand with the fierce
composure of Ashanti chieftains. On the weekends, middle-class
Grenadians—citified, revolutionized, interventionated—come
out with their ghetto blasters and bottles of wine to relax,
though they are an involved people, not inclined to forget about
their national tribulations. A Rasta, alone on a washed-up log,
has a new song to sing every three minutes. A shipwright climbs
a lignum vitae, hacking off a branch with his machete to replace
the curved bow section in the keel of his pirogue. There is the St.
George's Medical School, with bullet-pocked walls and its own
restaurant called No Problem; raw, undeveloped sections of
shoreline property wandered by cattle; the Africa Bar, as local a
dive as you're bound to find in the islands; a cluster of Creole
houses, alive with laundry and cooksmoke and cardplaying and
old women positioned throughout the day on windowsills. And
at the end of the day a white woman, a tourist, purchases a
Grenadian boy for ten minutes while she photographs his profile
against the slate-blue chalk of twilight.

For a popular, publicized beach, Grand Anse is not a bad
place to be. The alternative is Levera, at the top of the island,
offering the raw, hardcore Caribbean beach experience. It is a
difficult spot to get to, totally isolated, and unadulterated by any
enterprise. Many tourists wouldn't enjoy Levera or call it wonderful, but it is a terrific spot to spread your towel and ruminate
about what has brought you so far away from home. And to
marvel that on the trip northward through the island, you heard
someone playing a tuba off in the jungle when you braked at an
unmarked crossroads, observed a shot-up Soviet biplane on the
tarmac of an abandoned airport, and read this sign spray-painted
on the side of a banana station: GOD IS GOD . . . FREE US, CHRIS.
It's the perfect West Indian puzzle. Did the graffitist run out of
paint, or does a fellow by the name of Chris have yet another
plan for organizing paradise and making it fulfill the promise of
its beaches?

MWEMBE'S WOMAN

by Kathleen Coskran

The bentwood table and chairs were a good twenty meters from the snack bar and only shade at Hippo Point, but Kathleen Coskran, who was a Volunteer in Ethiopia in the sixties, insisted on sitting outside in this Kenya bar because her skirt smelled. "A kid got sick on me," she explained. "One pothole too many, but that's what I like about taking *matatus* — the intimacy. There you are, strangers riding thigh to thigh with no place to look but in one another's faces."

Kathleen Coskran has written about this African intimacy in *The High Price of Everything,* her first collection of stories, which won the 1988 Minnesota Book Award. When not teaching creative writing at Hamline University and the University of Minnesota in Minneapolis Kathleen spends a good deal of her time traveling, often to Africa.

"Every time I take a *matatu* I expect to crash," Kathleen said, continuing her story about African buses, "so I memorize the other passengers — the Masai woman wearing a beaded choker like a neck brace, the old mama chewing some leaf with the sweet aroma of compost, the guy in the suit balancing his wrists on the points of his knees so the sleeves don't wrinkle, and I think, if this is my day, here's a group I could go out with."

The waiter appeared with my beer and a slice of papaya with a green sliver of lime for Kathleen. She scored the yellow flesh with her pocketknife, dripped lime juice in the cuts, then lifted each cube to her mouth, smacking her lips in a decidedly un-Western manner. When she finished eating she folded the rind in quarters, and leaned back to stare at my gray beard.

"I was traveling in Uganda," she said, "and the guy on my left was smuggling sugar in from Kenya. I didn't know this until he dived out the window at a road-block. The woman next to me slipped a kilo of the con-traband sugar into her basket, then pulled my skirt over the rest just as a soldier stuck his semiautomatic in the window.

"The *matatu* was packed, but the soldier had eyes for me alone. 'Passport?'

"He took it, looked at my picture, looked at me, back and forth three times, then handed it back and walked away.

"That's why I like to travel," she said. "I don't know what's going on and I'm in the middle of it."

I arrived at Whispering Palms Hotel sweat-streaked and on foot, with a duffel bag and mattress on my back, but the guard let me pass through the first gate anyway. My age and white skin were enough to get me in, but my general condition made a uniformed man chase after me before I reached the graceful entrance with its fountains and statues. "Can I help you, madam?"

"Yes, I'm looking for the Cantina," I said. "Mwembe and Njoroge."

"It is there," he said, turning me around with a touch to my elbow. "On the road."

I walked back to the gate, nodded to the guard, and continued another hundred yards to a round cement-block building that served as a snack bar and dance hall for hotel workers. The Cantina. Several young Kenyan men lounged at one of the long picnic tables watching a buxom woman in an oversized Alpha Tau Omega T-shirt sweep the floor with a broom that was so short she was forced to stoop double. In spite of her hunched posture, she smoked, swept in time to Kenny Rogers singing "Lucille" on the jukebox, danced a step or two, and carried on a conversation that embraced everybody in the room. When I appeared she stuck the truncated broom under her arm and straightened up to observe my entrance. Everybody stopped talking. I was hesitating in the middle of the room and adjusting the slippery weight of the duffel on my back, wondering whom to approach first, when a skinny, grinning teenager hurried over with his hand out. "Can I help you?" he said in English.

I let the duffel slide to the floor. "Yes. I am looking for Mwembe or Njoroge. Maria sent me."

At the mention of Maria, he broke into a beatific smile. "This is wonderful," he said. "I am him. I am Njoroge."

He grabbed my bag and hoisted it to his shoulder. "Come, come," he said, taking my arm as he would for a long-absent, beloved friend. "We will find Mwembe." I was parched and exhausted—I'd just walked six kilometers under a relentless sun. I would have preferred to rest for a minute and get something to drink, but he quickly shepherded me out the door, across the road, and down a footpath ankle-deep in sand. The path was shaded by columns of coconut palms and looked inviting, but it was terrifically hot. After a few minutes Njoroge was clearly struggling with my duffel bag. "You carried this?" he gasped.

"Yes," I said. I took a handle and we squeezed together to carry the bag along the narrow path. It was a path I walked many times in the next ten days. Once I stopped and looked around, wondering if I should take a picture of it, should try to capture what a walk through a coconut palm forest on the way to the village of Kikambala is like. I didn't take the picture because it would never show enough—the deep sand, the fifty-foot-high coconut palms, the underbrush of crashed palm fronds, coconut shells scattered across the sand, the pokes of light through the trees. It was shady and quiet without being comfortable. So hot and dry in the sand. Writing this now, in northern Minnesota in December, I am struck again with how walking through that coconut palm forest was like walking through a northern woods among the jack pine full of snow. Quiet. White. Spikes of sun through the trees. Rustle high up. Monkeys in the trees instead of chickadees. So hot there. So cold here.

A coconut crashed to the ground just in front of us, with the force of a bowling ball falling a hundred feet. "Yikes," I said. "What was that?"

Njoroge laughed. "A coconut from up there." He pointed with his chin.

"That could kill you. Aren't they dangerous?"

He thought it was a hilarious question. "No. Nothing ever happens with them. We eat them."

We passed what looked like random clusters of huts and rectangular buildings scattered in no pattern that I could discern, along no path, facing at odd angles to one another. The village.

Just ahead a man was sawing a board that leaned against a tree. When he spotted us, he dropped the saw and hurried over. He was disarmingly handsome, with flawless ebony skin, a taut bony face, and a blinding smile. Mwembe. He was broader than Njoroge, taller, a man, not a boy. He laughed when I told him Maria sent me and that I wanted to stay with them, that I wanted to live in a hut, wanted to learn about the village, just as Maria had.

"This is good," he said. "Very wonderful."

"She has sent you a letter and some other things."

They took me to a long, corrugated tin building, one room wide, with four doors and a cement slab across the front. Mwembe unlocked the padlock on an end door and we went in. It was a small room, six by ten separated from the next room by a seven-foot divider. There was no ceiling. The room was open to the thatched roof and branches used as studs supported the tin walls on the inside. It seemed to be a kind of closet or storeroom: a couple of cardboard boxes on the floor contained a jumble of miscellaneous items; a narrow pad on a piece of plywood was covered by a bedsheet so thin the blue flowers looked like shadows, and a wire strung above the pad held an assortment of rags and clothes.

Mwembe and Njoroge sat down and opened Maria's letter and package. They immediately ate the candy she sent, then exclaimed over the letter and admired the socks and shorts. As I watched them, I gradually realized that the pad was a mattress and the storeroom was their home, where the two of them lived together, and, as it turned out, where I was to live for the next ten days. There were no huts for rent.

I went to Kikambala in an attempt to connect with "Kenyan life." I'd been writing stories of white women in Africa, but I hadn't been there in twenty years. I needed to know if I was getting it right, if the texture of life was as I remembered it. When I came home people asked me if I'd found what I'd gone for and were confused when I didn't have a definitive answer. I'd been away for three months—either I had found it or I hadn't.

It wasn't that simple. I wasn't an anthropologist, taking notes on courting rituals; I wasn't after facts or patterns or oral histories, but the fabric of stories, the kind you make up, not the kind you record. I could have taped the stories Mwembe and Njoroge told me—they think in fiction the way I do—but I wasn't after their stories. I was looking for my own.

My ten days there were as idyllic as they were confusing: they were idyllic because of Mwembe's enormous capacity for generosity and friendship and because of the profound simplicity of daily life in Kikambala. We lived in the air there, in the heat and the rain, with raucous monkeys, marauding goats, foraging chickens; we lived with sweat and constant physical labor to accomplish the simplest tasks. Illness and death were as close as the stars at night and the first piercing rays of the sun at dawn.

When I went for a last word with Mama Hashima, the feisty old lady who gossiped with us on the slab most nights, she was so ill she couldn't raise her head. "We must do something," I told Mwembe but he shrugged. She had malaria, so of course she was weak. I couldn't accept her illness, but it didn't occur to Mwembe to question it.

I had to be taught everything: how to chop an onion in my hand, how to cook beans over a fire, how to draw water from a well, even how to sit without moving or speaking and watch the clouds drift across the night sky, switching off the stars as if they were light bulbs, until the envelope of dark swallowed every part of us and it was time to sleep. Learning to live in Kikambala was like recovering from a long illness when you learn again to do what some stirring of the unconscious tells you you once did naturally.

The confusion came from the presence of three elegant beach hotels nearby and the profound effect the steady influx of tourists in search of exotic experiences had on the village economy. It took me a day or so to realize that many of the hotel guests were more interested in an exotic sexual adventure than an Indian Ocean tan and that, in the minds of the villagers, I was lumped with the most adventurous foreigners—I was living in Mwembe's room.

It seemed clear that neither Mwembe nor Njoroge expected anything from me that I didn't want to give. I had been sent by our mutual friend, Maria, but she hadn't told me she met Mwembe when she was a guest in the hotel or that she moved into his room *with* him. Mwembe showed me photographs of him and Maria with their arms around each other and her head on his shoulder. "I want to marry a tourist," he explained.

There was no place for my things in the room. Mwembe emptied the largest cardboard box and put it on the floor in the back corner. "For you," he said and left me alone to unpack.

He was waiting when I came out. "Can you wash your body with your hands?"

"Yes," I said. I didn't know what he meant, but I was ready for my own version of the exotic.

A woman appeared just then with a plastic basin full of water. I didn't realize until much later that Mwembe had ordered her to go to the well to draw my bath. She placed the basin on the ground behind a three-walled lean-to. I was embarrassed by the special service, but was so hot from my trek in that I couldn't bring myself to refuse the bath. I hung my dress over the gap in the lean-to and squatted at the basin to cup the water in my hands. I let it trickle over my skin and back into the basin a few times, then added soap and did a final rinse. I had no towel, but it was so hot that my skin dried while I rinsed my hair in the last drops of water. My pleasure in husbanding the water so that each drop was individually absorbed by my parched body was palpable. I wasted nothing. I washed my body with my hands.

The woman who brought the water lived in the room next to mine with her two daughters: Pando, who looked to be about three; and Happy, a baby who had an American father, according to Mwembe.

"Oh, where is he from? What is his name?"

Mwembe didn't know. He didn't know the mother's name either, so I called her Helen, after Helen of Troy, because she was so lovely—square face, high cheekbones, and perfect teeth. Most days Helen wore a red *kanga* bordered in black and green with the words SORRY FATHER repeated along the border and a pale gray blouse splotched with white flowers like bedroom wallpaper. She wove a couple of yellow beads into her braid, threaded wire through the holes in her ears, and wore blue and yellow beads on a string around her neck. The one time she left the village, she put on a tailored skirt and white blouse that made her look like a particularly elegant stenographer.

She slept alone most nights, but had a lover who appeared every three or four days, a gaunt man who always wore a long wool overcoat in spite of the heat. The overcoat was the uniform of his profession—he worked as a night watchman for a German in a big house on the beach.

Mwembe said the man was a deserter from the Kenyan army who fled when all his companions were killed by Somalis on the frontier. "We couldn't see where the bullets were coming from. They lay in the sand like fish on the bottom of the sea and they killed us." Helen and the deserter tried to be quiet when he spent the night, but I heard them anyway.

Another woman lived in the third room with her husband and baby boy, Tieno. This woman did nothing but sit on the cement slab in front of the house with her baby and ask me to give her things—the blouse I was wearing, my *kanga*, my bag, my skirt. She had huge pendulous breasts that hung to her navel. I went swimming the third day and hung my swimsuit to dry on a tree behind our house and she stole it. I wondered how she'd get those huge breasts in my skimpy suit.

A white-haired man lived in the last room. He mumbled in his sleep at night, but that was the only time I heard him speak. He was gone during the day, and in the evening he sat alone at the end of the cement porch.

By the time I got up at seven every morning, Helen had swept the compound in front of all our doors, been to the well for water, washed her own patch of cement, scoured the surrounding area for coconuts and palm fronds that had dropped in the night and dragged them in front of her door to make thatch with later in the day, and was washing Happy with detergent in a basin of water.

She supported herself and her children by selling the thatch she wove to local hut and house contractors. She sat on the ground with Happy on her back and cut lengths from palm fronds with a long machetelike knife called a *panga*. She stripped the leaves from the stalk, then hacked the stalk into three- or four-foot strips with her *panga*. Meanwhile she soaked fibrous stalks that she would use to weave it all together.

Pando cut palm stalks with a *panga* just like her mother; she cut small lengths, Helen long ones. Then they sat side by side, their backs straight as trees, held the stalks steady between their toes, and wove thatch. The two of them talked and sang as they worked, but their hands never stopped. Happy either slept tied to Helen's back or babbled to herself in a cardboard box that Mwembe brought for Helen to use as a playpen.

At night I switched the padlock from outside the door to inside and locked it. Mwembe told me never to open the door to anybody. "Trust no man," he said.

I felt a little like Snow White, but I was touched by his solicitude and agreed not to open the door when they were away. It was beach boys that he was cautioning me against. "I want to marry a tourist," Mwembe had told me the first day, "but I am not a beach boy. Oh, no, ask any man. Njoroge and I are not beach boys. But I want to marry a tourist."

He was clearly disappointed when I told him I was married, but he brightened up considerably when I mentioned my twenty-year-old daughter. "Yes, I want to see her," he said. He was twenty-two.

Njoroge was living with Mwembe because Njoroge's older brother's house had burned down some months earlier and Njoroge had had to give up his house to this brother. They both told me, in separate conversations, that the brother, who was married and had a child, hadn't rebuilt his own house because he was a beach boy, which I took to mean that he was lazy and got money too easily.

When they talked about beach boys, I imagined handsome youths in cutoff jeans and straw hats, probably barefoot or in Ho Chi Minh sandals, selling shells and seducing women, so I was surprised and a little disappointed when I met my first beach boy. He arrived on a girl's bicycle with the same straw basket swinging from the handlebars that I had on my Schwinn thirty years ago. It made him seem childish instead of alluring. His name was Gordon, and he was dressed in khaki shorts and a freshly pressed white shirt. He had what you would call a famous smile—all teeth and enthusiasm and, although he wasn't particularly handsome, he was charming: delighted to meet me, incredulous at his luck, couldn't have been happier. He made Mwembe promise to bring me to his house and to his shop as soon as possible, then established something of a conspiratorial relationship with me. "When will you finish my bed?" he asked Mwembe, winking at me.

Mwembe shrugged. "Soon."

"This boy, I have much work for him. Much work," the beach boy said, "but he is lazy. If he will come to my place, I have much work for him. You tell him to come."

I smiled, nodded, said that I would, and wondered why Mwembe had not followed through on this work. He obviously needed the money.

The beach boy shook my hand again with both of his and told me how very pleased he was that I was in his village. He couldn't wait to see me again.

"He didn't seem so bad," I said to Mwembe as Gordon pedaled off. "He was nice."

Mwembe frowned. "He wants you to stay at his house, but it's not good. Not good." He shook his head. "I tell him you are staying here, with me."

"I am fine here," I said, "but where are you and Njoroge sleeping?"

"We have two places, two rooms we can sleep in."

I had arrived in Kikambala thinking I could rent a room or hut, but there was nothing available, or so Mwembe had said. The longer I was there, the more I realized that nothing was as it seemed. I now think it would have been possible for me to get my own place, but Mwembe had a proprietary interest in me because of the honor my visit brought him.

Gordon returned the next day and reluctantly Mwembe agreed to let me go to Gordon's house, but only under his escort. We followed Gordon through the village, past Whispering Palms Hotel, and up a dry, unshaded hill to a four-room cement-block house with glass windows and a thatched roof. "See my big house," he said. In the third room on our tour of the house, we came upon his mother, a squat, bent woman who greeted me automatically, but without the expressive enthusiasm of her son. I belatedly realized she was blind and wished I had taken her hand or arm and tried to speak Swahili with her.

The fourth room was furnished with a horsehair sofa, the underpinnings of which protruded like extra toes, a coffee table, and two metal folding chairs. A fat white woman whose legs had been piped like dough into orange capri pants sprawled on the sofa with a Kenyan man in shorts. He greeted Mwembe and glanced at me. The woman kept her eyes at knee level.

"Hi," I said. Neither of them responded.

I refused the beer Gordon offered, so he brought me a Coke. Mwembe and I perched on the edge of the metal chairs while I drank the warm Coke and Gordon described his plans for me: he would show me many things, he would be my guide, we would go to Fort Jesus. "We shall go to disco, everything, yes?" He smiled his famous smile.

The white woman suddenly heaved herself up, left the room, then returned with a beer for the other man, which he took with a nod. The blind mother shuffled in, patting the wall with the side of one hand. All the chairs were taken, which gave Mwembe and me the perfect opportunity to vacate ours. We jumped up, thanked Gordon for his hospitality, and fled.

"Who was that other man?" I asked.

"Gordon's brother. Another beach boy."

"And the woman?"

"His wife." Mwembe shrugged. "She has an old husband in Germany, but she comes here every year for three weeks."

Helen brought over octopus and a plate of *ugali* one night. She said I needed some real *ugali*. The day before she'd brought cassava boiled in coconut milk; it was exquisite food, simply prepared.

Later, Mama Hashima from the hut behind our house joined us on the porch along with Helen and the deserter. Tieno's father and the old man sat at the end and smoked. Everybody else joked and laughed together in Swahili. I could follow the conversation enough to nod occasionally, but at one point they were laughing so hysterically I had to ask Mwembe to translate. "It is the tourists at the hotel," he explained. "The men want to buy boys." He repeated it in Swahili and Mama Hashima put her head in her lap and cackled over that one for a long time.

✤   ✤   ✤

There was a small, low table at the head of the bed where I left money. The boys took it to buy food, water, and mosquito coils; they put the change on the table, and we left it there until it was needed again. The basic food supplies—salt, sugar, coffee, and bread were stored in a small cardboard box, along with the matches and paraffin for the stove. There was a second box with a pot for cooking, three plastic bowls, three forks, one large spoon, two small spoons, two plastic cups, and two brown ceramic cups.

There was one butter knife and one sharp knife. I kept cutting myself with the sharp knife because it was so wobbly and dull and there was no surface to cut on. I couldn't peel and slice fruits and vegetables in my hand the way Mwembe could. He separated slices of mango from the hairy seed and offered them on the end of the knife like slivers of glistening sapphire. He handled papaya the same way, each slice plucked from a painting.

The third time I cut myself he snatched the knife out of my hand. "I'm going to kill this. It's *kali* for you."

"No, it's okay," I said. "A sharp knife is better than a dull one."

"No, it is *kali*," he said and ground the thin blade against the edge of the cement slab we were sitting on, to dull and nick it.

"Stop," I said. "You're ruining the knife."

He didn't stop until it was too notched and scarred to cut anything. He didn't want to see my blood again.

I wanted to say, Look, I am the mother of five and in my own kitchen I'm a whiz with knives, mixers, blenders, microwaves, garbage disposals, turning stoves on and off, and cleaning toasters. I can even handle an electric knife.

The night I did cook for them I made chili and fruit salad, with store-bought sliced white bread on the side. The beans were pebbly and the fruit butchered rather than sliced. Fortunately, it took me so long to prepare the meal that it was too dark for us to see what we were eating by the time I served it. It was the worst meal I ate in Kikambala.

We ate all our meals on the cement slab. The other families on our "slab" didn't—they ate in their dark rooms, with the door open so they could see—but Mwembe, Njoroge, and I sat in front of our door and ate out of the same bowl with our three spoons.

We were leaning against the wall of the house, eating bread and bananas for breakfast one day, when Mwembe spied this boy passing on the path that led to the *duka*. The child looked to be four years old.

"Shadrach," Mwembe called, "where are you going this morning?"

Shadrach stopped, put his hand under the elastic of his shorts, and turned his head, but not his shoulder, toward the sound of Mwembe's voice. He was frozen on the path.

"*Jambo*, Shadrach. *Harabi*."

The child squirmed, raised each big toe, folded the left toe on top of the right, and stretched his neck like a crane at sunrise.

"Come. Have some banana."

Shadrach put his other hand in his shorts and balled his fists together so it looked as if a tiny tumor had popped from his navel. His head didn't move, but the small body clenched and unclenched at the sound of Mwembe's voice.

"He's afraid," I said. "Let him go."

"But I like this boy," Mwembe said. "I like his head. He has a beautiful head."

Shadrach's head was an elongated ovoid. His small rounded chin widened to a perfect, close-cut dome. His ears curved tightly around his scalp, a calyx cupping the perfect flower. His solemn mouth and shaded eyes were limned across the shell of his skull.

"Where are you going?" Mwembe called again.

Shadrach's perfect chin flickered, pointing down the path.

"Go, then. Go to the *duka* for your mother."

I expected him to break into a run when he was released by Mwembe's friendly voice, but his left foot slowly lifted off his right, his knee bent, the right foot moved, the heel shimmered, and he inched down the path again, the shy boy with the beautiful skull.

"I like his head," Mwembe said.

That was life in Kikambala—slow-motion. I felt as if I'd entered the great heart of a whale whose every beat lasted a lifetime and in between I could find all the parts of myself and stitch them together before jumping back on my itinerary. Nothing happened there, but Mwembe taught me to breathe one breath at a time, not to break into a run, but to lift each foot and move with the grace of a beautiful child.

I was always thirsty. We bought water at Ali's *∂uka:* eighty cents a gallon. You filled your tin yourself from a spigot stuck in the ground. I didn't know if it was safe so I drank the water only as coffee the first few days, but the coffee didn't quench my thirst. If I made the twenty-minute walk to the Cantina for a Coke, I was parched and sweaty by the time I got back.

One afternoon Mwembe cut open an immature coconut and insisted that I drink all the juice inside. "Get a cup," I said. "We can share it."

"No, it is new for you."

I raised the rough skin to my lips and drained it. The juice was sweeter and richer than the watery stuff in mature coconuts and it slaked my terrible thirst. The flesh inside was like a jelly. We scooped it out with a spoon, ate it, and tossed the husk on the ground.

Mwembe threw all our garbage on the ground in front of the door: banana peels, potato peeling, crusts of bread, soaked coconut flesh, fish bones, cabbage scraps, eggshells, mango and orange rind—everything. The goats joined the monkeys and chickens in our rubbish heap to tidy up every morning. The goats ate all peelings except lemon; chickens loved tomatoes; nobody, not even the monkeys, ate the cabbage leaves; a goat carried off the leaves from the cassava plant that Mwembe cut so I would know what the plant looked like. The crows and chickens bickered over the coconut husk and picked it clean together.

One morning five goats came galloping up, as if word had gone out that a banana peel had just been tossed. Banana peels were the goats' delicacy-of-choice. They usually grazed their way over, sniffing and biting at everything along the way, but those guys were on the run. They didn't stay long, looked mildly embarrassed at finding nothing to scavenge and then galloped away.

It was chicken-mating season while I was there. The roosters chased the hens around ferociously. The hens even came squawking up on the porch, then they leapt down, circled through the trees, around the garbage, dove in the weeds, but the roosters were fast. After one particularly rowdy session a bedraggled red hen returned on her own to make her nest in the dirt in front of me. She stirred and scratched in the dust for half an hour, her legs up and flying, then she rolled in the dirt, pecked at it, turning around and around, squatted and wiggled for a minute, then was up and pecking again. Next she walked around the burn pile and had a go at a more promising site, same routine, same result, but she couldn't find comfort, couldn't drop the egg, couldn't stop trying.

The days were filled with repeated behavior. Things crashed from the sky all the time. I saw or heard seven or eight small explosions every day; usually it was a coconut or a whole palm frond—twenty to thirty feet long—falling more than fifty feet to the ground. Limes and immature coconuts also fell, but with less fanfare. The continual crashing to the ground contributed to the fatalistic feel of the place, and the debris and garbage every-where heightened the sense of living by rhythm and by chance. Let things lie until you need them; what will fall, will fall; God knows.

Mwembe sawed wood most mornings, working hard, he said, although every time I went over there he was talking to some-body. I commented on his many interruptions.

He smiled happily. "These are my friends."

"Yes, but you are poor. You must work."

"I am working," he said. "Take my picture." He transformed himself from a gregarious kid in a fishnet tank top and white sailor's cap to a serious workman, intent on the job; his friend put a steadying hand on the board so I'd include him in the picture.

Later I walked down to the beach. The tide was nearly at the line of the horizon, three hundred yards out. The deserted beach was beautiful as a postcard with flawless white sand and a line of coconut palms whispering in the wind, but I was uneasy being alone in so much space. I thought of the Peace Corps Volunteer twenty years earlier whose body was washed up and buried by the local people in an unmarked grave on a beach just like this one. Nobody knew he was missing until his up-country school called the Peace Corps office to complain that he hadn't been in the classroom for two days.

I'm not good in water alone and it was a long way out there, so I lay on the sand in the shade, but that brought no comfort either. The continual wind kept the sand rolling along the beach and I was coated with grit almost immediately.

Later, just before sunset, Njoroge and I walked down to the ocean again. "What was the first African country to get independence?" he asked. Njoroge was a natural teacher.

"Ghana," I said.

"No!" he shouted. "Everybody says Ghana, but it was Egypt, from the British in 1922. You must remember that Egypt is part of Africa."

"Of course," I said humbly. The tide was high and on the way out. We waded in a few feet; the water was uncomfortably warm.

"The Luo are our fiercest people," Njoroge said, a Kikuyu himself. "They are known for their *kali* temper." He waved to a group of girls sitting on the beach not far from where we were walking. "The Luo are also our most learned people."

We stopped to talk to the girls. There were five of them, lovely young Kenyan women, modestly dressed. After Njoroge introduced me, the most forthright girl looked me up and down with wide, sharp eyes. "Hello," she said in a voice that was not friendly. "Who is she?" she asked Njoroge in Swahili. "Why is she with you? Are you sleeping with her?" The girl didn't know I understood.

I shifted my weight back and forth in the sand. "The water is warm," I said, to change the subject. "Have you been in?"

"Give me money, miss," the girl said, then laughed and turned to Njoroge. "She is old," she said in Swahili.

We walked a half mile down the beach, then turned back. The girls were still there, some distance from us, when they spied two German women. They flocked up, smiling and curtsying. I heard the leader say, "*Jambo!* How are you liking Kenya?" The round-eyed hostility she had turned on me was hidden. They *jambo*ed those old ladies for all they were worth.

That everybody thought I was Mwembe's and Njoroge's sugar mama took some getting used to. I went to the Whispering Palms bar alone one day to get something cold to drink and to sit in a chair. I'd developed a pinched nerve and could hardly support my own back sitting on the slab in front of my room. I'd been frequenting the Cantina, but the only other white people there were German men with money and sweet words for the young Kenyan women. The white men regarded me with the particular interest that the Kenyans did, whispering out of the side of their mouths while staring and laughing. I thought I could blend into the tourist crowd at the hotel.

When I entered the poolside bar, a waiter was placing a tray of beer and soft drinks on a table for a quartet of women near the door. A lone swimmer was doing a lazy backstroke up and down the pool, and an assortment of plump, middle-aged tourists were sunning themselves wearing the barest suggestions of swimsuits. I took an empty table. It was pleasant; I was cool and relaxed under the shelter, happy to be anonymous for a moment, relieved to be sitting in a chair with a back.

"It is Mwembe's woman," somebody said in Swahili.

I looked up. Two waiters were leaning on their trays at the other end of the bar, talking about me. They made no attempt to lower their voices or serve me; one glanced at me just as I looked up. "She is cooking with Mwembe," he said.

I raised my chin to get their attention, to place my order, but both waiters stared past me. Finally I got up, walked to the bar, and asked for a Coca-Cola. I took it back to my table, drank it quickly, and left. I never went back.

At eight o'clock in the morning, the heat had already left me limp on the slab in front of the room. Mwembe hovered before me. "I cannot finish the cupboard without more nails. I am going to Mombasa for nails."

"I thought Njoroge was bringing you nails yesterday." Njoroge went to Mombasa every other day to buy supplies for the Cantina, where he was employed for about a dollar a day.

"He did not find nails," Mwembe said. "There is a nail factory in Mombasa, but it is too hard to find them."

"Okay," I said and leaned back on my pad.

He gave me the key to the room, but lingered anxiously.

"Don't worry," I said. "I will take care of everything."

He smiled with that straight line of perfect teeth and tucked his red shirt in his shorts—the shorts Maria sent that were too small for him. He wore them because they came from her. "Okay," he said. He was reluctant to leave me, conscious that the host should hover around his guest at all times.

When he returned hours later, he'd brought lunch: two strips of cassava, roasted and spread with *pilipili,* wrapped in leaves; one green mango, spread with *pilipili,* four small bananas; two hard-boiled eggs; one ripe mango.

"This is a delicious lunch," I said when he unwrapped the food. We were squatting in the dark room because it was cooler inside than out in the middle of the day.

"You call it cassava in your country," he said.

"I have never seen cassava in my country."

"That is the English word. We call it . . . ," and he said the Swahili word.

"I have had the best food in Kenya here in your house." It was true; we ate beans cooked in coconut milk with tomatoes, potatoes, and onions, meat boiled with spinach, rice and fish with tomato sauce and *pilipili,* peas and dried corn cooked with tomatoes, potatoes, and onions.

He rocked back on his heels, pleased. "That is good," he said.

"Did you get the nails?"

"No, there are no nails. Just as Njoroge told me."

"That's impossible."

He shrugged. "There is a nail factory right in Mombasa and I can buy no nails. If I buy one kilo, two kilos, maybe I can get nails, but for a poor man like me . . ." Mwembe was not one to complain. "Tell me about this mountain again."

I had told him about climbing Mount Kenya the week before I arrived in Kikambala. He had never heard of Mount Kenya, the second highest mountain in Africa after Kilimanjaro. He had never heard of Kilimanjaro.

"Where is that mountain?" he said.

I got out my map and showed him. He looked at the map for a long time, looked at Mombasa, Kikambala, the town where his parents lived. He traced the road to Nairobi; he had taken the train there with Maria and stayed at the Central YMCA; he spoke of that trip and the Central YMCA often. He pored over the map for half an hour in the dark room with a flashlight.

When I started to clean up from lunch, he jumped up to do it.

"No, I will wash the dishes." I'd watched the other women wash, and I was ready to draw water from the well, find coconut debris for a scrubber, and do it myself. I took the dishes outside and sat on a small stool in the dirt to the side of the house; I didn't want Helen or the other women to see me because they'd laugh or, worse, they'd try to do it for me. Mwembe didn't care if I was clumsy; he was content to lie on the porch and look at the map; he would be equally content to let me lie on the porch while he cleaned up. Work was not work to him; it was part of life to be shared.

One night Mwembe had a cold, or maybe the flu, and he and Njoroge came to me for *dawa*.

I unwrapped some Alka-Seltzer Cold Medicine. He gasped when he saw the big flat tablets.

"Don't worry," I said. "We put them in water, like this." I dropped them in a glass and both boys jumped like the tablets. The noise of the sitzing *dawa* was magnified in the small room lit by the flame of the lamp moving against the wall.

"This is very good medicine," Mwembe said solemnly. His whole body had grown limp and sad. By contrast Njoroge was hopping about like some insect, waiting to see what would happen when the tablets dissolved.

I gave the glass to Mwembe. "You must drink the whole thing for it to work." I was afraid he'd recoil at the taste or have some superstition against drinking such a strange concoction, but it was the only cold medicine I had.

He took it willingly and solemnly chugalugged it.

"Hey," Njoroge said, "I want to taste it."

Mwembe gave him the glass, with a third of it left.

Njoroge raised it in a toast and downed it like vodka.

"Hey," I said, punching him in the shoulder. "What did you do that for? It was medicine, *dawa*, for Mwembe. You're not sick."

Njoroge gave me the universal shrug. "It is nice medicine. I wanted to taste it."

I ranted about how Mwembe was cheated of the proper dosage, but neither of them was impressed. Mwembe didn't mind sharing with his friend Njoroge. I'm sure they wondered why I made such a big deal about common generosity. Of course, Mwembe would share anything he had with Njoroge. I stifled my urge to say, I know how your culture works, how unbelievably generous and gracious you are to one another, but sharing medicine is stupid; the sick one doesn't get a sufficient dosage and the healthy one . . . well, you know.

The next morning Mwembe arrived unsmiling again—still sick. "I cannot work today," he said.

I brushed off the mattress. "Lie down in here for the day. You'll feel better, get some sleep."

"No," he said, waving his fingers at me. "It is better to sit on the porch. If I go to bed I am giving this sickness the chance to get all over me, to cover me." His fingers fluttered weakly across his body. "I must stay up and fight it."

"But it is germs that have made your body sick. You need rest to fight those germs, to make your body strong enough to kill them."

He smiled at me tolerantly and rolled his eyes at Njoroge. Nonsense, his look said.

He stretched out on the cement slab when Njoroge left for the Cantina and was asleep in minutes.

There were no windows or ventilation in the room, so it was pitch black at night and stifling with the aromatic humidity of the boys' clothes dangling over my head. The room was lit by a single paraffin lamp until I went to sleep, then by the faint glow of the mosquito coil that burned under the bed. I imagined that the coil breathed poison into the narrow room, but I didn't care. It kept the mosquitoes off me, so I could lie naked on top of the sheet.

It was usually quiet, too; I heard only the faint sounds of the sleepers down the row of rooms, so I was startled awake by a pounding on the tin door one night. A man shouted, "Mwembe?" The padlock rattled in the loop. "Mwembe!" he shouted.

I lay quietly. I wasn't to open the door to any man.

"Let's go dancing," the man shouted in English and struck the door again. "Mwembe!"

I waited, but said nothing. He wouldn't be speaking English if he really wanted Mwembe.

"Let's go to the disco at Whispering," he called.

I imagined that Helen and her babies were lying listening to this, and the mama of Tieno and her husband, and the old man at the end. I waited a long time before going back to sleep.

The next morning Mwembe asked me if somebody had come in the night.

"Yes. It was quite late."

"It was this beach boy, this Gordon." He was clearly upset. "He shouldn't interrupt in the middle of the night or even early in the morning . . . you might be having a dream. He might be interrupting something really important. Nobody should interrupt a dream."

"It's okay," I said. "I wasn't dreaming."

"Let me tell you a story," he said. "There once was a man who was inventing the first computer. He worked and worked—for six long years, working very hard, he was very close to solving the problem, to getting it all finished. He had taken all his materials, notebook, his pens, papers, all his calculations, off in the bush, to work on it. His wife didn't know what he was doing every day and she became very curious. So on this day, when he was so close, only two weeks, three weeks, from completing the project, the wife followed him to see what it was that he was doing all the time, and when she got close to him she said, 'What are you doing?'

"He was so involved, so concentrated, he didn't say anything.

"Again she said, 'What are you doing? What are you doing there with all that writing?'

"Again he didn't say anything, didn't lift his head, and the third time she said, 'What are you doing? What are you doing?'

"At that, his head jerked up and he burst into tears and sobbed and sobbed, didn't stop crying. He got up and followed his wife home, and was still crying, still sobbing, into the house, and he cried all night and it was only the next morning that he was able to stop crying and to explain to her that when she spoke to him she interrupted his thoughts, interrupted his dream. He lost the rest of what he was thinking about and he would never find it.

"The wife started to cry because it would have been so much money, he would have been famous. Then she took all of his papers, all of his calculations to the university, to some scientists, to see if they could find the clues to what he had lost. The scientists took all his calculations and they solved the problem. They

were the ones who introduced the first computers to the world
and got all the credit and all the money.

"So," he said. "Do you see? You must let somebody finish a
dream."

Ali, the *duka* owner, who sold water as well as matches and
tinned foods, was the only man in the immediate neighborhood
who was rich enough to have more than one room for his family.
Ali's children stopped by our cement slab nearly every day.
Mwembe always tipped our pot of food to them and invited
them to eat; the girls laughed shyly and refused, but the little
boy, Nasser, always scooped out a bite or two.

I stuttered in my infantile Swahili with Ali's wife when I
bought something at the store; once she invited me in to see her
house, with its six rooms radiating from a central courtyard.

I bought three rolls there one morning; Njoroge hadn't shown
up for breakfast, but Mwembe was pumping the stove to heat
water for coffee as I spread tinned margarine on the rolls.

"Did he talk to you?" Mwembe asked.

"Who?"

"That *duka* owner. Ali."

"No, I didn't see him. Why?"

Mwembe shook his head seriously, without the usual white
grin. "Yesterday, he take me in his house and ask me something."

"What did he ask you?"

"He ask me to give him two thousand shillings."

"That's crazy. What did you say?"

"I just laughed, but it is not good." He filled the coffeepot with
water bought from Ali and put it on the stove. "It was very
wrong for such a man to ask me for two thousand shillings. He is
my father. I am young; he is old."

He rocked back on his haunches and looked at me. I could see
that he was disturbed by this incident—he had waited a day to
mention it. "It is very bad for him to ask me this, very bad. An
old man can ask to borrow ten shillings, but never so much
money from a boy like me."

The whole thing made me uneasy: Ali would never have asked
Mwembe for money if it weren't for my presence; he must have
assumed that I was rich and buying Mwembe's body or something. I tried to make a joke of the whole thing. "Maybe Ali is
just a crazy man."

Mwembe clicked his tongue. "Maybe he wants to take my money to do witchcraft on me. He thinks he can take what is mine to hurt me." The water was boiling; he filled our cups and handed me the red one. It was too hot for me to drink, but he gulped half his down, obviously preoccupied with this strange request from the richest man in the village.

"Okay," he said and smiled at last. "I will try to become a man who might have two thousand shillings to lend. If the *duka* owner thinks it is possible, then maybe God will, too, and it will happen." He was glowing. "Yes, I shall become a man who has two thousand shillings to lend."

On the last night we sat on the cement slab in the moonlight for a long time. Mwembe told me how happy he was to have me as a visitor, that it was good to have visitors, that any kind of visitor was wonderful because he wanted to be the sort of person people visit.

"I am lucky because I always have many visitors," he said. "Not just tourists, but other boys in the village always come to my house in the evening to talk. I like that."

He spoke modestly, to convince me how glad he was that I had come to him. He told of helping the mother of a friend to buy a little flour from time to time; he was pleased to be asked. "I feel lucky that there is no problem in my personality so that people come to me.

"By tomorrow, when you are gone," he said, "it will be very lonely around here. It will seem that the room is too big." He laughed, knowing that the room was very small, but he said it again. "The room will be too big for me and Njoroge when you are gone. We will never forget you."

I could only stammer out a few words—I would never forget them, they had been so unexpectedly, extravagantly kind.

The next morning they stood at the edge of the village and waved goodbye as I trudged down the road with my duffel on my back. I stopped once and looked back at the two of them standing there and thought of taking one last picture, but I didn't do it. The picture could never show enough—two young men lifting their hands to welcome me, opening their room to me, calling to me from the path to share their food, showing me how to breathe one breath at a time and how to move with the grace of a beautiful child.

SCHOOL OF EXILES

by Jeff Taylor

Jeff Taylor explained that it is a tradition when you shop at the Pécs Sunday market to have a Palinka. Taylor, who stayed on in Hungary after his Peace Corps tour was finished in 1992 to write a novel, continued to describe his fondness for Palinka. "You always shop better, or at least with less prudence, once you drink a Palinka."

Such imprudence has caused Jeff to buy a dulcimer, a cat, and a Russian sewing machine on different occasions, none of which he knows how to put to much use.

"I like coming here because this market is a microcosm for Eastern Europe," he explained. "You've got Poles, Romanians, Russians, Ukrainians, Chinese, and Gypsies. Over there you have the gaudy, semipermanent stalls run by the Hungarians selling cheap clothing, and beyond them, used cars. But right here," he added, pointing to wares laid out on car hoods, "you see the real incongruity of Eastern Europe. Underwear next to a doll's head next to a cam shaft for sale on the hood of the same car.

"It's for this that I think our generation came here to Hungary. Not for the beauty, because, in fact, its often down-right ugly Eastern Europe. We came for the incongruity. We are a generation who have been defined by the fact that we are inarticulate. If some-

thing really comes of the artistic ferment that is supposed to arise from so many of us being here," he said,
as he directed my gaze back to the underwear/doll's
head/cam-shaft car hood, "we will express ourselves
much the way this guy sells his wares."

Mohács, the town where I taught English in Hungary, is easily located if you follow the river Danube straight south from Budapest to where it crosses over into former Yugoslavia. Its situation at this vertex of river and border was to become very significant during my second year of teaching, but when I arrived Yugoslavia was one nation, a slightly richer country to the south of us. For an entire year, despite being a stone's throw down the road, I'd never crossed over because it seemed pointless to visit a country where I didn't know the language, and that, for at least the first hundred miles, would look like the one where I did. Prices were twice as high as in Hungary, and for the moment I was pleasantly enamored with Hungary, content to stay on my side of the border. At that time Yugoslavians were the pushy people who came up to our supermarkets on Saturdays, traded their deutsche marks on the black market, and bought trunkloads of salamis and cheese. I still referred to their language as Serbo-Croatian, and grumbled about the "Yugos" to myself when too many of them were crowded into the checkout lines. I had no idea which of those increasingly antagonistic republics lies to the south of me. As it turned out, both Serbia and Croatia do; the Danube is their border. The western bank, Croatia, would be the setting for the fiercest battles in the first year of the Yugoslavian civil war.

While traveling through Western Europe during the summer

after my first year, I caught news of Slovenia's independence and Serbia's bungled intervention, then the subsequent seizure of borders by the Croatians. Was the world really focused on my own sleepy border post? At home, my imagination was disappointed. No tanks were poised at the border. Any skirmishes between the Serbs and Croats were out of sight. Hungary was playing a subdued role in the conflict, since Serbia claimed (correctly) that Hungary's sympathies lay with Croatia. The indicators of crisis lay more subtly in the voices of those who strolled the main street. More pervasively than usual I heard a language not Hungarian, and they were not shopping, or at least not by the trunkload. The editor of the local newspaper whispered to me that a former police station held some refugees, and a much larger one sat hidden in the vast cornfields run by the state farming cooperative, but for safety's sake locations were secret.

The Croatians on the sidewalks looked nothing like what one could imagine refugees to be. They were better dressed than the Hungarians who were giving them refuge. Better dressed might not be the best phrase; rather, more tastefully or fashionably dressed. This had more to do with the Croatians being more urbane, since they had fled from towns considerably larger than Mohács. If they had been refugees in Budapest they would not stand out at all. Mohács was just a small town, like any, and styles drag and take on a sheepish conformity. The Croatians do their best to imitate the Italians. The men love baggy trousers, and the women wear loose-fitting leggings. When winter came, they wore leather jackets with fur-lined hoods, and in even the weakest of East European sunlight, they wore sunglasses.

Even though the Croatians kept a low profile, reports were circulating that as many as five thousand had taken refuge in Mohács, a big influx for a town of twenty thousand. Matt, a friend from the States who had come to teach with me at the local gymnasium, and I decided that we should offer to assist in some way. As far as the refugees' basic needs, though, little had to be done. The Hungarian government and the Red Cross had arranged housing, food, and winter clothing. The refugees suffered from boredom and thoughts that kept wandering back home. We decided to do the only useful thing we knew how to do—teach English. A quick inquiry revealed that the community of refugees had inconspicuously organized all the teachers and fourteen- to eighteen-year-olds into an ad hoc gymnasium. If we would agree to teach their students for two hours on Wednesdays, then officially it could be cited in their class books that the students had been progressing in English. Even in the wrong country, East Europeans fatalistically had everything recorded in their official book.

The school across the street from the Hungarian gymnasium was the Radnoti Miklos Ipari Szakkozepiskla, or in English, the Miklos Radnoti Industrial School. Young people who do not attend a gymnasium go to an industrial school, the American equivalent of shop class and study hall. It serves the purpose of keeping the kids off the street until they are eighteen. Most of the boys become auto mechanics and the girls hairdressers. Since they study little else for four years, this explains Hungary's high number of well-skilled mechanics and hairdressers. As if it had been painted into the walls or carved into the desktops, or perhaps even left in the stale air, the dreary industrial school's "hold 'em till eighteen" attitude hung around when the Croatians borrowed the building in the afternoons. I found later that attendance was miserable for students and teachers. Yet the experiment in maintaining normality had to be applauded.

One aside: the industrial school unsurprisingly was named for a poet. More streets, schools, and cultural centers in Hungary are named for poets than for politicians, kings, musicians, and scientists combined. In the case of this school, though, it would seem insultingly inappropriate for it to be named after Radnoti. Radnoti was not one to take more than a passing interest in motors or curling irons, but, instead, was one of Hungary's most sublime modernist poets. He had the audacity, in the twentieth century, to write delicate love poems to his wife. Radnoti, however, was a Jew, and the poems were found in a bloody notebook left on his corpse in a mass grave near the Nazi death camp where he spent his last months. The low, sulking school seemed a bleak reward for one of Hungary's Holocaust martyrs.

We did not encounter any of the initial goodwill that Americans routinely receive when they begin with a class of East Europeans. The kids appeared sullen and mistrustful; they slouched, crossed their arms, and kept their coats on. Their differences in skill were no help either. Two students were fluent: Viekoslav, who translated everything to everyone else; and a flippant girl who had cut off almost all her maroon-dyed hair and

never came to another lesson. A handful of others were somewhere in between, and the rest were beginners. We split up the
class: Matt took the beginners to his half of the room, and I
began to assess the talents of the others. I showed them a picture
of a woman doing housework. I asked them to tell me any nouns
that they could see. I was pleased to hear they knew "finger-
nails" and "dust," but an extremely tall boy with a Freddy
Kruger T-shirt told me they also knew the word *tits*. When I
asked for verbs, I got "to hoover" and "to tidy." The tall boy
answered, "to fuck." A short boy named Daniel with bowl-cut
greasy hair sat next to Freddy Kruger and hadn't said a thing. I
said, "Come on, Daniel, what verb do you think of when you see
this picture?" He stared at his folded arms and sneered,
"Killing."

We decided that we had to purge our lessons of any references
to war or violence. For most of the semester, given their differences in talent, we conceded to show them a video program
called "Family Album," and when they got bored with that, we
showed them *The Simpsons*. We had resolved that the best we
could do was keep their English from going into remission.

That fall and winter were the periods of the fiercest fighting in
northeastern Croatia. From September I constantly heard
Federal Army MiGs flying over us, continually violating
Hungarian airspace. After the first few weeks they'd attract as
much attention as jets from O'Hare violating Wisconsin airspace. By October I could hear bombs. I once checked a map to
find out how far we were from the towns where the major battles were happening. Osijek was thirty-five miles away, and
Vukovar, which the BBC said looked like Hiroshima after the
Serbs had finally taken it, was forty-five miles away. That's my
mother's daily commute from St. Joseph, Michigan, down to
South Bend, Indiana, where she teaches.

In November the Serbians dropped two bombs on the
Hungarian border town of Barcs, to my west. No one was killed,
but the Peace Corps evacuated the two volunteers it had located
there. It may have been a mistake, or a half-baked provocation.
After a couple days of hysteria the residents of Mohács reverted
back to assuring one another that the southern neighbors would
keep their domestic brawls on their side of the border. And,
indeed, the Federal Army was more careful from then on to see
that their bombs fell only on Croatian towns.

After hearing bombs all night I'd wake up to listen to the latest reports from the BBC. Sometimes, the attacks would be reported as rumors or allegations, and I would think, I can confirm them, they kept me awake all night. Then I'd do some shopping and go teach. Try as I might, I just could not imagine the bombings as real, when life appeared to be functioning so banally. In the teachers' room we would discuss it like last evening's soccer match, and I would yawn a little from the sleep I had lost, but indications of the bombings' actuality ended there.

In December we had two weeks of clean, dry cold, and the Danube froze. Matt and I were ice-skating one afternoon when the sound of bombing began. Bombs are not loud from ten miles; they had the gentle sound of a dirt clod exploding. A smooth-running Trabant is louder. Bomb sounds are soft but long, just long enough for you to consider what they are. We were ice-skating to the sound of bombs. I thought how odd Europe had become recently.

Some of the students genuinely began to warm up to us after the first week. Particularly Viekoslav, who had already finished gymnasium and should have started studying food-processing engineering at the University of Osijek. He usually visited with his sister Jelena, who was just beginning English, and his cousins Bruno and Ivan, who studied as intermediates but had learned all the English they knew from subtitled action films. They liked to go to bars, but they never drank alcohol, just a soft drink, a Coke or some nasty green kiwi-flavored syrup. I doubt they could really afford much else, but going out at night was a cheerier monotony than the one that filled their days.

My apartment was a generous gift from the school because it was located on the corner of the town's main intersection. My building was, in itself, as curious a revolution as anything that had happened in 1989. It was built five years ago and covered, or rather surrounded, an entire block. The ground floor was crowded by new shops, a travel agency, and a bank. In the courtyard sat the town's largest grocery store, bigger than a convenience store and smaller than a supermarket. Nonetheless, it was always well stocked with basic foods, and it experimented with Western imports like peanut butter, olive oil, and Heinz Barbecue Sauce. Food shortages, or lines for that matter, have not existed in Hungary since the fifties. The facade of the apartment block was rippled with variations of windows and balconies. It was painted in green, pink, and orange pastels, and somehow got away with it tastefully. The entrances were even wackier combinations of stairs and glass. The building showed the culmination of learning from forty years of mistakes with Stalin blocks, such as the uniform towers of the Liberation Housing Estate that sits on a muddy field on the edge of town with half of Mohács crowded into it.

My apartment's outstanding location played a part in the Croatians' dropping in so often. They had to drop by, of course, because I had no phone; most people don't. Hungary is the only industrialized country with more automobiles than phones. From my place we either went to a sad hotel across the street or to a bar. At the hotel we were the only people except for a man who played Croatian folk songs on his Casio by request. Hungarians rarely went into this bar because it was run by Gypsies. I think Hungarians need to hate the Gypsies the way they need to breathe. Our other option was Mohács' new glitter bar, the haunt of the local young and tacky. A tiny place directly under my apartment, with only six tables, it nonetheless could squeeze in a lot of taxi drivers and their girlfriends. The bar proudly displayed its bottles of Johnnie Walker, Jack Daniel's, and a tequila bottle with a sombrero instead of a cap. We would all crowd around one table. If Viekoslav had gotten ahold of Croatian cigarettes, he'd have me smoke them until I was sick. He wanted me to see how much better they were than Hungarian ones. I could only appreciate how much stronger they were.

Viekoslav was an incorrigible patriot, his most abrasive trait. To him, and his cousins usually nodded in agreement, the Serbs were the lazy ones who never produced wealth, but only taxed it away from Croatians. If there was a lucrative firm in Croatia, its director would still be a Serb. Croatian universities were also superior; Serbian ones let in anyone, even Gypsies. Sometimes this pride took an annoying turn even against his hosts. Although Viekoslav would quickly express gratitude to the Hungarians for permitting him to stay, it chafed him to have to live here when everything was supposedly better in Croatia. He often expressed his bafflement at why Matt and I would, one, come to Hungary, two, to Mohács. If I said Hungarians were hospitable then they were doubly so in Croatia. If I said life was comfortable here then it was virtually opulent in Croatia.

Waving his cigarette through its own impenetrable smoke, he would assure me that, above all, the cigarettes were much better at home.

By mid-December, we had reached the end of the first semester, and the Croatian gymnasium had informed us that the kids needed grades. Matt and I hurriedly devised embarrassingly easy tests over some of the ideas we'd covered in the first semester. Some kids who showed up to take the test, for example Daniel, hadn't been to class since the first day. Americans generally come to Eastern Europe unprepared for the amount of cheating that students here try to get away with. The Hungarians had a saying that, "If you're not stealing from the state, then you're stealing from your family." This mentality trickles down to the kids, so that cheating often becomes accepted if it allows one to get by. The Croatians were no different from the Hungarians.

Daniel had unabashedly brought in a full-page list of irregular verbs, a major part of the test, and was using it to fill in the chart on the test. I walked over to his desk and took away the cheat sheet. Normally, though, I would have ripped the paper to pieces in front of all the students, done the same with the test, informed the student that he had received a 1, and sent him out of the room. In this situation, though, I felt reluctant to do so. I simply had no idea what the boy had been through; instead, I opted to pleasantly urge the students not to cheat. In fact, Daniel was not alone; those students who had been coming all semester were whispering the answers to those who had showed up that day for the first time. I collected the tests and graded them. Some of the tests were pathetic. Some students obviously knew almost nothing but a small jumble of words. With nagging guilt, I gave everyone at least a 3 (on a scale of 1 equaling failing and 5 perfect), but I was deeply dissatisfied with my teaching accomplishments with them, and Matt tended to agree, given his experiences with his group.

Matt pointed out that we were teaching them virtually nothing, although the school registers would show that the students had had a year of English and should be passed on to the next level. We decided that, in order to really do some service to these students, we should treat them as real students with all the expectations we have for our Hungarian ones. We would have to go against the students' more prevalent wishes to have easy, entertaining classes, and give them grammar, vocabulary, and listening exercises.

Matt and I did not know what we had hoped to accomplish by teaching the refugee students, but given the increasingly deteriorating situation in former Yugoslavia, we decided it was not enough. We decided to make a documentary film. We had no idea what this would involve, but we went ahead and hired a cameraman and began filming during Christmas vacation. The whole film was a Sisyphean task, since we would compile many, many hours of footage, only never to edit it. Nonetheless, the camera gave us a reason to see the insides of the refugee camps on their most poignant day, Christmas Eve (in Hungary and Croatia, Christmas Eve is the big holiday, not Christmas Day). With the help of a Hungarian doctor, a friend of mine, who cared for the refugees, we toured one of the camps, an old student hostel.

They were just serving the traditional Christmas Eve lunch of spicy fish soup. The conditions were in no way appalling. The old hostel was simple cement walls with room after room neatly crowded with double bunks. The rooms were only about half full; the others were eating. Mostly older people were sitting or lying silently on their beds; almost all of the rooms had a small radio tuned to Radio Zagreb, which was playing Christmas music. The rooms were well swept and all the beds made. Periodically one of the older women would begin crying quietly. In some of the rooms small Christmas trees were on tables. In the last room was a larger one with some cut-out decorations, and a young woman, whose family had put it up, posed proudly next to it for the camera. A middle-aged man sitting cross-legged in his bunk showed us drawings he had made from memory of bombed-out churches. He told us of a priest from his village whom Serbians had killed by stuffing pages of the Bible in the cleric's mouth. The Serbians are usually Serbian Orthodox and the Croatians usually Catholic. The religious divide helps to aggravate the ethnic one. Finally, the man asked the doctor in Hungarian (many of these refugees knew Hungarian or were ethnic Hungarian) who we were. The doctor answered that we were Americans. He asked, "Then we don't have to be afraid of them, right?"

The second camp we visited would have been much the same, except that all its residents were moving. They were to be transferred to a permanent camp near Lake Balaton. Many of them rushed to the doctor to bid him farewell, wish him a "Merry Christmas," and thank him for his service. The doctor also bid them farewell, wished them a "Merry Christmas," and inquired about specific ailments, but this was obviously taking its toll on him. He turned to me and asked, "How do I wish them a 'Merry Christmas'? How?" They gathered near some buses, and I could see that almost all of them were older people, sixty or seventy years old. Again the doctor turned to me. "What kind of Christmas is this? They've worked their entire lives, and now they get on that bus with a few plastic bags. This is what they have for a life of work?"

We probably made poor documentary filmmakers because we were too compassionate to sensationalize this bitter moment by pointing the camera at these people. We tried to let them board their bus with as much dignity as possible. Here the doctor began telling me a story. An old friend, a Hungarian woman who lived in a village just across the border, rang his bell late in the night a week ago. She was bandaged around her neck and could only stutter out a frightened encapsulation of what had happened to her. When the war began her two military-age sons had fled to Hungary. Two weeks ago Serbian neighbors who had become Chetniks, Serbian irregulars, came to the door demanding to know where the boys were. She claimed she did not know. A few days later the neighbors returned and demanded an answer to the same question, and she explained that she still did not know. They made her and her husband get into a car, then drove them to a field outside the village. They had her and her husband kneel by a ditch alongside the road. They put a gun to her husband's head. She assumed it must be filled with blanks, because they wanted to frighten her husband, who suffered from a heart condition. She awoke in the same ditch to find all quiet. Her husband lay next to her. He had been shot in the head. Her own neck was fresh with blood, and the neighbors had also obviously left her for dead. She walked eleven miles from that field across an unguarded section of the border to Mohács, with a makeshift bandage from her shirt, to the only person in Hungary she knew.

Christmas Eve, around eleven o'clock, Viekoslav and his friends knocked on the door. They wanted to invite us to midnight mass at a church service for Croatians. We arrived twenty minutes early, but already almost all of the sitting and standing places were taken. Since Matt and I had both gone to Catholic schools, the mass was easy enough to follow, and the rhythm of the prayers made them recognizable. I got the impression that there was not a single atheist among all the refugees in Mohács. Every Croatian I had ever asked assured me that he or she was Catholic, not agnostic, was "raised Catholic," or was vaguely religious. They all answered simply, "I am Catholic," without any modifiers. It was what I would imagine Northern Ireland or the Poland of Solidarity to be like—where religious difference mollifies a secular divide.

On the way out of the church the young woman who had stood by her Christmas tree noticed us and invited Matt and me to visit her family the following day. The next day I went alone since Matt was ill, and I found them much as the day before. Most of them were sitting on their bunks listening to the radio. They knew only about as much Hungarian as I did, but we had no trouble communicating. They made me tea and offered some cakes. The young woman asked me if their Christmas tree was not, indeed, the most beautiful in the whole camp. I tried to think of topics we could talk of without causing distress. I couldn't think of any, so I switched tactics and began asking about their jobs and their house back home. The young woman showed me two snapshots of a white house, taken from within its courtyard, with a German shepherd in the foreground. She told me that they didn't know what had happened to her dog, but they feared that the house had already been plundered. Her mother worked in a factory and she in a clothing store.

I asked the young woman if she was married. She said she wasn't, but she had a boyfriend in Croatia. She told me that now he served in the Croatian National Guard, and she hadn't heard from him in over a month, but when the war ended they wanted to get married. We smoked cigarettes, and I asked her how they had met and what she liked about him. It was the closest I could find to a pleasant topic for us to talk about. She kept using the old tin can they used as an ashtray as an example of how miserable this place was. When I left I promised them I would visit them again the next day. I immediately went out and bought them a black ceramic ashtray.

Not all the refugees in Mohács were Croatian. Many were ethnic Hungarians. I had three in one of my classes in the

Hungarian gymnasium. I only figured this out two months into the year when I noticed that they spoke English with Slavic accents (Hungarian is not a Slavic language and produces a different accent), which they must have acquired from teachers with similar accents. They became three of the most talented students in the class. They, like the Croatian students, seemed to have benefited from not having dubbed films in Croatia. In Hungary most of the American movies and all the TV programs are dubbed. I found that the students from Croatia had a much better capacity to understand spoken English and had larger passive vocabularies.

I got to know one of them, Krisztina, very well because she volunteered to perform in my English play. Krisztina is the remarkable product of Central Europe, incomprehensible to an American Cold War paradigm. Her parents are Hungarians with Yugoslavian citizenship, but she was born in West Germany when her parents worked there as guest workers. By the time she was four, her parents had moved back to Yugoslavia to try to start a small soft-drink factory in the increasingly liberalizing atmosphere of post-Tito Yugoslavia. They asked their German neighbors to care for Krisztina and her brother so they could devote their full days to start the business. By the time she was eight, the factory had grown out of its garage, and her parents were earning enough to have her flown home from Germany every weekend. By this time, though, she was also very confused as to who her parents were. She was being raised by Germans and spoke German, and she could barely speak either of her father's languages. When she was fifteen she returned to Yugoslavia to study in a new Hungarian bilingual gymnasium, and by the time her parents sent her across the border to escape the war, Krisztina spoke German, Hungarian, and Serbo-Croatian as native languages, besides being the best English student in the class.

Furthermore, Krisztina's father's business had grown to be the largest soft-drink manufacturer in northern Serbia and eastern Croatia. He had bought Krisztina her own house and owned a twenty-room villa on the Dalmatian coast. Krisztina still has a million deutsche marks deposited in her name in a Slovenian bank account. When the war began her father refused to leave his beloved factory, so he sent Krisztina across the border to our gymnasium. Like the Kuwaitis, she holds the strange distinction of being a millionaire refugee.

The weekend before we began rehearsals for our play Krisztina went home to visit her parents for the first time since she'd left. After that first rehearsal Krisztina told me about her visit. She hitchhiked into Serbia, then crossed the Danube and hitchhiked home. By this time an eerie peace had settled in northeastern Croatia. The UN peacekeepers were supposedly in control, but Krisztina said that everyone knew that they had very little power. The Chetniks backed by the Federal Army could do as they pleased. When Krisztina was at home that first night, a drunk man with a beard banged on their door. As with most doors in her village, theirs had been shot up so much that it could not be locked effectively. The man strode in and pointed his AK-47 at her mother's head and demanded something to drink. Krisztina's mother made him coffee at gunpoint. Krisztina decided to return to Hungary the very next day.

Yet a month later Krisztina decided that she wanted to go home again, and once more she told her story to me without emotion. She went home by the same route, but this time rides were scarce on the Croatian side, and she walked most of the five miles from the Danube to her village. When she arrived on the village outskirts, she went first to her uncle's house, as that was closer, but there she was surprised to see her mother and father sitting in the living room with blank stares. "What happened?" she asked, and her father began to cry. Never in her life had she seen this quiet workaholic cry. "They took everything. Even the carpets," he answered. A band of Chetniks had come to their door that day and told them and the rest of the families on the street that they had to leave their houses in ten minutes in order to make way for Serbian families to move in. A half hour after they moved out, her father crept back to the house. Indeed, there were no Serbian families; they had only wanted to plunder the houses. Krisztina later saw it. They had even ripped the carpets up from the floor. They had taken every one of Krisztina's books, even the Hungarian ones, which they couldn't read. Her father drove her back to the Danube, where she would cross over into Serbia and then back into Hungary. The border guards, though, told her that no one but military personnel could cross the bridge. Krisztina showed her Yugoslavian passport and begged the man to let her cross, telling him that her school would be very angry if she didn't return by Monday. They finally agreed to let her cross, but on foot, and told her that she would never be allowed to cross back in again. Since that day Krisztina has not been home, nor has she heard any news from her parents.

On the day of the dress rehearsal before the all-important Hungarian National English Drama finals, I was in an ornery mood. Krisztina became the focus of my disposition because she wasn't singing loud enough and her acting was listless. After the first run-through I took Krisztina aside. "Look, Krisztina, what's your problem?" She looked at me with reddening eyes. "Jeff, my best friend died yesterday." She had just received the news from a newly arrived refugee. I thought to myself that if my best friend were to die, I would be unfunctionable, but, instead, Krisztina performed, and we would win the drama finals the next day.

We had another refugee, Leon, in our play. Matt and I met him with his sister as we were going from Pécs to Mohács on a bus. I asked him, in Hungarian, if his seat was free. He responded in English that he didn't speak Hungarian. When he found out that Matt and I were American he asked, "Man, why do you guys wanna live in Mohács?" His parents were living with friends in Mohács, but until then he had been living in Budapest and studying there at the prestigious Serbo-Croatian bilingual school, which had swelled with refugee students, but that week he had been kicked out for fighting with a teacher. In the second semester Leon started in my English class, and I found him to be extraordinarily talented when it came to picking up odd bits of slang. With mechanics, though, Leon had acquired something remarkably similar to the sloppy grammar of an American thirteen-year-old. I mentioned the possibility of his being in my play. Leon had no acting experience, but he was charismatic and extroverted, and he would be good as the writer character.

Leon initially showed up only infrequently at rehearsals, but as his part was independent from most of the others it was tolerated. Then one night he got to know Barnabas, the bass player. Barnabas was similar to Leon in many ways. He was talented in English, but otherwise a rather undisciplined student. Matt had written music for the play and asked Barnabas to play bass in the play's band. Barnabas gladly agreed since he really looked up to Matt. Both Leon and Barnabas consciously cultivated a Jim Morrison look (The Doors had just come out) with their dark curly hair, and liked the same mix of alternative and punk rock. To them, as to Matt and me, the definitive album of the times was The Red Hot Chili Peppers' *Blood Sugar Sex Magik*. Leon was always asking us what lines meant. Barnabas and Leon took to going out after rehearsals and drinking wine spritzers at a pizza bar. Matt and I sometimes stumbled upon them there. We would find them speaking in a language unique to themselves. Leon had learned a little Hungarian by then, but they mostly spoke English laden with all the slang we'd taught them. Verb tenses had been thrown out the door, as neither considered them very essential to communication. Barnabas would ask, "You liking the Nirvana, 'Smells Like Teen Spirit'?" "Oh yeah, it's a cool." Leon would answer. "You know bass player, he's a Croatian man."

At the drama festival they made a dashing pair, and many of the actresses from other schools asked me who the long-haired boys were. Peace Corps Volunteers don't often return home feeling they've produced much in their host country, but I, at least, get to take home the satisfaction of having taught these boys their common language and helped cultivate their friendship.

As the year closed Viekoslav had returned to Osijek because its western side (it straddles the Drava) had been secured for the Croatians, and the university was reopened. He returned to Mohács a few times, and he told me about how life usually went on as normal, but shells came over the river sometimes. His home, though, still lies in the Serbian-occupied area. Leon and his family also moved to Osijek. The Croatian government offered to relocate them there since his parents are teachers and taught the entire year in the ad hoc gymnasium in Mohács. Leon is starting at the art college in Osijek this year, and he has invited Matt and me to come down and stay with him in his dorm room. "We're gonna make a big party," he said. Krisztina is finishing her last year of gymnasium this year in Mohács. As a person of Hungarian nationality, she is entitled to study at a Hungarian university as if she were a Hungarian citizen, but she said she'll probably try to go to a university in Germany or England instead. A year later none of these stories seem so tragic. Even Krisztina believes that her parents are still alive, and that she will see them again when the United Nations gets firmer control over the territory. Her parents might be some of the luckiest refugees anyone could know. These three young people have all found ways to adapt to the crisis.

The mildness of the crisis, at least from what we saw in Mohács, was one of the reasons we left the videotapes of our documentary to gather dust in Matt's desk drawer. When the fighting in Bosnia started, and refugees began pouring out of there, our situation paled in comparison to that catastrophe. Yet not all Mohács' refugees have found a way to rebuild their lives. On the streets there I still see former students, the Croatian gymnasium still operates, and a full-time Croatian English teacher has been hired. Most of the parents get along finding some kind of work in Hungary or surviving on the savings they still have, but if they have not got that then their lives become increasingly desperate.

If you travel to southern Hungary you will certainly still see refugees in the bus and train stations, as I did in Pécs the other day. A middle-aged husband and wife were sitting on a bench in the crowded waiting room. They were well dressed, and the woman wore a fashionable leather coat, but they looked as if they had worn the same clothes for many days. The man dangled two plastic shopping bags between his legs. The woman's eyes became ringed in red wrinkles as she cried, but the man just stared blankly across the crowded waiting room. After a while the woman stopped crying and joined her husband in staring silently across the room. I don't know how long they can continue to survive in Hungary. As the war gets worse in Bosnia, and the United States considers involvement, perhaps some solution might present itself, and they can find their way home. They also might become one of Eastern Europe's host of minorities always living in somebody else's country.

MBEYA DREAMING

by Leonard Levitt

Leonard Levitt wrote one of the first books about the
Peace Corps. Titled *An African Season*, it covers
Levitt's first year of living and teaching in a rural
upper-primary school in Tanzania in 1964 and 1965.
In the book Levitt tries to figure out where he stood
in Africa, caught between the European farmers,
locked into their memories of a fading white man's
Africa, and the Africans, who moved in confused fits
and starts into the modern world. He never did work
it out, and at the end of his tour he realized that he
was alienated from both worlds. His youthful
American egalitarianism cut him off from the
Europeans, and his Western rationalism cut him off
from the Africans.

After he left Africa he returned to the United States
and a long and successful career as a journalist, most
recently at *Newsday* in New York. He also wrote two
other nonfiction books and a novel.

Today he says, "I would describe my writing as
divided between journalism and literary journalism.
The first, which is New York City urban and gritty,
pays the bills. The second allows my soul to soar.

"'Mbeya Dreaming,' I like to think, is of the latter
category. It grew from a grant from the Rockefeller
Foundation for the Humanities that allowed me to

return to Africa and find the students I had taught a generation before as a Peace Corps Volunteer."

Finding them proved to be easy for Levitt, but what had happened to them and to their country was much more difficult to comprehend. "Coming to terms with what I was witnessing raised questions for me about my original reasons for joining the Peace Corps, which was the most painful of all."

i

We leave for Mbeya from the white-tiled, Chinese-built Tazara railroad station at the edge of Dar es Salaam. Dar has been a disappointment, no, a disaster, with nothing as I remembered it. I'd remembered a city of white, sun-baked buildings, of streets filled with honking cars and music pulsing from transistor radios, of people calling, laughing to each other in rhythms of expectation. Now the stores are bare; factories abandoned. Buildings are stained brown and yellow, with panes of glass missing from windows. People queue around the corner of a bakery, waiting for bread.

I had even miscalculated the shifting of the monsoon. It had shifted early this year, the dry, cool wind off the Indian Ocean becoming a thick, pulverizing heat, a heat so fierce we must spend the midday hours indoors.

Mbeya, I assure my wife, Susan (and reassure myself), will be different. Cool and high in the mountains, Mbeya was the gateway to Tukuyu, where years before I had been a teacher at the Mpuguso Upper Primary School, an experience so rich it had changed the direction of my life and now brought me back to Africa.

Mbeya was also the gateway to my understanding of Africa. It was here, fresh from college at age twenty-two, that I spent my first months in what was known then as Tanganyika. It was a lovely little town, set in a valley of bare black hills, its streets lined with jacaranda trees, their velvety petals filling the branches and covering the ground purple beneath them. It had a tiny airport, where a DC-3 from Dar es Salaam arrived each morning around eleven; two paved streets; and a country club, called the Mbeya Club, which, with its tennis and squash courts and nine-hole golf course with black tar greens, remained a last remnant of British colonialism. Across the tarmac road that ran alongside the first hole down the hill and out of town sat the elegant Mbeya Hotel, which hosted dignitaries out from Dar and from as far away as Nairobi.

Of course, there was no Tazara railway then. The tarmac road out of Dar es Salaam ran west only a couple of hours to Morogoro before turning to dirt and stones, while the red-earth stretch that ran the forty miles between Mbeya and Tukuyu was a three-hour horror of potholes, impassable during the rains.

Then, a decade later, in one of his ideological peregrinations, the *Mwalimu*, President Julius K. Nyerere, turned eastward toward China. As presidents of African nations go, the *Mwalimu* (a Swahili word denoting respect and meaning "teacher") was on the benevolent side. At least he genuinely sought to improve his nation's lot, attacking what he called Africa's three scourges—"poverty, ignorance, and disease," a slogan that still rings in my ears. Unfortunately, he never figured out how to accomplish this. Having studied in his youth at the University of Edinburgh in Scotland, he came under the sway of some nineteenth-century Fabian Socialists and spent his adulthood attempting to adapt their shopworn theories to Africa.

The *Mwalimu* even gave a name to this philosophy: African Socialism, or in Swahili, *Ujamaa*. Alas, its result is that Tanzania, as the country is now known, is the world's largest per-capita debtor, and, as I discover, is in every way near ruin.

The *Mwalimu's* Chinese phase, which was characterized by him and his followers all wearing Mao shirts and which culminated in the building of the Tazara railway, proved as disappointing as the others. By the 1980s when I return, the Chinese have departed precipitously, the Tanzanians having rushed to take over the running of the line before its completion, with predictably catastrophic results.

Although we have purchased first-class tickets, Susan and I stand behind two locked iron gates in a line with the hundreds of African passengers traveling second- and third-class, men in Western trousers and women in traditionally African *kangas*, seated on the floor amidst trunks and suitcases, holding babies and carrying wrappings of fruit, loaves of bread, and hard-boiled eggs. The train has no dining car, we have been instructed, so their food must sustain them through the next morning when we arrive at Mbeya.

These are apparently experienced Tazara travelers, as they wait silently and patiently for the gates to open. This occurs, with Chinese-like precision, on the dot of ten. The line surges forward out onto the hot, white platform to the train.

Our first-class tickets place Susan and me in a six-seat compartment in the front of the train. Entering it, I throw our bags up onto the luggage rack. Susan and I then sit staring out the window across the platform. Time passes. It is growing hot. The train sits. We are to depart at eleven, but at noon we are still motionless.

For perhaps the hundredth time since my arrival I ask myself what I am doing here, why after twenty years I have returned with my wife to Africa; what it is I hope to discover, to recapture. And for perhaps the hundredth time I remind myself that I have returned to find my students from Mpuguso, "the boys," as the African teachers and I referred to them. So moved, so awed had I been by these boys—some of them no less than my age at the time, all of them determined to secure an education against the most heart-wrenching of odds—that at the end of my two years teaching I had, of all things, written a book about them and Mpuguso school.

It was a youthful, sunny book, filled with dreams and imaginings, at a time when, not unlike Africa itself, the whole sphere of the world's possibilities lay stretched out, uncharted, before me. If as a young man I'd gone off to Africa uncertain of my direction, I'd returned home, my career launched as a writer.

As I muse upon this, I find myself gazing out the train window across the station yard, at a clump of coconut trees towering above us. As I stare, the train still motionless in the midday heat, I notice two men, Africans, shinning their way up the thin gray stems. They are older men, hard and lean, each with gray hair, each wearing only a pair of shorts over their black bodies.

They are climbing on adjacent trees, their arms and legs wrapped spiderlike around the narrow stems. They are climbing in tandem, each of them reaching upward in two graceful motions, first loosening his thighs while clasping the stem with his hands a few feet above him and pulling up his lower body.

As I watch them high in the trees, two Indians enter our compartment, a father and son in his teens or early twenties. Both are portly, with stomachs swelling over their trouser belts. Each carries two large suitcases. The father barks orders in Gujarati. The son hoists the suitcases onto his broad back, then tosses them up onto the rack above us.

Twenty years before I had not been prepared to deal with the Indians of Tanzania. They did not fit into my bipolar view of Africa in which there were simply the Africans and the British, the blacks and the whites, the oppressed and the oppressors. Though they were ubiquitous as shopkeepers and traders not merely in Mbeya or Tukuyu but also in every outpost through which I traveled, I simply ignored them.

"So you are going to Mbeya, is it?" the father says to Susan and me in a cheery, singsong voice.

Looking at Susan, he says, "But you know, you cannot sleep here in this compartment. It is only for men. You will have to sleep in another." He gestures with his head down the corridor. "That is for women."

Susan turns to me with a stricken look. She had been no less enthusiastic than I about my returning to Africa. Although she had loved that early book about Mpuguso and had told me, half jokingly, this was the reason she married me, I saw she now held herself back, fearing that over the years I had come to exaggerate the role I'd played in the boys' lives.

"No one told us we could not stay together when we bought our tickets," I say hopefully to the Indian, implying that he has made a mistake.

"Ah, yes, but it is true."

Seeing Susan's expression, he says to her, "But you can stay here with us in the compartment until then."

He smiles again. "My son and I are also traveling to Mbeya. Where we live. I have just returned from Canada, where my two elder sons have gone.

"Soon," he says proudly, nodding toward this sloppy-looking youth, "he and I will be going there as well." He stops and looks

about, then lowers his voice. "There is no place for us here anymore in Tanzania.

"Ah, but you must be hungry," he says, his voice rising cheeri-
ly again, his declaration moments before a tentative step in testing the waters of our sympathies. From a leather satchel he
removes mangoes, dates, nuts, and breads and offers them. He
barks another order to his son, who stands up and leaves the
compartment. Minutes later he returns with an African waiter in
a dirty white apron.

In stentorian Swahili the father orders food from him.
Holding up his hand, refusing my offer to pay our share, he
announces smilingly, "Ah, but you are our guests."

I also order from the waiter in Swahili, but in a softer tone. I
am amazed each time I speak it that after twenty years it comes
out right, or at least understandable.

"Ah, so you know Swahili?" the father says in English after
the waiter has departed. He says this warily, as though my
knowing Swahili is a warning, an alert that in this zero-sum
game of racial sensitivities the tide of my sympathies may have
shifted to the African side.

We sit opposite each other in our compartment, each of us
staring out the window up at the two Africans in the coconut
trees. The African waiter returns, carrying dishes of meat covered in gravy with roasted potatoes. Where does this food comes
from, I wonder, since the train has no dining car?

Afterward, the waiter returns and removes our dishes. It is
long past noon. We are two hours late in starting out. I look out
the window again across the station yard to the trees where the
two Africans are now high amidst the green coconut leaves.

Suddenly the train lurches forward. We roll out of the yard. The
track curves. Through our window I catch a glimpse of the train's
rear cars. They are teeming with passengers, Africans who are
hanging out the windows, spilling out between the coaches.

We roll past the coconut trees, past the high grass at the station's edge, past a gate crossing where a short line of bedraggled
cars is stopped, past the mud huts and banana trees on the city's
outskirts and out into the countryside. We move slowly. People
come out of their huts to stare at us as we pass.

Unlike the road to Mbeya, which runs west from Dar through
Morogoro and up the escarpment to Iringa, then south along the
edge of the Rift Valley to Mbeya, the Tazara runs south down

the coast, then west across the great Selous Game Reserve and up into the mountains so that we will approach Mbeya not from the north but from the east. Presently, we slow down and stop. We are a few miles outside Dar es Salaam at a miniature replica of the white-brick station in Dar. Outside our window ragged boys run along the platform shouting, *"Ndizi! Nyama!* Bananas. Meat." Through our window the Indian father and son shout out to them. The boys approach, holding up clumps of green bananas and fatty pieces of meat on skewers. The son stretches out a thick arm and hauls in the bananas, pieces of meat, and a coconut, then tosses out a few coins that clatter onto the platform as the boys scramble for them.

The father barks another order to the son, who pulls down a suitcase. From it he removes a thick knife, which he uses to slice the coconut. "For you. For you," he says, smiling and shoving it at Susan and me. "Our guests."

The train starts up again. We roll farther into the countryside, past mud huts and furrowed fields, stopping every few miles, it seems, at another white-brick station, another miniature version of Dar es Salaam's. Our compartment is sweltering. The heat seems to roll in through our window in waves.

The father begins to talk of Mbeya. He says he is a retired schoolteacher who had taught for twenty-five years at the H. H. Aga Khan School. I recall the school, a white-domed building at the bottom of the hill of one of Mbeya's two main streets. The Indians owned the *dukas*, or shops, that lined them, and were the *fundis*, or craftsmen, who formed the sinew of the economy.

As though for the first time, I recall something of their brief, tortured history in East Africa. Brought by the British from the subcontinent a century before to build their railroads, they had remained in the unenviable position of middlemen — even in the hue of their skin — between the ruling British and the indigenous African population despised equally by both.

In Mbeya, the Indians spoke their Gujarati dialect, prayed at their mosque, and kept their children apart from the Africans, sending them to the H. H. Aga Khan School. Sunday evenings, the entire community gathered in front of it — men in Western suits, women in saris with braided black hair, children, grandparents, and great-grandparents — and promenaded through the town.

I ask the father about the few Indians I had known in Mbeya.

Our director's secretary had been an Indian, a slender, quiet girl known to me only by her first name, Nilu. "Ah, she is gone," the father answers. "Gone to Canada."

I ask of Makanji, whose two wooden stores had stood opposite each other down the street from the Mbeya Club, which sat atop a hill and whose rear bay window overlooked the sloping golf course. Only that year, the year of our arrival, the year of *Uhuru*, or independence, had the club accepted its first non-white member—an Indian, not an African.

Makanji, one of the town's more prosperous merchants, had a teenage daughter in school abroad. Once I had been on a plane with her to Mbeya from Dar es Salaam as she returned home. She had sat a few seats ahead of me, a dark, skinny thing in preposterous high heels, wearing scads of lipstick and smoking a cigarette, a pose that, with her community's strict Muslim ways, she could strike only surreptitiously in Mbeya.

"Oh, Makanji is gone as well," says the father. "They left for Canada many years before."

"And what of the De Sousas?" I ask. The De Sousas were Makanji's rivals. They were four brothers who with their churlish father ran Mbeya's largest department store. One of the brothers, whose first name I had long forgotten, was the only Indian with whom I could claim anything approaching a friendship.

He was a porcine little man with a high-pitched voice whom I had met when we arrived in Mbeya and were boarded for two months at the Mbeya School, a mile outside town where the tarmac ended. Like the rest of the country, the school was in transition. Some of the British staff remained, along with two junior African teachers. The British were condescending toward them and contemptuous of us Americans for not sharing their disdain. Still, they treated us graciously, as kith and kin, even offering us a discounted fee to join the Mbeya Club. They believed, sentimentally and mistakenly, that our numbers provided sustenance for their dying way of life. To the contrary, our arrival presaged their end.

Mbeya's short rains had begun, and each afternoon before they struck we played loud, madcap games of soccer on the school grounds, running about in our tattered shorts and torn sneakers. Our games attracted crowds of passersby. Barefoot Africans joined in, slipping in and out after a few kicks and continuing on their way. European farmers appeared, though they were too standoffish to join and stood chatting on the sidelines. On weekends the portly Indian merchants from the town came to play, which is where I met my friend De Sousa.

Like the British, De Sousa had been delighted by our arrival in Mbeya. But he viewed us in more practical terms — as a source of new wealth for his business. When I left Mbeya to begin teaching at Mpuguso and mentioned to him I was writing away to London for subscriptions to some English periodicals, he wrote away for me to arrange it. When I asked him why he went to such trouble for a meager profit, he said, with the disingenuousness that made him, and all the Indians, so vulnerable to caricature, "Then you will do more business with us, is it?"

Yet it was not merely our money that drew De Sousa and other Indians to us. There was a social equality we Americans offered them, an awareness that despite our similar skin color we were different from the British. I bantered with De Sousa in a way no Englishman would have. We swapped dirty jokes. He became a regular at our afternoon soccer games, waddling up and down the field, side by side with us in our tattered, torn shorts, in his stylish whites and imported black, cleated shoes.

And yet for all this, my memory of him is tinged with regret. As I said, the four brothers worked at their store behind a wooden counter with their churlish father. Whether because the old man barely spoke English or because he had grown choleric or senile, he would stare past me whenever I asked for an item, then would shuffle away without speaking.

Whether he acted this way to me alone, to other Americans, or even to the imperious British, I did not know. But having in my two months in Mbeya already gained something of the British hauteur, one day when he turned away from me I called out to him across the counter, "When I ask you for something you answer me. And call me sir!"

There was a stunned silence in the store. Then from all four directions the brothers ran toward me, jabbing their fingers and jabbering in Gujarati.

"You get out of here from this store!" my friend De Sousa screamed in English in his high-pitched voice. "You cannot talk to our father like that! You dare speak this way to us only because our skin is brown."

It was, of course, this last remark that wounded, his accusing me of the very thing I had come to Africa to disprove, or at least to ameliorate. Whatever insult the old man had caused me, I knew immediately I had gone too far. He was an old man. More important, he was their father. And though I told myself I had addressed him as I would any rude shopkeeper, I knew also I would not have spoken to him as I had, had I not observed the British doing the same, and to great effect.

Yet at the same time I was young and headstrong. Because I knew I could never convince De Sousa of the fallacy of his brown-skinned logic, and with his last phrase ringing in my ears, I stormed out of the store.

It should have ended that way, I suppose, barring my apology, in permanent estrangement, but it did not. And, sadly, it was the De Sousas, not I, who effected the rapprochement.

My friend De Sousa's mustached older brother initiated it. It was he—the first non-European member of the Mbeya Club— who mentioned to an Englishman there of his family's disagreement with me. It was all due, he said, to a "misunderstanding." That was the word he used, *misunderstanding*, a word behind which each of us could hide, one from which each of us could retreat.

"But I don't understand," I told the Englishman when he repeated the brother's conversation to me. "I was clearly in the wrong."

"What you Americans don't understand," he answered, "is that they want your bloody money!"

"Ah, so you know the De Sousas?" says the Indian school teacher. "I knew them well."

"Are they still in Mbeya?" I ask.

"No, they are dead."

"Dead?"

"Dead. They are all dead. They died of heart trouble. The old man also. They had too much money. They drank too much liquor. There were too much women." The Indian schoolteacher laughs.

"And what of their business?"

"Oh, the widows started fighting. They all fought among themselves. It was very unpleasant. Now they are dead as well."

"And the store?"

"Oh, the store is still there. You can still see it. But it is boarded up now.

"Look!" He points outside through our window. We have entered the great game reserve of the Selous and are passing a herd of wildebeests. The land is parched. Much of the grass has been burned, for we are at the height of the dry season just before the short rains. Our window is open but it is hotter outside than in. Dust blows through it into our faces.

"Maybe you will see a lion," the Indian says, smiling. "You can take a picture."

But it is too early and too hot in the afternoon for lions. By the time they awaken in the early evening when the air has cooled, we have passed through the Selous. And so the afternoon glides by. The Selous behind us, we again begin stopping at stations every few miles, each of them tiled replicas of the ones preceding, each with names I have never heard before.

Later, as it grows dark, a passenger from one of these stations enters our compartment. He is an African, but not, I can tell, a Tanzanian. He is in his early twenties, wearing khaki trousers, a white T-shirt, and white tennis sneakers with untied laces that dangle to the floor. He says nothing to us as he enters, but sits down opposite Susan and me next to the Indians. From a green canvas bag he pulls out a book, holds it up in front of him, and begins to read. It is a textbook, and as I am seated opposite him I can see the title on the book's cover, printed boldly in English: *American Imperialism in Southern Africa.*

The young African says nothing as he reads. Five, ten, fifteen minutes pass. The Indian schoolteacher tries to talk to him. He speaks in English, in the same singsong, cheery voice he has used with Susan and me. The young African continues reading. The Indian tries again in Swahili. The young African ignores him.

I open a pack of Trident gum and offer a piece to Susan, another to the father, the son, then to the African. Looking up as he reaches for it, he smiles, then laughs and in thickly accented English says the only words he speaks to us the entire journey, "Ah, sugar-free!"

Ah, sugar-free! That Madison Avenue colloquialism, uttered with such familiarity. How is this African in his T-shirt and unlaced sneakers so familiar with "sugar-free"? Equally intriguing, where has he obtained the money for his first-class ticket?

Who is he? I find myself wondering. Is he farcical or sinister? Is he, with his *American Imperialism in Southern Africa,* one of the ridiculously semieducated revolutionaries in Paul Theroux's *Jungle Lovers*, trained abroad in guerrilla warfare for an unexplained local cause? Or is he the brooding, impenetrable young officer Ferdinand of V. S. Naipaul's *A Bend in the River* who is destined to rule his nameless country and whom Naipaul's Indian narrator must accommodate to survive?

Listening to the Indian schoolteacher struggling to make conversation with this African half his age, I find myself recalling my incident with De Sousa. No, the Englishman's cynical assessment at the bar of the Mbeya Club years before had been incorrect. The De Sousas' "misunderstanding," their attempt to accommodate me, stemmed not from their venality but from their vulnerability. No, the De Sousas had allowed for my insult simply because they were afraid. Because of their perilously Indian position in black Africa, they were simply afraid to offend.

The train rolls on. The night shadows appear. Susan is staring at our compartment door, awaiting the conductor, who will tell her she must move to a compartment down the hall. When he appears, she rises without a word and announces bravely, "It will be just fine."

Later, too, the young African climbs up to the baggage rack and turns down the upper berth into his bed. A trail of light lingers outside as the two Indians and I sit across from him, silently watching him undress. I watch him pull off his white T-shirt, displaying a smooth, hairless chest. I watch him take off his sneakers, wrapping them inside his shirt and trousers, and place them as a pillow under his head. I watch him slide out of his khaki trousers, revealing a pair of white jockey undershorts. With *American Imperialism in Southern Africa* lying innocently beside him, he falls asleep.

Night falls. The train rolls on. In the darkness we appear to be climbing. The stations seem closer together. At each there are the same crowds, the same shouts of boys, now only shadows, running along the platform.

The Indians and I have selected our berths. I am below the young African opposite the Indians. A breeze comes in through the window. It is growing colder. In the distance I can make out the glow of a mountain fire. They are burning the land, preparing it for planting before the short rains.

The train's whistle wails out into the night. Lying in my bed, I feel the years peeling away. I see the bare black hills and the jacaranda trees in bloom. And in that whistle I imagine I hear the word, over and over, "Mbeya, Mbeya."

ii

I am up with the first streaks of dawn. I slide out of my berth beneath the sleeping African, slip past the two snoring Indians, and step outside the compartment into the darkened corridor. The air is still cool from the night. Through the windows I can make out the shadows of the mountains in the distance.

One by one the passengers from our compartment emerge, first the Indians, father then son, then the young African. They take their places in the corridor, a few feet apart like sentinels, staring, like me, silently out the windows.

I look down the corridor waiting for Susan to appear from her compartment. When she does, she forces a smile. She has been up all night, she whispers. There was an argument over the window. She and another European woman had wanted it open. The African women had wanted it closed. They could not agree and kept opening and shutting the window through the night.

It is now seven o'clock. In the gray light of morning the mountains in the distance seem bare, with no trees. The train continues to stop at small white-tiled stations, with names I still do not recognize — Ilonga, Malamba, Chimala, Lumba, Inyala.

Presently, we pass over a concrete overpass, something I have never seen before in Tanzania. "Ah," says the Indian father. "We are approaching Mbeya."

"Do you remember anything?" Susan asks, touching my shoulder. "Does any of it seem familiar to you?"

I shake my head. Staring out the window, I find myself searching for signs, for landmarks — the airport, the road to Tukuyu; the steep hill up into town, the golf course of the Mbeya Club running alongside it. But like Dar es Salaam, nothing is the same. Nothing is as I remember it.

At nine o'clock we pull into a large brick station, as large as that in Dar es Salaam. It, too, is tiled and all white. Carrying our suitcases, we walk beside the two Indians. A group has come to meet them, prying their suitcases from their hands and carrying them to a waiting car.

"We will see you!" the father shouts to Susan and me as he

and his large-bellied son disappear inside the car. "You will come to our house! You will be our guests here in Mbeya!" We never see them again.

Instead, I search for a cab for Susan and me. Finding one, we jump inside. Who is already in the backseat but the young African from our compartment? I nod to him but he stares past us. Where is he going? What is he doing here in Mbeya? Where is he getting his money?

"The Mbeya Hotel," I announce to the driver, and we bounce off down a pothole-filled tarmac road past unfamiliar brown, dusty fields. We pass patches of brick and mud huts, some of which are gaily painted on the outside, with the words, bizarrely scribbled or scripted in English, Tanzania Bar, Texas Hotel, Africa Bar, Cowboy Inn.

Lightheaded from lack of food and sleep, I feel I am dreaming—or sleepwalking—as though my returning to Mbeya has been a terrible mistake.

We come to a crossroad on the edge of town. It is my first landmark, the airport road. Presently, we begin climbing a steep hill, then veer off to the right into a dirt driveway. In front of us stands a stone building with a plate-glass window and a crack running its length through it. Above it is a sign reading MBEYA HOTEL.

Our driver lifts our suitcases out, carries them to the front door, then drives off with the young African in the back.

I open the door and we step inside. Behind a low wooden counter stand two Africans, a man and a woman. The man is wearing tapered olive-green trousers, the zipper of his fly bizarrely stitched outward so that it appears to be open. The woman is wearing platform shoes and a skirt above her knees. Above them on the wall, as in every public building throughout the country, is a portrait of the *Mwalimu*, standing slim and gray-haired in a white Mao shirt.

As I wait for the Africans to acknowledge us, I notice a poster on the wall with circles, squares, and connecting lines, and with English titles beneath them. The poster appears to be an organizational chart. Written across the top are the words Tanzania Railways Corporation, Mbeya Hotel, and beneath them, Hotel Staff Establishment.

Beneath that is written Hotel Manager, and beneath that, Hotel Accountant. There, the chart branches into two forks. The left fork, in descending order, reads, Receptionist I, Kitchen Assistant, Chef, Bar Steward, House Keeper, Room Attendants. The right fork reads, simply and inexplicably, Receptionist II, Head Waiter.

I glance from the chart back to the two Africans, who have stopped talking and are staring at us.

"*Jina langu Bwana Levitt*," I begin, explaining I would like a room for myself and my wife for the next couple of weeks.

His face expressionless, the African in the tapered trousers says in English, "You are Mr. Levitt?"

"Yes." I smile.

Turning to Susan, his face still expressionless, he says, "And this is your wife?"

"Yes." I smile again.

Still expressionless, the African turns to me and says, "You are Mr. Leonard Levitt?"

My jaw drops in astonishment. Without thinking I nod my head.

"And are you," the African continues, "the Mr. Leonard Levitt from Mpuguso school?"

I am speechless. What can this mean? Again, without thinking, I nod my head.

The African breaks into a smile. "And you wrote that wonderful book about Mpuguso?

"Mr. Levitt, do you recognize me?" the African shouts. "I was a student at Chimala Middle School. I came to Mpuguso during a track and field meet and met you. I read your book."

Standing before this African in his bizarre tight trousers, I feel tears coming to my eyes. Can this be possible? With Susan as my witness, does someone here in this dusty, unrecognizable town I had last seen twenty years before remember me?

"I also watched you teach the boys their exercises. "*Simba!*" he shouts, beating his chest. "*Simbaa!*"

Simba! the Swahili word for "lion." *Simbaa!* Oh, I remember *Simba*. Besides my regular classroom duties, I had taught physical education to the smirking, oldest Standard 8 boys. Partly to wipe the smirks off their faces, I had taught them calisthenics.

Down at the soccer field, where the cows grazed between the goalposts, I had herded the boys into a circle, and demonstrated jumping jacks, shouting out loud to them as they spread their legs and raised their arms above their heads, "One! Two! Three! Four!"

Next, I ordered them to extend their arms, stiff and straight, at shoulder height. A minute passed. There was not a sound. I saw some of them looking questioningly at each other. Their smirks were gone, replaced by grimaces.

I then had them lie flat on their backs and lift their feet inches off the ground. Five seconds passed. Ten. Now I heard gasps of pain.

I rolled them over into push-up position, had them bend low to the ground without allowing their chests to touch.

"Up!" I shouted at them.

More gasps as they raised themselves.

"Down!" Down they went.

"Hold it there!" I shouted to them. "Ho old it!"

More gasps, groans.

"Say it!" I shouted. "Ho-old it!"

Their bodies extended in push-up position, they had roared back, "Ho-old it!"

Startled by the noise from this pent-up release, they had broken into grins, the tension broken, their pain dissipated.

"*Simba!*" I shouted to them, still in push-up position. "*Simbaa!*"

"*Simba!*" they roared back. "*Simbaa!*," their shouts, their laughter reverberating across the field.

Now recalling the episode with this nameless African in the Mbeya Hotel, I, too, want to shout, to laugh. Those calisthenics had become part of Mpuguso's regimen, spread by the Standard 8 boys to the school's lower forms. On Tanzania's national holiday, which is known as *Saba Saba* day, I had led our Mpuguso schoolboys in a celebration in Tukuyu, where before the entire town and all the schools of the region we had performed our calisthenics, culminating with the boys' shouts of "*Simbaa! Simbaa!*"

"I also went to the English debates when you were the debate master," the African continues. "Mr. Levitt, do you remember those debates? Do you remember when you were the debate master?"

Again I nod my head, my composure beginning to return. Indeed, I do remember those debates. Each Saturday night, after the boys had swept the dining room, they had trooped down from their dormitories. The long wooden benches on which they had eaten their dinner were turned toward the stage. There, two boys debated in bombastic, polysyllabic English such topics as

"Resolved: It is better to marry an educated girl than an unedu-
cated girl." Or, "It is better to have one wife than many wives."

After the debaters had finished, to applause, jeers, shouts, or
groans, the debate was thrown open to the floor. One after the
other, the boys would rise. Actors and orators all of them, even
the youngest, some of them only ten or eleven years old, they
showed no hesitancy in waving their arms and launching into
histrionics.

Yet it was at one of these debates that I was left unnerved,
frightened, the only fright I'd ever felt in Africa. The speaker, I
remember, had been a short, stocky Standard 8 boy, with an
occasional stutter, named Peter Mwakyusa; the subject,
"Resolved: Africa belongs to the Africans, not to the Indians or
the Europeans!" In a ringing peroration, Peter, overcoming his
stutter, had shouted, "And why do I believe Africa belongs to the
Africans, not to the Indians or the Europeans? Because my
father lived here and my grandfather before him and his grandfather before him. That is why I believe Africa belongs to the
Africans!"

There was a tremor through the dining hall as he finished.
There then burst applause and shouting, yelling and screaming,
louder and longer than any I'd ever heard, as though Peter had
drawn from a deep, dark African wellspring of emotion and
brought up something in the boys that was wild and untamed.

Afterwards, as debate master, I took center stage. I would
begin by criticizing the boys' bombast, their pomposity of language, their misapprehension that the longer or more arcane the
word (*missive* for *letter* was a favorite; *raiment* for *garment* was
another), the better their command of English. Often, I accompanied my criticisms with a curl of my eyebrow, a twist of the
corner of my mouth, a sudden pirouette and jab of my finger. I
was a pretty fair actor myself.

"Mr. Levitt. My name is Azim Mwinyimvua," announces the
African before me. "But here I am known as Bwana Simba."
Stretching out his hands to take mine and Susan's, he says to us,
"Welcome to Mbeya! Welcome to the Mbeya Hotel. Welcome
Mwalimu!"

Bwana Simba, it turns out, is nothing less than the highest
title on the Mbeya Hotel's organizational chart—the hotel manager. He motions to the woman in the platform shoes, who hands
him a key from a hook on the wall. He then informs Susan and

me he will give us the hotel's finest suite. He summons a barefoot man in a baggy white uniform to carry our suitcases, and leads us off.

We walk down a narrow hallway through the lobby, past two Africans kneeling on the floor, scrub brushes in their hands. One of them, a strapping fellow Bwana Simba introduces to us as Bwana Juma, is wearing cut-off shorts and black rubber hip boots. The other, a gray-haired man, also in shorts, wears scruffed black shoes with no socks. The two are dipping their brushes into pails of soapy water, and scrubbing at a long ratty carpet with holes and faded spots that fills the lobby.

To the right of the hallway, chairs and tables have been arranged against the windows, making a portion of the lobby into a lounge. The glass in some of the frames is cracked. In others it is missing entirely. There are flies everywhere.

To the left of the hallway is the hotel dining room, and off it, another lounge area, with a long bar and *choo*, or toilet, which with the heavy evening bar traffic is forever overflowing onto the floor.

The windows overlook a dry courtyard. Bwana Simba opens a side door on the right and leads us down a path. There is a garden, or what was a garden, which has turned to brown grass and dust. A herd of goats is grazing, munching on the grass and at the few remaining flowers.

We pass some cabins, which are the hotel's guest rooms. Bwana Simba stops at one in the rear of the yard. "This is one of our finest suites," he announces. As though in apology, he adds, "I would give you the hotel's deluxe suite, but the Minister of Defense is staying there now." He lowers his voice. "There was a report of trouble on the border with Malawi and the minister has gone there to survey the situation. He did not return from the border last night, but we must keep the room open for him."

As though to make up for this, Bwana Simba says he will assign Susan and me our personal houseman. "He is my best houseman. He is a very hard worker."

As for our cabin, it is indeed, as Bwana Simba has proclaimed, a suite. It has a bedroom with a sagging double bed, a sitting room with a couch, and a bathroom with a chipped old tub. Above the bed is a *chandalua*, or mosquito net, though as Susan runs her hand through the white netting she discovers a hole the size of her fist.

There is also a lightbulb. Since it is the suite's only lightbulb, at night we must unscrew it and take it with us as we wander from room to room.

So pleased am I to have stumbled onto Bwana Simba that I do not notice the walls of unbaked brick. "Look," says Susan. She points to a corner of the bedroom which is being eaten away by red army ants that cover the wall. When we inform our personal houseman of this, he arrives with an aerosol can of Raid. But by the time he has sprayed and departed with his can, the ants have already returned.

It is now nearly eleven o'clock, and as we have not eaten Bwana Simba offers to serve us tea in the dining room. He calls to another servant in a white uniform, who, Bwana Simba tells us, "will be your personal waiter. He is also from Iringa. His name is Bwana George. He is a very hard worker and he speaks American English."

Bwana George is a reed-thin, gray-haired fellow who delights in speaking what he believes to be American English by rolling his *r*'s from the back of his throat as though gargling. He serves us tea in a heavy chipped cup and milk from a pewter creamer with the emblem of the East African Railway Hotels, the agency established by the British generations before in colonial days to run all its elegant hotels throughout East Africa.

As we sip our tea I notice a mural on the walls of the dining room. It is a series of black-and-white photographs of the British in safari regalia, shouldering their rifles and straddling carcasses. Their white skins startle me. It is the only physical trace of them I have seen in Tanzania.

After our tea Susan and I walk into town. As I have not yet found my bearings Bwana Simba escorts us to the tarmac road and directs us up the hill. As we walk an assortment of vehicles — cars, trucks, buses, taxis — in varying states of disrepair struggle past us, creeping up the hill at two or three miles per hour, spewing out gray-black exhaust in their wake.

Across the road lies a field bare of grass and dotted with half-completed mud huts built with corrugated tin roofs. A web of footpaths crisscrosses it, Africans passing in all directions. At the bottom of the field I can see a horseshoe-shaped stadium. Green billboards ring the outside, with Swahili slogans painted on them in large printed white letters, the words visible to travelers on the road. *"Nchi Maskini Haiwezi Kuendelea Kwa Msingi Wa Fedha,"* reads the first. "A Poor Country Will Not Progress If It Depends on Aid," I translate for Susan. "*Nchi Maskini Haiwezi Kugitawala Kama Inategemea Misada Toka Nje*," reads a second. "A Poor Country Is Unable to Rule Itself If It Relies on Foreign Aid." How ironic, how amusing, as the country is the largest per-capita aid recipient in the world.

At the top of the hill another tarmac road crosses the first, running down a smaller hill. Ragged wooden *dukas* line the street, set back on raised wooden terraces. Once Indian-owned, the shops have African tailors now sitting outside them, working on Singer sewing machines. Others are boarded up or shuttered closed.

Susan and I walk in silence, the only white faces in the traffic of people as I search for De Sousa's and Makanji's stores. We pass a shoe store with an empty display window; a building with a sign reading TANZANIA BREWERIES CORPORATION, MBEYA BRANCH; a bookstore containing Russian-language picture books and the Swahili writings of the *Mwalimu*, including a translation he had done at Edinburgh of none other than Julius Caesar.

To the left we pass the African market. Women in dust-covered *kangas* are sitting on their haunches selling bananas, onions, pieces of roasted meat, and the last small oranges of the season. The sun is hot. Waves of dust blow across the street. There is the smell of garbage. Flies are everywhere.

At the bottom of the hill we notice a store whose sign reads DOCTOR'S OFFICE. Through the glass-front window, we can see packets and tubes of medicines displayed. In this country with no foreign currency to purchase medicine we see Neva Shampoo, Galloway Cough Syrup, Junior Aspro, Sloan's Liniment, Castor Oil, Clearasil, Dill Water, Calpolo Suspension, Baby Rhinol, and Gripe Water.

Susan and I stare at each other without speaking. So this is what it has come to. No medicines in the stores. No currency to buy them. Wordlessly, we turn and retrace our steps up the hill. As we approach the top we pass a building I had not noticed on our walk down the hill. It is of stone, set back toward the hill. I cannot explain why but I find myself staring at it. A dirt path leads to its heavy wooden door. Taking Susan's hand, I walk toward it.

The door is ajar and we step inside. It is musty and dark. Holes of plaster pock the walls. Chairs and couches are turned toward the rear, facing a large bay window overlooking the hill.

Staring out the window, I see the half-completed, tin-roofed mud huts and off to the left, the tarmac road running down the hill alongside them. As I stare, the scene focuses into sharper relief. The tin-roofed mud huts are on what was once the golf course. The tarmac road is the road out of town that ran along the course's first hole. Suddenly, I realize I am standing inside the remains of the Mbeya Club.

iii

A few days later Bwana Simba bounds up to Susan and me. "Mr. Levitt, do you remember your fellow teacher Bwana Mwandunga?" Mwandunga had been my next-door neighbor at Mpuguso, living in the two-room brick house next to mine. He was a short, stocky fellow with a round face and a Micawberish bearing, with a tall, attractive wife and two small children, Elizabeth and Bernard. I had taken snapshots of all of them and one of the photos, of Elizabeth and Bernard, had been used as the jacket cover of my book.

"Well," says Bwana Simba, "do you know that Mwandunga lives not far from here, in Icolo?" I am about to point out that Icolo, Bwana Simba's "not far from here," is actually south of Tukuyu near the Malawi border, a distance of seventy or eighty miles, but before I can do so, Bwana Simba announces he has found me a driver, a former government worker who, miraculously, owns a new Datsun. For a thousand Tanzanian shillings, about $120 at the official exchange rate, he has agreed to drive Susan and me to Icolo to see Mwandunga.

We leave early the next morning, pass the cutoff to the airport, pass the painted brick and mud huts of the Tanzania Bar, Texas Hotel, Africa Bar, and Cowboy Inn. Passing them, I notice another, an apparently Swahili word written across some huts that I had not noticed before—the word *Bucha.*

"What is *Bucha*?" I ask our driver. "I do not know that word."

"You do not know *Bucha*?" the driver laughs. "*Bucha* is not Swahili. It is English. *Bucha* is 'meat.'" *Bucha*, I realize, is the Swahili transliteration of "butcher."

The road to Tukuyu is all tarmac now. There are no large

stones to swerve around, though there are potholes, deeper than any of years before. With Mbeya behind us the haze begins to lift. Blue mountains come up on the left with white tips of clouds on their peaks. To the right, the land is green, with black-brown furrowed fields. Small herds of cattle cross the roadside, led by old men and small boys.

Suddenly, as we round a bend, there lies an overturned bus. It is on the side of the road, on its back, windowless, its wheels off the ground, the ribs of its frame sticking out like the carcass of a huge animal.

"Do you know what happened?" says our driver. "This bus company was owned by an African. His driver told him the brakes were going on the bus. The driver said he did not want to drive it anymore because the brakes were bad. So the owner said he would drive it himself. It was several years ago. A Sunday. They came around the turn and the bus did not stop. The brakes did not hold. It went over. Twenty-eight people were killed."

He turns to us and shakes his head. Susan and I look at each other. The bus has been lying there for how many years? I wonder.

The driver turns back to the road, staring straight ahead, grasping the steering wheel with both hands.

A little farther on we pass a mud-baked school building at the edge of the road. Literacy, education had been one of the Mwalimu's priorities. One of his proudest boasts was that under African Socialism there was a school in every village.

Because the school is so close to the road, we can see in through the classroom windows. But there are no students inside. Instead, they are all outside at a nearby soccer field with rickety wooden goalposts at either end, running about in their white school shirts and white shorts.

In each village we pass it is the same—a school by the roadside with its classrooms empty, its students all outside playing soccer.

We reach the village of Kiwira, the midpoint to Tukuyu, in less than an hour. At its marketplace, people stream across the tarmac, sucking on long pieces of sugarcane. Then, a few miles farther, in the distance I see Tukuyu. It is just as I remember it, its outskirts on the ridge of a hill, ragged wooden stores and tailor shops, like those of Mbeya, sitting on raised sidewalks on both sides of the road. Ahead, at the bottom of a hill on the right lies its marketplace. The day has already grown hot and the crowds wandering through the streets on the ridge of town move listlessly.

Our driver suggests we stop at the market to buy oranges or mangoes. We will be gone all day, he warns, and it is growing hotter. But the marketplace, like that in Mbeya, is nearly bare. There are no fruits, except some small red-brown bananas. It is too late in the season. And so we pick up and carry on.

Soon we are out of town again, passing mud huts hidden by thick banana leaves. A few miles more and the road begins to descend. From the highlands of Tukuyu it will drop four thousand feet to Kyela, on the shores of Lake Nyasa, where the land is flat. Then around a bend, we catch a glimpse of the lake, a speck of blue. The sun is climbing higher. We are already perspiring. It is not yet ten o'clock.

A few miles more and we have completed our descent, down into a Hades-like haze. The road is now flat and the heat comes up in waves. Our driver is not sure where the turnoff to Icolo is. We stutter along but somehow find it, a narrow dirt road on the right that crosses a bridge over a narrow, brown river, the Songwe, which runs alongside us.

The land here is lush and fertile. Long, low mud huts line the road, with cattle lying on the ground in the heat under thickly green, low-hanging banana trees. Ahead on the right is another school. We stop the car. A crowd of schoolchildren gathers around us. From inside the building I can see eyes peering out of windows.

I walk up to the office and ask directions for Bwana Mwandunga. They know him here and tell us he is at his office some miles away, but that his house is but a few hundred yards farther along the dirt road. We return to the car. By now the crowd has swelled and leads us along the road.

From a mud hut on the roadside a woman appears. She is tall and attractive and is wearing a *kanga* wrapped around her. She is, of course, Mrs. Mwandunga. She is exactly as she looked when I had last seen her.

"*Hujambo, hujambo,*" I call out to her. Hello, hello. I am still some yards away. She turns and stares at me. Suddenly she cries, "Ha! Levitt!" and runs toward us.

"*Nimefika.*" I have arrived, I call to her, grandiloquently.

"*Yuko wapi jirani, Mwandunga?*" I say. Where is my friend Mwandunga?

And suddenly, he materializes. Short and stocky with a round face, he, too, looks exactly as he had twenty years before.

"Ah, Levitt," he says in English, smiling to Susan as I introduce them. "What have you brought me? Where is my *zawadi*, my present." Knowing Mwandunga as I do, I return to the car to fetch a faded brown, long-sleeve sweater I have brought for just this occasion. He takes it from me, holds it out in front of him, and studies it, for what I am not certain, then tries it on and, hot as the day is, continues to wear it.

"Ah, Levitt, why didn't you let me know you were coming? I would have prepared. I would not"—he points at himself—"have worn these old clothes."

He then invites Susan and me into his hut. Inside it is cool and dark. Mwandunga brings us wooden chairs to sit on. His wife serves us tea, apologizing that there is no sugar. Such is the state of Tanzania's economy that these staples no longer exist.

Susan has brought her camera and I ask whether she can take his picture. He nods, orders the others away from him, dusts off his sweater, then sits stiffly and solemnly in his wooden chair as Susan takes it.

I ask him if Mrs. Mwandunga would like her picture taken. She refuses, pointing to her clothes and saying she is too dirty. She then gets up and walks off a few yards. I see her washing her hands from a basin, taking scoops of water into her hands and tossing the water over her face.

Above Mwandunga on the wall I notice a picture hung on a nail. It is of a young girl and a young man. "This is my daughter, Elizabeth," Mwandunga says.

"Little Elizabeth!" I say.

"Yes," he smiles. "She is in Dar es Salaam. And that is her fiancé." He smiles again as he pronounces this last word, indicating his pleasure at this, his expertise in English. Fiancé.

"And of course, you remember Bernard," he continues. I smile. Bernard, his youngest, on the jacket cover of my book.

"Bernard," says Mwandunga triumphantly, "is in secondary school."

I nod my appreciation.

"Levitt, it is not like when you were here. These days there are very few secondary schools in the region. So there are far fewer openings. It is not like when you were here, Levitt. It is much more difficult now. Bernard is one of the . . ." He struggles for the word.

"Bernard is one of the elite," I help.

"Yes," he laughs, playing with a new word. "Elite. Bernard is one of the elite."

Months later after Susan and I have returned home, I receive a letter. It is from Bernard, one of the country's two or three percent who have been accepted at secondary school, one of the elite.

"Dear Mr. Levitt," it begins.

"I am over joyed with the idea of writing to you. Really this is what I have to write to you. I look at your photograph now and then. Heard you came to Tanzania, why not pass here Mr. Levitt? A word of greeting would suffice.

How do you do! How is Mrs. Levitt? Is she well? I pray she smiles. Is your home a happy one? I like happy homes, happy husbands, happy wives, happy Children and that's what I call a good home. I have nothing to offer to Mrs. Levitt. However I promise to send my photograph soon or later."

The letter was signed, "Mwandunga's Junior."

Meanwhile, a crowd has gathered outside Mwandunga's hut. Mwandunga tells me they are his relatives. He says he has been in Icolo for some years now as a school inspector, monitoring the quality of the curriculums of the primary schools in the region. I nod my head. I do not say this strikes me as somewhat bizarre, as Mwandunga himself has only a Standard 8 education, never having attended secondary school.

"Do you know, Levitt, that one of your students is also here in this village?"

"Who is that?"

"Peter Mwakyusa."

"Peter Mwakyusa!" Peter Mwakyusa, who during the Saturday night debates had fired up the school with his wild burst of African nationalism.

"Yes, he is the party secretary for Icolo. His office is just down there." Mwandunga points down the dirt road we have come on. "I will send word to him that you are here. He will want to see you."

Like Mwandunga, on the surface Peter Mwakyusa has not changed. He is still short and stocky, and has the same short haircut he had as a schoolboy.

"So, Levitt, you have returned to us," he says paternally,

almost patronizingly. He says this matter-of-factly, with no emotion, as though my returning here to his village at this remote corner of the country is the most natural of events.

We shake hands. He takes two or three steps back and literally looks Susan and me up and down, as though appraising two animals. "Are you still teaching, Levitt? I remember your teaching. You were a fine teacher. A fine teacher."

"No, I am a journalist. A writer."

"A writer? Why not a teacher? Why did you stop? *Hakuna maua*. No more buds, no more flowers."

Taking me by the hand, he begins leading Susan and me about the village. "I am the party secretary here," he explains in English as we walk off the road, past his office, and through fields as villagers appear and stare at us. He explains he is the secretary of one of three local areas, responsible, he says, "for knowing everything of the twenty-five thousand people in my district.

"I am interested in knowing the will of the people," he adds, "so I can determine their needs."

"And what of *your* life, Peter?" I ask. "Are you married? Do you have children? How long have you been here in Icolo?"

He shakes his head. "No, I am the party secretary. Personal matters are not important."

There is a *mkutano*, a meeting, in progress that Peter says he must attend, and invites Susan and me to accompany him. There, in a clearing some yards away, under tall, leafy trees protecting the people from the afternoon sun, is a long table with wooden benches at which a dozen or so officials are seated. Beyond them are perhaps a hundred villagers seated on the ground, old men in varying states of dress, from Western trousers to cloths slung over their shoulders to turbans wrapped around their heads.

Leaving Susan behind with our driver, Peter leads me to an open space on one of the benches and we sit down together. Peter points out the official at the center of the table—a tall young man in a white Mao shirt that hangs outside his trousers.

"That is our Area Commissioner," says Peter approvingly. "He is very radical."

"You mean he is against the government?" I say facetiously.

"Oh no, no." Rising from our bench, Peter walks up to the Area Commissioner and whispers in his ear. The Area Commissioner nods his head.

Meanwhile, one of the officials at the table has finished speaking. Seated on the ground, the old men have raised their hands and are asking questions. They are speaking both in Swahili and Nyakusa, the local dialect. I cannot understand what they are saying, but they appear to be growing angry, with more of them raising their hands.

I am struck by this scene, this picture-postcard version of the *Mwalimu's Ujamaa*, the African equivalent, perhaps, of a Vermont town meeting, and I wonder if Susan might take a picture of it. But first, I realize, I must obtain permission from the Area Commissioner. Taking out my notepad, I scribble in Swahili, describing myself to the Area Commissioner as Peter's former teacher, and ask Peter to hand the note to him.

Too late, I realize I have made a mistake, for in writing the note in Swahili I have implied the Area Commissioner does not know English. By then Peter has passed on the note. I watch the Area Commissioner pick it up, glance at it, and jot something of his own on it. He places a pin through the note and passes it back to Peter.

Peter hands it to me, unopened. I pull out the pin. Scrawled on the back of my note are three words, in English, all capitalized. They are: "Is Not Allowed."

The meeting continues. The old men continue to raise their hands. The questions appear interminable. But finally, it is over. The Area Commissioner stands up and walks straight to his car. Without a glance at anyone he drives off.

Peter does not mention the Area Commissioner's refusal, but begins leading me again through the village, past the mud huts and the kraals where the cattle are lying and amidst the banana trees.

Like the Area Commissioner, he does not speak to anyone. When I ask him whether Susan can take his picture with some of the villagers, he says, "But I am the party secretary! Why should I be taken with them? It is not dignified. You should know this, Levitt. You know Africans better than anyone."

I have no idea what he is talking about. "Peter," I laugh, "you are the first politician I have ever met who does not want to have his picture taken with his constituents."

But Peter does not respond to this. Instead, he begins berating me for not understanding him, for not understanding Africans. "What we believe, Levitt, is that if a man is rich and has much land, he exploits the others who have less land than he. Why should one man have much land and others have none? The land belongs to everybody. Shouldn't they all be equal?

I wonder where he has picked up such nonsense.

"You see, Levitt," he continues, "we are not like the Chinese. The Chinese have to be taught about socialism. They had it imposed on them. With Africans socialism is natural. We have a word for it. It is called *Ujamaa*. The word is new, but to us Africans it is natural."

"But what if a man works very hard and sells his crops and makes money from them?" I say for the sake of argument. "And another man does no work and produces no crops. Why shouldn't the first man take his money and buy the land of the second man and produce more crops and make more money?"

"But that is not the African way, Levitt. You know Africans. You taught us. You know this about us."

Again, I have no idea what he is talking about. He is mad, I find myself thinking. They are all mad. What is it that he thinks I know of them? That equality does not mean equal opportunity but equal ends? That being equal means being the same? That there are no differences between people, in their character, in their intelligence, in their motivations?

Is this what is meant by African Socialism? Is this the logical conclusion of the *Mwalimu's Ujamaa*? Here in this remote village, is this the final mutation of Fabian Socialism, as interpreted by none other than my former student Peter Mwakyusa?

And it is so sad. They have worked so hard. They had believed so much, the *Mwalimu* as much as any of them. For the first time I find myself feeling sorry for him. Yes, he had truly wanted to help his countrymen. He had truly wanted to eradicate poverty, ignorance, and disease. Yet it is now all a pretense, a sham. I think of the organizational chart on the wall of the Mbeya Hotel, the walls of our room covered with ants eating away at them, the single can of Raid. I recall the line of decrepit cars and buses creeping up the hill into town; the ridiculous signs on the walls of the stadium across the road. *Nchi Maskini Haiwezi Kuendelea Kwa Msingi Wa Fedha.* A poor country will not progress if it depends on aid. *Nchi Maskini Haiwezi Kugitawala Kama Inategemea Misada Toka Nje.* A poor country is unable to rule itself if it relies on foreign aid.

I recall the boarded up Indian-owned stores, the bottles of

Neva Shampoo, Junior Aspro, Sloan's Liniment, and Galloway Cough Syrup that now pass for medicines. The schools on the roadside with no pupils inside them. The overturned truck that has lain there for years. I imagine the corpus of Tanzania, lying inert beside it, with all the transfusions of foreign aid unable to resuscitate it. I suddenly have the premonition that in not too long a time the grass and weeds will grow up and cover everything.

It is growing late in the day now and time for us to depart. Peter escorts Susan and me to our car. But the car has a flat tire. While we and Peter watch, our driver replaces it with the spare. Now the driver says we must hurry. If another tire goes, there is no spare. He says he is afraid of the darkness. We must, he warns, return to Mbeya before nightfall.

We say our goodbyes to Peter, who stands expressionless behind us in the road as we pull off.

But at the bridge over the brown river Songwe, two soldiers stop us. They are young, in their teens perhaps, boys really, in green fatigues and high black boots, with rifles slung over their shoulders. They want to see Susan's and my identification. They want to examine Susan's camera.

They search our belongings—the camera case, Susan's pocketbook. They pat under the dashboard. They say they want to see if we are sending messages across the Malawi border. To whom? Why?

They want to know about the package of rice Mrs. Mwandunga has prepared for us. They say they are checking smuggling from over the border. There are shortages of rice around the country, they say. Speculators—Indian businessmen—have driven out to the rice-producing areas. They then return to the cities where they sell the rice on the black market.

Our driver is nervous. He speaks to them so quickly I cannot understand him. The soldiers say they want to send us to Kyela so that we can report to the Area Commissioner. The Area Commissioner is the last person I want to see. Our driver continues talking, gesturing, pleading. In the end they let us go.

The sun is low in the sky now as we head back to the main road and begin our ascent into the mountains. Now in the fading light around the roadbends we see blocks of wood, stones, and even small boulders that someone has placed like a barricade across the road so that we have to slow down and swerve around them.

"*Wanatengeneza bara bara*," our driver explains. They are preparing the road. This is why he fears the dark. This is why we must return to Mbeya by nightfall. "At night," he adds, "thieves and highwaymen take over, trying to stop rich Indians and steal their belongings or even their vehicles. Last month outside Mbeya they stopped an Indian and robbed him, took his watch and his car, even his clothes. The next time he did not stop at the barricade. He tried to go right through it. He broke his car. Then he got out and ran."

The flatlands of Kyela are behind us now, the blue lake becoming smaller around every curve as we wind higher and higher. We are racing both against the fear of night and of another blowout.

It is dusk as we pass through Tukuyu. We pass the shadows of the marketplace at the bottom of the hill, the ragged wooden store buildings on either side of the street, the raised sidewalks and wooden railings in front of them. A fog has come in off the mountains, and the town seems gray and shabby. In the dusk the wooden railings seem like hitching posts in an old western movie.

In their white school uniforms, swarms of schoolchildren, girls and boys, are walking through the streets, apparently returning home after their long school day.

Then, off the road on Tukuyu's outskirts, I make out another group of schoolboys. They are older, tall and ungainly, and they are standing in their white uniforms in a circle in an open field. Because of the fading light, I am not sure at first what they are doing. Then I see they are moving in unison, raising their arms over their heads and at the same time spreading their legs apart, as though they are jumping. Though our windows are closed, I can hear their voices. Am I imagining it, or do I actually hear the words they are shouting out in English, "One, Two, Three, Four"?

We pass them by, their shadows in the distance, beneath the blue, dark mountains. As we do, Susan opens her window to look back one last time. It is then I hear another sound, a long, low growl that rolls out into the night behind us, a sound of which there can be no mistaking. Susan hears it too and turns to me. I feel a tremor running through me. The sounds we hear, the last sounds as we leave Tukuyu behind us in the night, are the boys' voices, shouting out into the darkness, "*Simbaa! Simbaa! Simbaa!*"

NOTES FOR MY NEXT TRIP TO THE ISLANDS

by P. F. Kluge

P. F. Kluge places his work in two categories: cold weather and hot weather books. The cold weather books include *Eddie and the Cruisers*, set in the author's home state, New Jersey, and the just-published *Alma Mater: A College Homecoming*, a nonfiction profile of Kenyon College, Gambier, Ohio. The hot weather books include *The Day That I Die*, a novel, and *The Edge of Paradise*, nonfiction, both set in Micronesia, where he was a Peace Corps Volunteer in the late sixties; and two novels, *Season for War* and *MacArthur's Ghost*, both derived from study and travel in the Philippines. The fifty-one-year-old author now divides his time between Kenyon College, where he teaches, and Manila, where his wife, Pamela Hollie, represents the Asia Foundation. He claims not to know where home is, has difficulty locating clothing, books and other personal effects, and longs for the day when he will live long enough in a place to find his name in the current phone book. He is always, he says, looking for new material. "Notes for My Next Trip to the Islands" is Kluge's way of letting his imagination return to where he began to see the world as a writer.

Almost twenty years ago, on a long voyage in the southwest Pacific islands of Palau, somewhere between Sonsorol and Tobi, a frozen human turd appeared in the ship's freezer, where food was kept. We never found out who put it there and why, though we talked about it plenty. We'd been eating unspeakable chow while cruising the Pacific: chopped-up hotdogs on sticky rice, peanut-butter-and-jelly sandwiches. The freezer-turd might have been a diner's protest. That was one, but not the only, theory because we were running out of water. A few dribbles came out of the shower, if the ship rolled far enough to one side, but you never knew, so you soaped and washed one part of your body at a time, slowly, which made it real rough on the guy, a voyage before, who'd been vomited on by a seasick priest in the upper berth. And the toilets—well, they stank and clogged and that led to the second theory. Someone punctilious and considerate had deposited that turd in the freezer, storing it there against the hoped-for day when it could be appropriately disposed of, in ship's plumbing that worked. It's funny, the shit I remember, when I think about returning to paradise.

You'll need a good map to find the place I'm aiming for, a map diligent and inclusive enough to put a name to something that, left alone, could easily be a printer's error, an imperfection in the paper. I am headed for Micronesia. The Peace Corps sent me there—to Saipan, in the northern Marianas—in the late sixties. Since then, it's been all my fault, a dozen returns, more than curiosity can justify, more than nostalgia can explain, more even than the professional writer's elastic definition of experience can begin to accommodate. The last time—I thought it would be the last time—I was there to write a book, to get it all down, to be done with it and move on. The book's been published, yet I still think about returning. I never learn. The places I thought were the beginning of my traveler's life have dominated its middle and, unless I'm wrong, will be in at the finish. So this is about visiting and revisiting, about leaving a piece of yourself behind, about not letting go.

Now the map test. Put a finger on the Hawaiian Islands and move west, into Micronesia. Pass through the Marshall Islands. Dip down into the eastern Carolines, through Pohnpei, Kosrae, Chuuk—Ponape, Kusaie, Truk, if your map is old—and continue on to Guam. You've covered Micronesia, east to west. This return, though, I will travel Micronesia from north to south, starting in Saipan, moving through Guam and Yap to Palau. Then I'll have gone as far as airline tickets can take me, leaving the realm of schedules and entering the zone of luck. If I hit it just right, though, there might be a boat headed south to Pulo Anna, Sonsorol, Merir, Tobi, and—look closely now—a place called Helen Island on some maps, Helen Reef on others, if it appears at all. An island at the end of the line, at the edge of the map, a traveler's reductio ad absurdum.

I heard about Helen twenty years ago when I was a Peace Corps Volunteer hanging around Koror, district center of Palau. I talked to people who'd visited, caught something in their voices, when they told me what they'd seen. Koror was a cluttered, funky place, all potholes and power failures, a tin-roofed, tropical rattle-trap that no one who lived there or visited could call a paradise. But when talk turned to Helen, hundreds of miles to the south, old dreams resurged: an empty, solitary island, a sanctuary and haven, a shipwreck fantasy come to life, a rumor, a mirage. I interviewed everyone I could who'd been to this magical place. In government offices I burrowed through years of field-trip reports. The island drew poachers, pirating vessels that filled up on giant clams, reef fish, nesting birds, and turtles. And the Palauan protectors were often little better, killing and capturing birds, drinking and partying, trashing the place. These visits were rare, though, and I suspected that something that I wouldn't forget was waiting for me down there.

It was a rough trip. I remember halfhearted copra loading on Sonsorol—the copra trade was dying—and a dispute about whether loading was the job of the island men or the ship's crew, and in the end we left dozens of burlap sacks out on the beach, in the rain. On Pulo Anna, I watched a Peace Corps Volunteer, a woman, leave after two years, and Pulo Anna was the sort of place you couldn't kid yourself about revisiting: the PCV knew she'd never see the place again and so did the people who said goodbye to her, and I remember her crying at the ship's railing, the island women crying on shore. On Merir—population three—we explored the center of the island at midday, only to be attacked by swarms of mosquitoes that were on us like a pack of angry hornets, chasing us down toward the beach. Time passed slowly between islands. The ship was filthy, the cabins were wretched, the food was slop, the showers were dry; we were behind schedule, we were crowded, we were lost. But a reward was waiting. One afternoon we spotted a ship on the horizon; approaching, we saw that the horizon was a reef and the ship a wreck, the rusted *Nagasaki Maru*. Two more recent wrecks were impaled, farther down the reef, and at the very end of the vast lagoon, there sat an island, an eight-acre raft of sand and palms. When we came ashore the next morning, I felt I'd traveled as far as it was possible to travel, coming to the loveliest, smallest, emptiest of places. A grove of tall coconut palms covered the wide end of the island: a shady and majestic place that swallowed you as soon as you stepped inside, where it was dark, cool, and damp. Outside the grove, back in the sunlight, the island narrowed, covered with brush and sea grapes, toward a spit of sand where a cross marked someone's grave, a fisherman's or poacher's probably. Did I say the island was empty? Helen was a bird island, frigates and goonies, a nest in every tree, a bird on every branch, regarding our approach with little, too little, fear. Helen Island was a turtle island, too. I didn't see it, but I spoke to people who had: on moonlit nights so many turtles came ashore to lay eggs, crowding onto the sand, that the beach turned black. That was it. That was all: one day, years ago. The island vanished before we were out of the lagoon; it slipped over the horizon and under the waves. Then we lost the *Nagasaki Maru,* gone in a wink, all of it. But there hasn't been a week since then, I haven't found myself wondering about Helen Island. And I can never face a map of the Pacific without glancing down into that empty blue space between Palau and Indonesia to see if Helen Island is still there. If I find it, I reach out and touch and cover it and connect. A fingertip suffices.

I am going back. I might as well face it. Once I looked at the world the way a hungry diner looks at a great menu. In time, I guessed, I would have a taste of everything. There was no place in the world I wouldn't go. And if someone had whispered that I would never see, say, Antarctica, I'd have been mortified at the loss of biting winds and midnight suns, black cold islands, calving glaciers sending icebergs out to sea. Now, years later, there's a long list of promises I haven't kept. Time runs out on the climb up Mount Kilimanjaro, the voyage up the Amazon, the reverent pause by Tolstoy's grave. This next, last trip to the islands gets harder to defend. To see new places would be to grow. But to lose touch with the islands would be to die.

I will not tell them I am coming. That's the most important rule when it comes to visiting islands. Forewarning would imply that arrangements are necessary, reservations welcome, but when you visit an island you acknowledge that the place has a life of its own, something that is—or ought to be—unaffected by your own coming and going. "The same tide that carries them in, carries them out" is the island saying about visitors. Accept it. You come in on the tide, quietly slip ashore, and take your chance on life as you find it. There are old friends on Saipan and Palau whose lives have continued in my absence, and I do not want to see them waiting, behind customs and immigration, when I come walking in. All Americans in the Pacific are haunted by the specter of MacArthur wading ashore at Leyte: a tableau that the Peace Corps, in its own media-conscious invasion, did little to refute. So I'll come back quietly. I lived here once. I left. I'm back again. What I want to pretend, I guess, is that I've never left at all.

❊   ❊   ❊

I'll travel light the next time I return and—how many places can you say this about?—I'll return lighter, because a couple pairs of shoes will die out there. My leather shoes are doomed, a vector for mold, and those running shoes will get sliced up on a reef, covered with bat shit in a limestone cave someplace. They'll stay and so will the books I carry, glue melting, pages loosening and turning into mulch. A camera will mark me as a tourist; ditto golf clubs, scuba diving and spearfishing gear. But isn't there a message in all this? A warning? Shouldn't I think about all the other trips that I could be taking: shorter distances, cheaper tickets, easier accommodations, better food. Trips to places with physical attractions that Pacific Islands can't match: mountains, deserts, lakes, valleys. Trips to places with cultures that fill museums and cuisine that makes great restaurants, cities that fine sensibilities spend lifetimes trying to capture. Isn't there something suspect about my going back to Micronesia, a lack of heft and depth, a paucity of wardrobe and equipment, a sense of a grown man returning to say . . . summer camp? And yet, walking through the apartment for the last time, pulling plugs, closing windows, I'll find island memories in every room. They're in the kitchen, where—though no one goes to Micronesia to eat— I've missed sashimi dipped in soya, lemon juice, and hot peppers, sampled on a boat, the victim fish still panting on the deck. And *kelaguin*, mixed, shredded meats of coconut and chicken, doused with lemon juice and hot peppers. And *demok*, a Palauan soup made of chicken giblets, coconut milk, and the leafy green tops of taro plants. In the living room, memories too, paintings and pictures of the islands, in colors brighter than what I see on the sidewalks of Evanston or the shores of Lake Michigan. The blues are bluer out where I'm headed, the greens are greener, everything primary, low on nuance, but bright as morning. Memories in the bathroom, blades and clippers that remind me my beard grows faster in the islands, my nails grow faster, too. Memories in the den, the TV room, where I'm ambushed three or four times a year by Cousteau diving down to the Japanese fleet that sank in the Truk Lagoon, or the Marshallese flogging commemorative coins on late-night cable, or the Americans recapturing Saipan in "Victory at Sea," or Lee Marvin and Toshiro Mifune stalking each other on a small island, in *Hell in the Pacific*, back in Palau. There are memories in my office, fiction published and fiction rejected, from the time I was hoping

Micronesia would be the place—the only place—I'd ever write about. Several drawers of magazines and newspapers, from the time I'd write an article for any place that would send me back, pay my expenses, or part of my expenses, or at least look at what I'd written, when I returned. There are memories in my bedroom, too: of sleeping mats and mosquito coils, cool linoleum floors, rolling ship berths, and a carpet of breadfruit wood shavings around an unfinished canoe in the outer islands, Lamotrek, or Eauripik, or Ifalik, I'm not sure which. Places I've slept. This is my baggage, this is what takes the place of camera and speargun. Memories.

For the quarter million tourists who visit the island annually, Saipan is a two- or three-day stop. For me, it's been between two and three years, and still counting. What the tourists—mostly Japanese, mostly office workers and honeymooners—see are attractions that can be ticked off, one by one. There are pleasant sandy beaches on the west side of the island, where they can wade out to pose for pictures against tanks and landing craft left over from the invasions. At dusk, it's happy hour at luxury hotels along the invasion beach, poolside cocktails and music from imported Filipino bands. There are golf courses, more every time I return, mounting evidence in support of my theory that its weakness for golf and sashimi will be Japan's undoing. At the northern end of Saipan stands Suicide Cliff, a breezy, shell-shocked escarpment from which hundreds of Japanese soldiers and civilians flung themselves when the battle for the island was lost. Down below, near where their bodies landed, signs guide visitors in toward command posts and caves built by the Japanese, bunkers and revetments constructed by the victorious Americans to store munitions for the planned invasion of the Japanese home islands. The road along here is lined with memorials and peace monuments in memory of civilian and military dead, Okinawans, Koreans, Japanese. Take all of these attractions, add a couple of doses of duty-free shopping, a side trip to the A-bomb loading pits and airstrips on the neighboring island of Tinian, throw in a taste of island nightlife, of pistol-shooting galleries, poker-machine rooms, strip joints, and a tourist can claim to have done Saipan. But a tourist visits a place. I visit a way of life, a place that used to be home. It's like stepping back into my childhood home, my parents' house, back through time, remembering how it was but forcing myself to confront what is, what new owners, decorators, renovators have accomplished . . . and destroyed.

The Saipan the Peace Corps sent me to was a war-surplus kind of island where people rode along in jeeps and lived in wooden-sided tin-roofed houses or reclaimed Quonset huts. They worked for the government, sort of, if they worked at all, and on weekends they drank beer and fished. It was a tightly woven island then and everybody seemed to be connected at the distance of, say, cousin. People lived on the beach side of the island, the west side, in a half dozen villages connected by a good paved road the American military had left behind. Outside this populated littoral were whole chunks of island waiting to be discovered: hidden beaches that took a half day climbing down to; overgrown Japanese farms with toads in water cisterns, snails in what was left of elegant gardens, handsome porches tenanted by crabs that scuttled away, when you came barging out of the boondocks; and caves—God, were there caves!—fortified by the Japanese, blasted shut by the Americans, but now rocks and earth had settled and you could crawl into caves that were tombs, shrines of helmets and mess kits, shoes and sake bottles, and bones. There were secret places everywhere, it seemed. What I didn't know back then was how fast the secret was getting out, and how far it was traveling.

On my first days back I'll drive around the island, thankful that the curve of coast, the presence of Mount Tagpochau at the center of the island, of Suicide Cliff at the north end enable me to find my way in a place changed utterly, an island where growth and greed, profit and progress are all tangled together in wild mutations no one could have foreseen. It started, I guess, in 1975. Saipan had been the capital of the Trust Territory of Pacific Islands, a United Nations trusteeship administered by the United States through the Department of Interior. The Trust Territory—"T.T."—was an ungainly amalgam of more than two thousand islands scattered over an area the size of the continental United States, a mixed flotilla of languages and cultures that included the Marshalls, the Carolines, and the Marianas, all of it run by the United States in a fashion that combined good intentions, a short attention span, and an underlying, self-interested estimate of the islands' past, present, and—possibly—future military value. United States control and largesse united the area; so did a common, usually mild, opposition to the United States. When the clock ran down on the UN Trusteeship and it was time to negotiate their political future, the islanders went their own ways, cutting separate deals with Washington. The Marshalls became a republic; so did Palau. Truk, Ponape, Yap, and Kusaie banded together as the Federated States of Micronesia. The islanders—who could blame them?—sought as much independence as they could risk with as much outside aid as they could get; they aimed to combine political sovereignty with economic dependency. The people of the Marianas were less conflicted. They voted to join the United States outright and forever, as U.S. citizens in a U.S. commonwealth. Now Saipan feels like an American place.

I'll spend my first days back cruising the hotels along the old invasion beach, the gaggle of nightclubs, duty-free shops, malls, and mini-marts on the island side. Athlete's Foot. Winchells Donut. Saipan transformed into Florida . . . for the Japanese. Inland, harder to find, there are garment factories' hangar-sized operations where imported workers—Filipinos and Chinese—turn out sweaters and flannel shirts labeled MADE IN USA. I'll drive down old dirt roads into workers barracks, factory compounds, mini-Levittowns for hotel employees. On the less developed east side of the island, I'll see new houses everywhere, mansions for Japanese investors, tax-avoiding Americans, and land-rich Saipanese. It's a good thing that I knew the island in another time, pre-prosperity, pre-Commonwealth, before this odd confluence of American politics and Japanese wealth, before this time of buying in and selling out. Tourists live in the present tense; they take the island as it is, two or three days at a time, and that's it. I travel in past, present, future.

One by one I find the people I used to know. Or they'll find me. There's a Palauan fellow who took me in after a typhoon carried off my home; he married a Saipanese woman who worked in my office. There's a former Peace Corps Volunteer who stayed on as a lawyer, another who writes speeches for local politicians. There's a woman, once a bar owner, who now works behind the perfume counter at Duty Free and a man, once a government photographer, who's very big in local government. They keep coming at me, every day I'm here, old friends and casual acquaintances, like faces at a high school reunion, men and women who were once my students, my neighbors, people I argued with or bummed rides from. We survived typhoons together, we survived elections. We've grown jaded, wised-up, wise; we've mellowed, we've soured; we haven't learned a thing. We'll ask about one another's health. If I am their prodigal, they are mine.

Once, when pressed, I defined heaven as a street lined with congenial taverns — dark wood, booths, decent bar food, the right music on the jukebox — and every time I walked that street I'd find an old friend I'd lost, someone I wondered about, not knowing if it was ever in the cards for us to meet again. In heaven we meet. We stare. We hug. We turn inside and talk. Coming back to these islands is as close to heaven as I've gotten.

There'll be a little more of heaven on some delicious afternoon, a Saturday or Sunday, sitting at a table in back of someone's house somewhere along the beach. There'll be fish and chicken on the grill, a bucketful of iced-down beer, kids and dogs around, cars and boats and parts of cars and boats. We'll sit there, "talking story," while the afternoon heat recedes. We'll talk of money and deals, sudden riches and new schemes. We'll sit there at sunset, mulling over courtships, court cases, the talk of the island. The smaller the place, the longer the memory: we'll have lots of catching up to do. Talk of outsiders: Filipinos, Koreans, Chinese, as many outsiders now as locals, third worlders clinging to an American lifeboat, climbing over the gunwales, threatening to swamp the Commonwealth. Night falls and we'll still be talking while dogs fight over table scraps — amazing how island dogs clean off a fish, never swallowing a bone — while lights go on in the big hotels, planes curve in toward the airport. Talk of local folks who struck it rich, who made and lost fortunes, moved to California, bought land in Seattle, landed in jail, prospered, vanished. We'll linger late into the night. Sometimes there'll be silences, wonderful relaxed silences, and I'll hear waves lapping the beach, music from a neighbor's radio, or someone will pick up a guitar. And though I'll be leaving soon, I'll feel that I've been home.

I'll leave quietly this next time; airport farewells have a discomfiting finality and make me feel that I might not be coming back again. So I'll slip into a line of sunburned Japanese office workers and head through customs and immigration, casually as if I were bound for Guam, twenty minutes south, for some weekend shopping. I'll feel good about having seen Saipan again. I'm not pleased with the way the island has changed: the unearned affluence, the cynical air, the threefold exploitation of American connections, Japanese investors and tourists, Filipino laborers. I'm not comfortable in an island of agents, landlords, arbitrageurs, and middlemen. But all this is countered—not erased—but countered by what endures and renews me, when I return: the dalliance of birds in the breeze off Suicide Cliff, the blaze of flame trees along Beach Road, the sunsets out beyond the hotels, the tanks, the reef, the heavy-scented, half-liquid feel of the night air, and the feeling of connection I get, sitting out late at a picnic table with old friends, trying—probably failing—to make sense out of a life that, my return convinces me, we're all in together.

Airports in the islands used to be like harbors, ramshackle, cluttered, close to the sea. On Saipan, you'd land on a strip the Seabees built, right after the Americans captured the island. Coming in, you'd see Japanese bunkers and pillboxes left and right. On Yap, the airstrip was something that the Japanese had left behind, along with a half dozen shot-up planes, scattered in the fields around the runway. The pilot used to do a flyover first, just to make sure no pigs were foraging in his landing path. In Palau, you landed on a red-clay ridge and picked up your baggage in a bulking bombed-out building that had been a Japanese communications center. Half the island seemed to come out to the airport on plane days and there was always someone you knew waiting there, even if they weren't waiting for you, even if they weren't waiting for anyone, just hanging around to see who came walking off the plane.

There are new airports now: a duty free shop on Saipan so outward-bound Japanese can load up on whiskey and cigarettes. Yap boasts a functional, typhoon-proof structure replacing the tin-roofed, earth-floored terminal that kept us out of the rain. And in Palau, my last stop, I'll confront an ugly, ill-constructed, litigation-plagued two-story structure with impassive customs and immigrations officials. Sometimes it's as though too many planes have landed; it's almost that simple. A hotel van will take me from the airport, over nicely paved roads, down to where a bridge now spans the channel between the islands of Babeldaob and Koror. You zip right across, where once you lined up, cracked a beer, stretched your legs, and waited for the rusty landing craft that ferried passengers back and forth across the channel.

The new Japanese-run Palau Pacific Resort will siphon off most of the people who come off the plane. I'll settle into one of Palau's cheaper places, hop in a rental car, and begin the homecoming game, trying to stay ahead of the news of my return, like a swimmer keeping in front of the ripples made by his own dive into a pool. "You're back!" people exclaim. "Why?" Why indeed? And then—it's never where are you living now or where is your home?—but *where do you stay?* or *where are you stationed now?* as if we're all still in the navy.

You can discover better places than Palau, more congenial, more welcoming, I suppose, but if you come to Palau when you're young, as I did, you stay hooked forever, hooked on sad old Koror, on the tumbling limestone islands—"Rock Islands," "Floating Garden Islands" to the south—or on the battlefield islands of Peleliu and Angaur, or the mountainous sprawl of Babeldaob. More than the place, the people draw you in. They had a cockiness and arrogance and sense of self that led me to hope they could hold their own in times ahead. Many of the men were sharp-eyed operators who put on conspiracy as nonchalantly as other men slapped on aftershave lotion. The women were shrewd and sharp-tongued, as skeptical as their men, skeptical *of* their men. There was nothing pretty in Koror's melancholy mix of Japanese colonial and U.S. Quonset architecture, but the place still spoke to you, especially if you were a reader or maybe a writer: it whispered Greene, Conrad, Maugham. Palau was where island travelogues segued into something deeper—drama, melodrama, thriller, or romance.

Politics is Palau: spend a week there and you'll be more deeply involved in Palauan turmoil, get further into the players and the game, than you'll ever get back home. The other chunks of Trust Territory have made arrangements with the United States. Palau—though it is called the Republic of Palau—remains a United Nations Trust Territory, the last on earth. Some people see Palau's recalcitrance as proof of Palauan integrity, a people's wish to avoid careless change, loss of control, abuse of land, and dilution of culture. That's one argument. Another, less flattering, is that Palau's turmoil reflects a self-interested desire to cut a more lucrative deal with the United States and to take maximum, ruthless personal advantage of the money that comes in, once the trusteeship ends.

Anyway, returning to Palau, hearing what recent moves have been made, what alliances and betrayals occurred while I was away, I'll get the feeling someone who follows a soap opera must get, when returning from a long vacation, reading one of those magazines that summarizes what they missed on *As the World Turns*. But it's not that simple. Imagine that there are two or three competing soap opera magazines, each with its own detailed, nuanced plot summary, imagine that there are disagreements about the characters, the events, what was said and when. Now you're close to the feeling of Palau.

When I was a Peace Corps Volunteer, and for years afterwards, I believed that something would come of all this fret: that Palau would find a way of dealing with the United States, and with the late twentieth century, that was better than Saipan's, better than Hawaii's. I'm less sure now. But still I'll listen to what they say, dining in restaurants that attract competing factions, cruising nightclubs and catching confidences over the clang of electric guitars, nodding agreeably as I lean against pickup trucks in tavern parking lots, catching the night air and glancing up at the night sky at the stars that once—no more— the people talking politics could steer by.

After a while, a matter of weeks, I'll get bored on my next trip to the islands. I'll have listened too much, I'll have tired of island politics, the knowing look, the real story, the inside track. And— I hate to admit it—the heat will get to me, the heat that hammers you half an hour after sunrise, chases you into the shade and behind air conditioners, and turns life outside into a slow-motion torture exercise. I'll start missing places that have less politics and more seasons. It will be time for me to leave, to end my next trip to the islands. But I won't go. I'll stick around Koror, hoping for a miracle that will take me south. A miracle.

What I've had so far is a fine returning, checking in on places and people, connecting then and now. But it's a good trip that will never be a great trip unless I break out of the circuit of islands that are connected by airports. What I've done so far is too much like driving across the United States without getting off interstates. You can travel through the islands that way and have a fine time if you don't know what else is out there. Saipan is fun, that's for sure, but there will be a morning that I drive to the top of a hill, park at the side of the road, and—you have to know where to look and you have to do it at dawn—I'll spot the nearest of the northern islands, a chain of volcanic hulks that trails off to the north: Anatahan, Alamagan, Pagan, Agrihan, and some others, uninhabited—or occasionally or lightly inhabited—high cones with emerald slopes, rocky shorelines, black sand beaches. There's an old Japanese fighter strip on Pagan that's been in and out of service over the years; otherwise, you can't get there by plane. You probably can't get there at all. That's the exasperating side of Micronesia, that's what sends you away determined to come back and do it right next time, because you've been sitting in a half-assed town, living in some hotel that's not great, and you're riveted by places temptingly, tantalizingly out of reach. Granted, it may console you to know that the same difficulties that keep you away prevent other people from getting there. But that doesn't stop you from yearning.

I'll make my stand in Palau. I will wait for a boat headed south, a government boat, some yachties, the Coast Guard, I don't know. I will wait while I get tantalized, misled, rescheduled, and generally jerked around wait at the mercy of mood, mechanics, politics, and weather. Eventually I will suspect that I'm waiting for nothing because an island named Helen, small and undefended, has surely been raided and ripped off. But maybe I'll get lucky on my next trip to the islands. Maybe I'll be able to head south again, see that island at the edge of the map and the end of the world rise over the horizon, glimpse first that rusted ship, the waves breaking against the reef, that grove of palms at the end of the lagoon, catching the late afternoon light, all the world's absences and silences. Maybe I'll have a chance to walk ashore again and find the place that I remember.